THE ABBOT AND THE WIDOW

TALES FROM THE MING DYNASTY

THE ABBOT AND THE WIDOW

TALES FROM THE MING DYNASTY

Ling Mengchu

Translated by Ted Wang and Chen Chen

Introduction by Teresa Chi-ching Sun

EastBridge

Norwalk

EastBridge

Signature Books

Chartered in the State of Connecticut, EastBridge is a nonprofit publishing
corporation under section 501(c)(3) of the United States tax code.

EastBridge has received a multiyear
grant from the Henry Luce Foundation.

The cover design reproduces a section of the twelfth century scroll, *Springtime on
the Bian River*, by Song dynasty artist Zhang Zeduan. The original scroll is over 17
feet long (208.5" x 10.06") and hangs in the Palace Museum in Beijing.

Woodcut illustrations retouched by Shirley Chien.

Library of Congress Cataloging-in-Publication Data

Ling, Mengchu, 1580-1644.

[Pai an jing qi. English. Selections]

The abbot and the widow : tales from the Ming dynasty / Ling Mengchu ;
    translated by Ted Wang and Chen Chen ; introduction by Teresa Chi-ching
    Sun.

p. cm. -- (Signature books)

ISBN 1-891936-39-5 (alk. paper) -- ISBN 1-891936-40-0 (pbk. : alk.paper)

I. Title: Tales from the Ming dynasty. II. Title. III. Series.

PL2698.L55A28 2004

895.1'346--dc22

2003026392

Printed in the United States of America

In remembrance of our friend
King Hu
godfather of martial arts films
who always loved a good story

CONTENTS

Preface

Chen Chen

It is with pleasure that we present this volume of short stories—the first of a projected series—selected and translated from among a total of two hundred such tales written almost four hundred years ago during China's Ming dynasty by two writers, Feng Menglong and Ling Mengchu.

Feng Menglong (1574–1646) wrote 120 tales evenly divided among three books—*Instructive Tales to Enlighten the World, Popular Tales to Admonish the World,* and *Lasting Tales to Waken the World*—that have been commonly referred to as the "San yan," or "Three Tales."

Ling Mengchu (1580–1644), inspired by Feng's volumes, also wrote two books of forty tales each, naming them *Slapping the Desk in Astonishment: Book One* and *Slapping the Desk in Astonishment: Book Two.* They were popularly known as the "Er pai," or "Two Slaps."

While the ten tales in our first volume of translations have all been selected from the "Two Slaps" by Ling, the second volume is planned to include eight or more tales from Feng's "Three Tales."

Neither of the two translators, Ted Wang or myself, have graduated from Chinese or English departments; nor have either of us, during our professional careers, been associated with Chinese studies or Sinology, be it in history, politics, anthropology, or literature. We are not generally familiar with the "Who's Who" of Chinese studies, either in China or the West. With no restraints from peers or from arcane academic conventions, we embarked on this adventurous endeavor with absolute freedom. Should we offend any scholarly sensibilities with this publication, the offense is unintentional.

Our intention, as lovers of Chinese and English books from the time we each emerged from infancy, is to treat an interested English-reading public to a delectable selection of toothsome stories. We believe that students of Asian studies will be able to informatively spice up their reading lists with these tales. More importantly, the tales may be of interest to readers who are related in some way to Asia, be they multigenerational Chinese Americans—whose forebears came to the Americas in the nineteenth and twentieth centuries—or people related to China by marriage, adoption, vocation, or history, such as old China hands, the progeny of missionary families, and others. There may also be not a few people among the general readership who simply would like to read some really good stories, the durability of which is shown by the fact that the tales have survived some four hundred years in a country with a redoubtable literary legacy.

My acquaintance with the Ming tales began in China before I entered my teens with editions censored, of course, for sexual content. I read and re-read them because of their brevity and varied content, especially in later years after I obtained the complete and uncensored volumes of these tales. However, it was not until I settled down in the United States and finished writing my memoir, *Come Watch the Sun Go Home*, that I conceived the idea of translating a selection from these tales wider in range than the sporadic and individual renditions I was told were currently available.

This ambition could not have taken off without the main force behind these volumes: my long-time collaborator Ted Wang, a veteran translator known for his eloquent and elegant style and whom the renowned late film director King Hu called a *qi cai* (wonder talent) of Chinese to English translation.

Ted Wang was familiar with the English and French classics, but had never come in contact with these nonclassic Chinese tales. From the moment he read his first tale, he was captivated by the richly detailed descriptions of an erstwhile everyday life unknown to most contemporary Chinese, the characterization of the protagonists, and the narrative skills. We agreed it would be a great waste if these delightful, vivacious, folksy, and even ribald tales were not made available to a wider English-reading audience.

We worked up some six or seven tales randomly selected from all five books and showed the translations to a few interested parties. It so happened that Ted met our then future-publisher-to-be, Doug Merwin, and told him about our project. Doug kept it in mind and, when the time came, launched it.

Thereafter, Ted and I embarked on a fairly intensive period of translation— on top of the work we each do for a livelihood—and I re-read all two hundred tales several times to gauge their respective merit and value for current and future selections. What naturally came to mind were the English and Italian classics *Canterbury Tales* and *The Decameron*. When these were presented to their respective readers in fourteenth and fifteenth century Europe, China's popular literature had already emerged from the era of the "The Legends of Tang (618– 907) and Song (960–1279)" told in teahouses and evolved into the rudimentary dramatic shows famed as the "Miscellaneous Plays of Yuan (1271–1368) and Ming (1368–1644)," starting some three hundred years before Shakespeare and, in later years, overlapping with his emergence in England. The Yuan and Ming plays were also performed at teahouses and fairgrounds, like their predecessors, the storytellers' tales.

This development of drama in turn enhanced and improved the narrative content and techniques of storytelling honed by centuries of practice. Since most of the storytellers were semiliterate, they passed on their stories primarily by word of mouth and with the help of prompt books. These stories gradually emerged in written form, and some were even presented before emperors for their entertainment, and then recycled back to the populace through the palaces' back doors.

Thanks to the efforts of writers like Feng Menglong and Ling Mengchu, we can now share with our readers these fascinating tales about merchants, scholars, housewives, magistrates, craftsmen, courtesans, abbots, nuns, and even children, spanning a broad spectrum of Chinese urban and rural life, including seafaring travel some four hundred and more years ago. While a few of the tales deal with supernatural powers, the majority are about everyday people in everyday situations, about their lives and loves and triumphs and tragedies, and about their strengths and weaknesses, virtues and vices. Throughout the translation process, I could not help but marvel at the techniques employed by these long-ago writers, at the precision of their narrations, at the structuring of the plots and subplots, and at their skillful use of suspense, flashbacks and flashforwards—in many ways as smooth and seamless as any of their twentieth–century counterparts. In some tales, the characters are so well crafted that each has a distinctive speech pattern.

While no good literary translations should be verbatim, we have kept as close to the original texts as feasible for informative and entertaining reading, but stayed away from untranslatable plays on words, flowery poetic flourishes, and extraneous narrative elements. For exact research, scholars in Chinese literature should go to the original Chinese texts.

Both translators wish to thank my cousin Dr. E-tu Zen Sun, Professor Emerita of Chinese History, Pennsylvania State University, for the unstinting and invaluable support she has given us since we first started on the translations several years ago. We laypersons have had to ask her an array of questions about things ranging from China's imperial and academic systems all the way down to details like dwellings and tools. She patiently read all the manuscripts we sent her and, to our embarrassment, even corrected our typos. E-tu's informative and instructive involvement bolstered our confidence in this endeavor.

Along the way, we engaged the assistance, as "readers," of six of our friends who, by gender, ethnicity, age, profession, and general interest, represent to some extent the diversity of the readership we envision. They furnished us with candid feedback after going through the draft manuscripts, and their positive reactions gave us great encouragement. Those we wish to thank are: Russell

Good, Sue C. Hoy, Janice Lance, Sally Morgan, John Wang and Robert Zivnuska.

We were also fortunate to secure enthusiastic support from Dr. Teresa Chi-ching Sun who wrote, at very short notice, the enlightening Introduction to this volume. Her essay greatly increases the instructive aspect of this series of books and lends academic clarification and dignity to the "fun" that this project is meant to provide.

Introduction

Teresa Chi-ching Sun, Ed.D.
University of California, Irvine

Popular fiction in Chinese literary history has had a long and delayed development. Traditionally, the Chinese had ignored this particular genre ever since their civilization came into being. Fiction and drama writing were regarded as a sort of trivial craftsmanship that had no place in the "grand hall of literature," and the stigma of this tradition is to be seen to this day in the name by which novels are still referred to—*xiao shuo* (little talk). It was not until the coming of Western literature to China that the Chinese, amazed by the value other cultures placed on the art of fiction–writing, began to perceive their own precious literary legacy. Thereafter, fiction assumed a prominent position in Chinese literature.

There is little doubt that one factor in the development of literature in China was the interdependent nature of literary talent and public affairs within the Chinese political, cultural, and historical context. Up to the turn of the twentieth century, the influence of Confucianism as the intellectual and moral source of Chinese civilization overwhelmingly dominated social mobility. The goal of life for almost every intellectual during China's imperial age was to cultivate oneself morally according to the Confucian teachings and thus be able to serve the imperial house by governing the populace according to these teachings. The educated elite won respect from their families and fellow scholars by rising in public officialdom through a system of imperial civil service examinations, during which they displayed their knowledge of the Confucian classics by producing essays in a literary writing style, and thereby acquired a position on the social and political ladder. Acquisition of knowledge of the classics as well as of the written medium in which these classics were couched demanded long-term devotion from the literati. In this process, they zealously perpetuated this literary style within their elitist circle in the writing of poetry, prose, essays, tribunes of opinion, and official documents. This jealously preserved literary writing style differed considerably from the colloquial language spoken by the common people, a language which was deemed unworthy of the efforts of scholars. Such discrimination left little room for any acceptance of fiction and drama as literary genres.

During the Ming period, however, parallel with the formal writing style, a trend toward writing in the colloquial language arose. This fresh literary activity was due mainly to economic prosperity and ubiquitous commercial development, which prompted creative story–writing among individual authors for the entertainment of the middle class in urban centers. The vigorous development of such story–writing attracted the interest of intellectuals, many of whom applied their literary talent to—and executed in the colloquial writing style—numerous works of fiction, drama, and short stories. Their formal writing training considerably enriched and articulated the colloquial writing style, and their education helped them perceive with deeper insight the life of the common people around them and touch upon their sorrows, joys, separations, and reunions. Most of these authors were disappointed scholars who had failed the civil service examinations or were unable to climb higher within the bureaucratic system, and they wrote novels to amuse themselves or, in many cases, to keep food on the table. Thus, with the diversion of a group of creative and talented writers away from the formal writing style and the Confucian tradition, a new literary genre took shape. The tales they wrote were interesting and popular among the common people, yet the genuine artistic value of the genre began to catch the attention of literary critics only toward the end of the Qing dynasty. It is unfortunate that the splendor of their achievements had to wait until centuries later to be recognized and perceived by their fellow Chinese. Among their more outstanding productions are such masterful works as *Journey to the West* (Xi youji), *Tales of the Marshes* (Shuihu zhuan), *Romance of the Three Kingdoms* (Sanguo yanyi) , and *The Golden Lotus* (Jin ping mei), all of which have been translated into other languages and widely read by people around the world.

A great many short stories were also written along with the full-length novels listed above. In the closing years of the Ming period, two large sets of such stories appeared in South China along the lower reaches of the Yangtze River. Known popularly today as the "Three Tales" (San yan) and "Two Slaps" (Er pai) and based in large part on the tales told by storytellers in teahouses and other places of popular entertainment, these two sets of stories acquired a unique position in the repertoire of Chinese fiction. Their writers did much to develop the creative aspect of short stories. They showed considerable maturity in terms of narrative enrichment, plot arrangement, and the articulation of narrative language and delighted and fascinated generations of readers with short and medium-length narratives of many different aspects of society in Ming and earlier times.

The "Three Tales" consist of three volumes, each containing forty stories and entitled respectively *Instructive Tales to Enlighten the World* (Yu shi ming yan), *Popular Tales to Admonish the World* (Jingshi tong yan), and *Lasting Tales to Waken the World* (Xing shi heng yan). These titles clearly reveal the elitist background of the writer Feng Menglong (1574–1646), as they declare his intention to educate the general public with sincere moral messages—a typical response to worldly affairs on the part of Confucian scholars. Most of these realistic stories end happily with victory for the virtuous and punishment for the wicked and regale readers with the triumphs of folk justice. Feng based many of his stories either on the manuscripts used by storytellers of Song and early Ming times, or on fragments of folktales, or hearsay, or unconfirmed historical occurrences. A few were tales of his own invention. Whatever their origin, his stories displayed considerable maturity of form as he combined oral storytelling skills with literary techniques. He was an innovator, not just an imitator.

The "Two Slaps," or *Slapping the Desk in Astonishment: Book One* and *Slapping the Desk in Astonishment: Book Two,* consist of a total of eighty stories in two volumes. At a time when the Three Tales mentioned above were creating quite a stir in the popular book trade, another writer, Ling Mengchu (1580–1644), was stimulated by the short-story writing trend to write his own tales. Also a poor scholar and frustrated official, Ling wished to create tales in his own manner. This he did by shaking off influences from Feng Menglong's writing style, deviating further from the Confucian norm than Feng, and writing stories centered around a different theme—wonder and amazement, without giving especial consideration to moral messages. With his literary pen he elaborated realistic oral accounts of the marvels and unusual events he encountered or heard about while wandering on the streets of cities during the turbulent years of the late Ming period. These ranged from romances between successful scholars and ladies from upper-class families and the adventures of merchants and travelers, to murders, unjust trials, and the seamier doings of beggars, thieves, prostitutes, and lascivious monks and widows. His aim was always to excite the readers' emotions and elicit exclamations of "how astonishing!"

At the time of this writing, more stories have been translated from the "Three Tales" than from the "Two Slaps." Those included in the present collection are a long overdue contribution to the treasury of translated Chinese literature.

THE ABBOT AND THE WIDOW

TALES FROM THE MING DYNASTY

How Fortune Smiled on Wen the Luckless

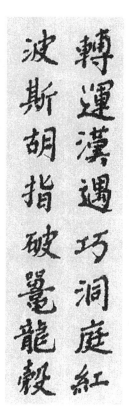

During the Chenghua reign [1465–1488] of our present Ming dynasty, there lived just outside the city of Suzhou a man named Wen Shi, who was nimble of mind and quick to learn whatever he set himself to doing. He had a fair command of music, chess, calligraphy and painting, and could perform on the flute and the lute as well as sing and dance.

While he was still a child, a soothsayer had foretold that he would become a rich man with tens of thousands of taels of silver. Feeling himself secure in the knowledge of his own talents and the soothsayer's prophecy, Wen did nothing to augment his estate. As time went by, however, the considerable inheritance left to him by his forebears dwindled until practically nothing was left. Realizing now that there were limits to his fortune, he sought to engage in commerce, but his endeavors met with little success.

One day, having learned that paper fans were selling well in Beijing, Wen hired a clerk and purchased a stock of folding paper fans. He had the most refined of these painted or inscribed by well-known artists, for which favor he presented them with gifts, and this greatly enhanced the value of the fans. On those of middling quality, he asked some good imitators of the aforementioned artists to paint something for a small fee. These were at least painted by hand, and could therefore delude the average buyer. The lowest quality fans were left blank, to be sold as they were. Even then, Wen counted on doubling the amount of money he invested in them.

Wen selected a date, packed up his fans, and set out for Beijing. As luck would have it, however, Beijing had a very wet summer and the selling season for fans was much delayed as a consequence of the cool weather. As soon as the rains ceased, Wen ordered his clerk to unpack the merchandise and display it to fashionable young men who desired fans from Suzhou. When the cases were opened, however, Wen's heart sank. Humidity had caused the ink on the fans to stick the folded surfaces together. Wen attempted to pry a few of the fans open, but when the folds were separated, the paintings on them were marred by unsightly patches, some bare and others with superimposed layers of paint. Only the unadorned fans, which were of little value, remained saleable. Wen disposed of these for a sum sufficient to defray the cost of the journey home, but forfeited his entire investment.

In the next few years, similar misfortunes befell all of Wen's ventures. Not only did he continue to lose money, his associates and even the clerks he employed suffered. People dubbed him "Wen the Luckless." His family inheritance withered away, so that he was unable even to find himself a wife. Thereafter he got along by knocking about and drumming up here and there a bit of business, none of which was of any consequence.

Wen had a clever tongue, and his pleasant and witty conversation ensured him a welcome at his friends' houses, and he was invariably invited to outings or excursions. But such occasions provided him only with a meal or two and did not afford him a proper living. Meanwhile, his erstwhile affluence caused him to be rejected by those who earned their subsistence by dancing attendance on the rich and supplying the latter with sundry services. A few people who pitied him tried to obtain a position for him as a private tutor, but respectable families declined to employ him on account of his lack of proper credentials. Thus, Wen found himself spurned by people high and low, all of whom derisively referred to him by his nickname "Wen the Luckless."

One day, Wen learned that a party of local seafarers, several dozen in number and led by a certain Zhang the First, were preparing for an expedition across the ocean. He thought to himself, "Here I am, in dire straits and with no means of keeping body and soul together. Why shouldn't I join them on the voyage? I shall at least see something of the world and thereby not have lived in vain. Should they permit me to join them, which I am convinced they will, I shall not have to spend my days at home worrying about food and kindling wood."

Zhang the First happened to pass by as Wen was thinking these thoughts. Now, Zhang was a merchant who made his living by trading in foreign lands and possessed a keen eye for rare treasures and exotic jewels. He was also adept at recognizing men of good will and was willing to lend them a helping hand. Hence he had earned the nickname "Zhang of the Discerning Eye."

Wen recounted his wishes to Zhang, who at once said, "Very well. We frequently become bored on our journeys, and if you should come with us, your conversation and pleasantries will help us pass the time. There is one thing, however. Everyone is taking some merchandise along, and it would be a pity if you brought nothing, for you shall have wasted the trip. Let me confer with my colleagues. We might put some money together for you, so that you could purchase a few things." Wen demurred, "I thank you for your generosity but I doubt the others will show the same willingness to assist me." "Let me talk to them first," said Zhang, who thereupon took his leave.

At this point, a blind fortuneteller came by. On a sudden impulse, Wen extracted a coin from his purse and asked to have his fortune told, whereupon the blind man said, "Your destiny is an unusual one, for it holds a vast fortune for you, one that is of no small significance." Wen, however, thought to himself, "I am joining that expedition merely to obtain some pleasure and to while away the time. I shall not be engaging in commerce since I have no financial wherewithal. And even if I did raise a little capital, it would hardly suffice to make me a fortune. This man is a scoundrel!"

Zhang the First soon returned from his mission. He was clearly vexed. "Hardly had I mentioned money," he said, "than they began to distance themselves. They are indeed absurd. All said they welcomed you aboard, but none uttered a sound when I spoke of giving you some assistance. However, two of my close friends and I have put together between us one tael of silver for you. It is not enough to obtain any merchandise, so I propose that you purchase some fruit and viands for the trip. The ship's company will, of course, supply you with your everyday provender."

When Wen, with many expressions of gratitude, had taken the tael of silver, Zhang added, "And make haste, for we are about to set sail." To which Wen replied, "I have little to prepare in any case. I shall be right there." After Zhang had left, Wen looked at the silver in his palm and laughed. "What little can I purchase with that?!"

Wen Shi walked briskly to the marketplace and there saw many baskets filled with bright red tangerines. They had been grown on Mount Dongting beside Lake Tai and were as succulent and delicious as the most renowned tangerines of Guangzhou, but at only one-tenth the price. Wen reflected, "I can purchase more than one hundred catties of these with that tael of silver. They will serve at least to refresh me during the journey, and I can present some to my shipmates to repay them for providing me with passage on the ship." He made his purchase, had the tangerines packed in bamboo crates, and then hired a porter to carry them to the ship together with his personal effects.

At the sight of the tangerines, however, those of the ship's company already on board clapped their hands together and scoffed, "Here come Master Wen's treasures!" Sorely embarrassed, Wen Shi boarded the ship in silence and never dared to mention his tangerines again.

The ship sailed before fair winds for many days, and large distances were traversed almost unnoticed. Then suddenly the lookout sighted a place with many buildings, tall city walls, and a bustling population, apparently the capital city of some country. The sailors found a safe harbor, dropped anchor, and moored the ship securely.

Some of the passengers disembarked and ascertained that many among them had previously visited this land, which was called Ji Ling. Chinese goods sold here brought in three times their purchase price, and the same applied to goods shipped from Ji Ling back to China. A single round trip enabled a trader to obtain an eight or nine-fold profit, for which reason Chinese merchants were most eager to come to this country, even at the risk of their lives. Most of those on board who had traded here before had their own agents, guides, and lodgings.

Thus everyone went ashore on his own business, leaving Wen, who knew no one and had no place to go, to guard the ship.

As Wen sat there idling the time away, he thought of his tangerines. "I have not inspected those crates since the day we set sail," he said to himself. "I hope the fruit has not rotted in the heat." He asked a seaman to open up the hold and uncover the crates. The tangerines at the top were in excellent condition, but Wen was still uneasy and had the crates brought up and their contents spread out on the ship's deck. It was then that Wen's fortunes began to change.

From a distance the tangerines looked like crimson flames, like a myriad stars glowing in the sky. People on shore were drawn by the flood of color and came to inquire, "What good things are those?" Wen did not reply. Instead, he picked out one or two that had been squashed somewhat, peeled them and popped them in his mouth.

By now a crowd had gathered, and people exclaimed in delight, "They can be eaten!" One of the more curious stepped forward and asked, "How much for one of these?" Wen did not understand their tongue, but the seaman did, and he raised a finger in jest, saying, "One coin apiece." The inquirer flipped up his gown to reveal an embroidered scarlet money belt. Extracting a silver coin from it, he said, "I wish to taste one." Wen took the coin and hefted it. It weighed about one tael. "I know not how many he expects to purchase for this much silver," he thought. "Nor do I have any scales. Let me give him one to start with."

Wen selected a large red one for the buyer. The man took the tangerine and bounced it in his hands, saying, "Excellent!" He then broke it open, releasing such a fragrance that even the bystanders uttered cries of admiration. The buyer, however, knew not how to eat it. Without separating the segments or even spitting out the seeds, he stuffed the tangerine whole into his mouth and, with sweet juice coursing along his neck, gulped it down. Then he laughed and exclaimed, "Marvelous, marvelous!" He reached once more into his money belt and drew out ten silver coins, announcing "I wish to have ten more, to present to my headman." Delighted beyond words, Wen selected ten of the best for the man, who left forthwith.

Having observed this, the spectators followed suit, some buying one tangerine, others two or three, and all using the same silver coins.

In this country, silver is used to mint coins bearing different designs. Those cast with a dragon and phoenix design have the greatest worth, and are followed in order of value by those depicting human figures, beasts, and trees. The ones of the lowest denomination bear a reed design. All of them, however, are of the same weight. The people who bought tangerines used coins bearing a reed design, and all were highly pleased with themselves, since they assumed they had obtained something good in exchange for a small amount of cash. In their quest for trifling advantages, they were of the same cast of mind as the Chinese.

Very soon, two thirds of the tangerines had been sold. People who had come without money felt such regret that they hastened to retrieve some from their homes. But when Wen saw how few of the tangerines remained, he told the purchasers, "I am not selling any more, as I need the rest for my own use." One client, however, doubled his payment and bought two tangerines for four silver coins, muttering all the while, "A pity I arrived so late!" Another person reproached him, saying, "I, too, want to purchase some. But now you have doubled the price!" To which the other replied, "Did you not hear him declare that he would not sell any more?"

As they argued thus, the first buyer sped back on a black horse. Dismounting and plunging through the crowd, he cried in the direction of the ship, "Do not sell any more! I want them all. My headman desires to buy them as a present for our khan!" Hearing this, the people stepped back, but stayed to look on.

Being a man of sharp wits, Wen saw at once that here was a good customer. He poured all the remaining tangerines out of the last crate. There were only fifty-two left. As he counted them, he observed shrewdly, "I have already informed everyone that I am not selling any more, as I need the rest for my own use. But if you pay more, I could let you have a few. The price, meanwhile, has risen to two coins for each tangerine."

The first buyer took a large sack of coins from the back of his horse and offered to pay one coin bearing a tree design for each fruit. Wen, however, declared, "No, I wish to be paid with the same sort of cash you used last time." The buyer then took out a coin with a dragon-phoenix design and asked, "How about his kind?" Again Wen replied, "No, I only want the kind you used previously." The buyer laughed. "One dragon-phoenix coin is worth a hundred of the other," he said. "I was merely jesting, for I would never give you that one. You are a fool to take the lesser coin instead of the one more valuable . But should you sell everything to me, I would be willing to add to the price one more of the coins you so desire."

Wen counted out the remaining tangerines, of which there were fifty-two, and took precisely one hundred and fifty-six coins for them. The man even bore away the crate, for which he left another coin, and tied it on his horse. Then, brandishing his whip, he rode away with a broad smile on his lips. The onlookers, seeing there was nothing left to buy, soon dispersed.

When the last of the onlookers were gone, Wen went into the ship's cabin and placed one of the coins on a scale. It weighed more than eight *qian*, seven *fen*. All the rest of the coins were of the same weight, and Wen now possessed approximately one thousand of them. He presented two of the coins to the ship's crew, then packed the rest in his bags, smiling as he did so and saying to himself, "That blind fortuneteller spoke the truth after all!" Greatly elated, he waited for his shipmates to return.

You must be mistaken, Storyteller! If silver were of such inconsiderable value in that country, why would habitual seafarers not do their trading in the following manner? They could sell the silks and satins they brought along in exchange for silver coins, and thus make a hundred-fold profit.

Esteemed Listener, I must inform you that people in that land are wont to pay for merchandise such as silks and satins with goods, whereas our people must also accept such goods if they are to make a profit. They would gain nothing by selling for cash, since they would receive in exchange dragon-and-phoenix coins, which are large in denomination but weigh no more than the other coins. Wen, however, was merely selling fruit for petty cash, and he profited from this exchange since he was only concerned about the weight of the coins.

Wrong again, Storyteller! If what you have said is true, why, then, did the seafarers not take foodstuffs and make their profit by selling these for coins of lesser denomination? Why would they invest in goods that required a much greater outlay?

Esteemed Listener, the truth is that Wen merely had some extraordinary luck. Should he have attempted to take along tangerines on a second such trip and the ship were delayed by adversities, he would have seen his cargo dissolve in a watery pulp. Wen was not a man blessed with consistent good fortune, as the incident of the paper fans would indicate. Add to that the fact that tangerines are even less easy to store than paper fans. Hence it is evident that your reasoning holds no water. But let us go back to our story.

When Wen's shipmates returned to unload such merchandise as they had sold to local merchants, Wen related to them what had happened during their absence. All expressed astonishment, saying, "You are indeed fortunate. Among us all, you are the only one who disposes of no capital, but you are also the first to have made a profit." Clapping his hands together, Zhang the First cried, "People say you are unlucky, but I believe your luck has now changed!"

He then advised Wen, "You would stand to gain little if you did not buy merchandise with the coins you now possess. I would suggest that you purchase Chinese goods from some of our shipmates and exchange these for some of the rare and exotic products of this land. You would gain a large profit by selling them in China, and in any case it would be better than letting your silver lie idle in your bags."

Wen replied, "I do indeed have bad luck. Whenever I invest any money for profit, I invariably forfeit everything, including my investment. This time, owing to your gracious assistance and by a touch of good fortune, I have gained some profit with no investment on my part. I have no desire to test my luck again. Should I lose what I have already gained, it is inconceivable that I would encounter another good deal like that of the tangerines."

Yet his companions insisted, "We all need some silver and we all possess merchandise, thus an exchange would benefit both you and us." But Wen remained adamant, "As the saying goes, 'a man bitten by a snake fears ropes for three years.' The mere mention of merchandise makes me quake with apprehension. I think I shall keep the silver coins I have already acquired." To which his companions could only say, "A pity, for you are letting pass a chance to multiply your gains."

Wen Shi then went ashore with his companions and watched them barter with the local merchants. And thus, during the next two weeks, he saw many good things, none of which, however, tempted him, as he was well content with his present circumstances. When all had concluded their transactions, the company returned to the ship, burned incense, drank toasts to the gods, and set out to sea.

After they had sailed a few days, the weather suddenly changed.

Black clouds blotted out the sun, somber waves surged to the skies. Dragons and serpents cavorted on high while fish and turtles cowered in the deep. Ships scattered like so many crows before a blizzard, and islands quivered like startled waterfowl. Within the ship, people were as grains flung about on a winnowing tray; outside, the ocean was a seething cauldron of violent waters. Seasoned mariners blanched before the fury of the Wind God.

The sailors shortened sail, after which the ship was buffeted hither and thither by the winds. Eventually, land was sighted on the horizon, and the crew maneuvered the ship in its direction. What they found was a deserted island where trees grew in profusion and wild grasses covered the ground. The only signs of life were the tracks of sundry small animals. None on board knew to what country the island belonged, or indeed if any human being had ever set foot on it since Creation.

The sailors dropped anchor and drove stakes on land to make fast the ship. To the passengers in the ship's cabin, they announced, "We will wait here for favorable winds."

As for Wen, now that he had some money, he was impatient to go home. Feeling restless, he told his companions, "I shall go ashore to look around." His shipmates asked, "What is there to see on a deserted island?" Whereupon Wen countered, "What better have we to do for now?" His shipmates, however, were exhausted after being tossed about in the storm and yawned incessantly. As they declined to accompany him ashore, Wen decided to go alone. Bracing himself, he leapt from the ship onto the shore.

This one action resulted in the discovery of a thousand-year-old turtle carapace, and a needy unfortunate acquiring considerable wealth. Had this storyteller been Wen's peer, and had he been possessed of foresight, he would have gone with Wen though he were a cripple who could hobble along only with the aid of crutches!

Undeterred by his shipmates' refusal to accompany him, Wen clambered to the top of the island, often drawing himself up with the assistance of vines and branches. The ascent was not overly arduous, since the island rose to no great height, but there were no paths through the tall grass and tangled brush.

From the crest of the hill, Wen gazed over the vast ocean around him. He felt like a drifting leaf and was suddenly overcome by feelings of melancholy, and he wept. "I am not unintelligent," he said to himself. "But I have had naught but bad luck all my life. Though fortune has granted me one thousand silver coins, who knows whether I shall live to enjoy them? Stranded as I am on this forsaken island in the ocean with no solid ground underfoot, my very life rests in the hands of the Dragon King of the Seas!"

As he brooded over his fate and fortunes, he spied a hump in the grass some distance away. Stepping closer to see what it was, he came upon an empty turtle carapace as long and as wide as a bedstead. He was greatly amazed, "I can hardly believe there has ever been a turtle of such size! No man has ever seen the likes of this; nor would anyone believe me if I should tell them! Since I have sailed across the ocean but have nothing to bring back, I shall take this and show it to people, so that no one may accuse me of bragging and say 'those Suzhou people are all liars.' Moreover, I could have the carapace sawn in two and affix four legs to each half to fashion a pair of beds, which would be most unusual." Thereupon Wen removed his leg bindings, tied them end to end, threaded them through the holes in the carapace, made a few knots, and proceeded to drag the carapace down the hill.

When Wen arrived at the ship, everyone on deck laughed uproariously at the sight. "Well, well, Master Wen," someone remarked. "What have you in tow this time?" Wen replied, "I will have you know that this is my merchandise from overseas." His shipmates looked more closely at his trophy, and one exclaimed, "An enormous carapace, indeed. But why do you bring such a thing?" Wen replied, "It is unusual." Someone said laughingly, "Why do you bother with a useless object like that, when you have already refused to purchase useful things?" But another man commented, "It might yet serve some purpose. No bigger turtle carapace could be found with which to practice divination." A third opined, "If it were broken up and used in apothecaries' prescriptions, it would equal several hundred small carapaces."

"Never you mind whether it's useful or not," said Wen. "What counts with me is that it is unusual and it cost me no investment." He then asked two sailors to carry the carapace onto the ship. It had looked large enough on the island, but now, in the confined space of the ship, it seemed even bigger. Nothing less than an ocean-going vessel could have held such a gargantuan object. All aboard the ship grinned broadly, and one man even said, "If people at home should ask me, I shall say Master Wen is now trading in big turtles!" Wen retorted, "Laugh if you will, but I have a use for it!"

Wen was so delighted with his find that he did not mind the jests and bantering. He swabbed the carapace inside and out, wiped it dry, then stowed his belongings in it. Having done that, he trussed the two ends with rope so that it resembled a large chest. To his shipmates he said, "I have already made use of it, have I not? " And the latter conceded, "Indeed you have. You are most resourceful!"

By the next day the wind had fallen. The ship set sail and a few days later raised the coast of Fujian. No sooner had it anchored than it was besieged by a band of petty solicitors, who vociferously recommended this or that trading house and shoved and pulled prospective clients. These solicitors desisted only after the merchants on the ship had all found and departed with agents with whom they had previously had dealings.

A good number of the ship's company went to visit a large trading house owned by a Persian merchant. Having been apprised of the arrival of these travelers, the host hastened to summon caterers, paying them a considerable amount of silver to prepare a banquet of several dozens of tables. He then came out to meet the visitors.

This Persian, whose Chinese name was Ma Baoha, traded only in rare merchandise brought back by seafarers, and his financial assets were beyond counting. All who traded overseas knew him, and among the ship's company

Wen alone had never made his acquaintance. Now, as he observed his host, he found that this Persian had resided in China for so long a time that his attire, manner of speaking, and gestures were quite like those of his Chinese visitors, although he appeared somewhat odd with his shaven eyebrows, trimmed beard, deep-set eyes, and prominent nose.

Ma exchanged obeisances with his visitors; then all seated themselves. After everyone had drunk two cups of tea, Ma rose and showed his visitors into a large hall where tables had been set for a munificent banquet. Such entertainment, it seems, was the custom at this port. Whenever a ship put in, local merchants had first to wine and dine the visitors before entering into trade parleys with them.

Ma set forth a cloisonne platter, clasped his hands in obeisance, and said, "Be so kind as to display your lists of merchandise, so that the seating may be arranged."

Here, I should explain to my listeners that the Persians lay great store by profit, and it is a long-established practice among them that traders whose lists contain special merchandise worth ten thousand taels or more should be seated at the principal tables. The remaining guests are placed in order of the value of their wares, regardless of age or status.

Since the traders from the ship all knew the approximate worth of each of their company, they seated themselves accordingly. Wen alone was left standing, as he knew not what to do. Their host remarked, "I've never had the pleasure of meeting this guest. Perhaps he is new to the overseas trade and has little merchandise to offer?" Wen's companions replied, "This is Master Wen, a good friend of ours who sailed with us for the pleasure of the trip. Although he has some silver, he was unwilling to purchase any merchandise. Regretfully, he will have to make do with the lowest place." Greatly embarrassed, Wen proceeded to the designated place, while his host seated himself at the top of the hall.

As the merchants drank, they vaunted their wares, one enumerating his opals and another describing the emeralds he had acquired. Wen, perforce, held his tongue and felt some regret. "I should, perhaps, have taken their advice after all and obtained some merchandise. Though I possess a fair amount of silver now, I have nothing to say here." Then he consoled himself with the thought that he had little call to be discontent, since he had possessed no capital to begin with but had succeeded in advancing his fortunes.

With such thoughts in mind, however, Wen was in no mood to indulge in any drinking. His companions, on the other hand, played drinking games and consumed vast amounts of their host's wine. Ma, being an old hand, observed Wen's discomfort. Yet it was not for him to broach the subject, so he merely urged Wen to empty a few cups of wine and left it at that. The visitors eventually rose, saying, "The hour is getting late and we must return to the ship. Let us discuss the merchandise tomorrow." With these words they took leave of their host.

Ma had the remnants of the banquet cleared away and then retired for the night. Rising early the next morning, he walked to the waterfront to greet his guests. The first thing that caught his attention as he boarded the ship was the enormous turtle carapace in the hold. Astonished, he inquired, "To whom does this treasure belong? I did not hear any mention of it yesterday. Is it for sale?" The merchants smiled and pointed at Wen, "This treasure belongs to our friend Master Wen." And one added, "And a difficult thing to sell it will be."

Ma glanced at Wen, and his face became flushed with embarrassment and annoyance. "I have known all of you for many years," he protested. "So why have you made a fool of me? Why have you caused me to insult my new client by according him the lowest place at my table?" Seizing Wen by the arm, he continued, "Our parleys must be deferred while I go home and make amends for my behavior." All were mystified and intrigued by this turn of events. Some who were better acquainted with Wen, or merely curious, followed Ma and Wen to find out what was going on.

They saw Ma take Wen by the hand and lead him to the seat of honor in his house. Disregarding the small group of people who had followed them in, Ma said, "I have deeply insulted you and pray you to be seated here for a while." Much bemused, Wen reflected, "I can hardly believe that the carapace is a treasure. Am I perchance about to have some more good fortune?"

Ma left his guests briefly, then reappeared and bowed them into the banquet hall. Several tables had been laid anew, and the first table was even more lavishly laden than on the previous day. Ma raised his wine cup and, bowing with folded hands toward Wen, announced to the assemblage, "This gentleman deserves to be seated at the first table, for his single treasure is worth more than your entire cargo of merchandise. I was exceedingly discourteous to him yesterday." All present heard these words with amusement, astonishment and incredulity, but they lost no time seating themselves.

After three rounds of toasts had been drunk, Ma came to the subject, "May I inquire whether you intend to sell your treasure?" Wen, who was not lacking in shrewdness, replied at once, "Why not, if I am offered a good price?" At this, Ma's countenance beamed with smiles. He stood up to say, "Then please name your price. I shall pay whatever you ask for, without haggling."

Wen, however, had not the least idea what the carapace was worth. Demanding too little would only expose his ignorance, but should he ask for too much he would run the risk of turning himself into a laughingstock. He pondered till his face became red, yet still could not come up with a price.

At this juncture, Zhang the First caught Wen's eye. Placing one hand behind his chair, he extended three fingers, executed a slashing motion with his forefinger, and then asked, "What say you to this figure?" Wen shook his head, thrust forward one finger and answered, "I dare not even name this amount." Their host had observed their exchange and inquired, "How much will it be?" Guilefully, Zhang replied, "Master Wen has indicated that he would demand as much as ten thousand taels."

Their host smiled, "Then I take it you do not intend to sell and are merely humoring me. A treasure such as that would never go for the paltry price you have just mentioned." All present were flabbergasted. Some stood up and drew Wen aside. "A stroke of fortune!" they exclaimed. "That carapace must be worth a great deal! But to be frank with you, we know not what price to set on it. We suggest you start high and let him bargain the price down."

But Wen was too abashed to do so and hesitated again and again. His companions urged, "You should be more worldly-minded."

Their host asked once more for a price, saying, "I can see no harm in your telling it to me." Wen thereupon quoted the figure of fifty thousand taels, but Ma only shook his head and remonstrated, "That is not possible!"

He then led Zhang the First aside to confer with him in private. "You are an old hand at trading overseas and enjoy the reputation of knowing the value of things. How is it that you refuse to put a price on this object? The only explanation is that you do not intend to part with it and are simply making sport of my humble establishment." To which Zhang the First replied, "If the truth be told, my good friend Wen came with us only to see something of the world and entertained no intention of purchasing any merchandise. The object in question was discovered by chance on a deserted island where we sought shelter from a storm. It was not purchased. Hence he has no knowledge of its value. He would be well content if you should give him the fifty thousand he has requested, for such a sum would suffice to provide him for the rest of his life."

Ma said, "In that case, you shall fill the role of principal middleman, and will be thanked appropriately. But on no account must you renege on the deal."

Ma ordered a clerk to bring writing utensils—brush, ink stick, ink slab, and paper. He then folded a sheet of fine paper manufactured of cotton fiber and tendered it to Zhang the First with the request, "Be so kind as to produce a contract, so that we may proceed with the transaction." Zhang the First pointed to one of his companions and said, "Master Zhu is better suited to this task than

I am." Whereupon Zhu ground a fine slab of ink, laid out the paper, and wrote as follows:

Contract Witnessed by Zhang the First et al.

Whereas Merchant Wen Shi of Suzhou has acquired in foreign lands the Carapace of a Large Turtle, and whereas he is willing to cede the said Carapace to the trading house of Ma Baoha the Persian for the sum of fifty thousand taels of silver, the merchandise and the monies specified above shall be exchanged by the parties concerned upon the conclusion of the present Contract. The terms of this Contract are irrevocable, and should either party renege on them, he shall be penalized to the amount of twice the aforementioned sum. This Contract is binding and final.

The contract was made out in two copies and the date inscribed at the end. Zhang the First and ten or more of the guests were listed as witnesses. Then the two copies were placed side by side and the title characters "Contract Agreement" written on the juncture of the two sheets of paper, so that half of each character appeared on both copies of the contract, after the date on the first copy. The names of Wen Shi, as seller, and Ma Baoha, as buyer, were inscribed under the title characters, and both men affixed their seals thereto. Then the witnesses signed their names, starting with the last man on the list. When Zhang's turn came, he jested, "The witness fee had better be a good one!" Ma smiled and replied, "To be sure! To be sure!"

When all this had been done, Ma retired to his chambers and soon returned with a large chest. "Let me first disburse the fees," he said, "after which I wish to say something."

The guests crowded around as Ma raised the lid of the chest. It contained one thousand taels of silver, separated into twenty packets of fifty taels each. Ma proffered these to Zhang the First with both hands, saying, "As the eldest in your company, please verify and distribute these monies among your fellows."

The truth was that despite the banquet, the contract and the general commotion, all the guests had remained somewhat skeptical, and it was only when they set eyes on the glittering silver that they became fully convinced of the reality of the transaction.

Stupefied and speechless, Wen looked on as though he were drunk or in a dream. Zhang the First tugged at his sleeve and said "It is for you, my friend, to decide how the silver should be shared." Only then did Wen manage to utter the words, "Let us attend to that after the principal transaction is concluded."

Ma smiled and addressed Wen. "There is something I would discuss with you. The entire payment, in silver, rests in packages on shelves in my chambers. These have been previously checked and are of correct weight. I suggest that you and two of your friends go in to examine and weigh one of the packages at random. You need not do so with each and every package." He then added, "That is a goodly amount of silver, and moving it will require more than a little time. How will you load it onto the ship all by yourself? Moreover, you have a sea journey ahead of you, and there will be many inconveniences."

Wen, after giving these words some thought, said, "Your concerns are most reasonable, so what do you suggest I do?"

His host replied, "In my humble opinion, this is not the time for Master Wen to return to Suzhou. I have here a silk and brocade shop in which I have invested three thousand taels of silver. The shop and its annexes consist of approximately one hundred rooms and comprise several halls and storied buildings. My humble suggestion is that you take the shop and its merchandise plus the attached properties in lieu of five thousand taels. This would become your property, and you could reside here and engage in commerce. The silver could then be transferred to you by consignments and in an inconspicuous manner. Later, if Master Wen should wish to return to your native town, you could travel unencumbered, leaving your property in the hands of a trustworthy manager. Should you not find this acceptable, I could transfer the silver to you forthwith, which would pose no difficulty for my humble establishment, but might cause you problems of both transportation and storage."

Both Wen and Zhang stamped their feet in approbation, saying, "You are clearly a man of much experience, since everything you have said is most reasonable."

Wen continued, "I have no family of my own, and have exhausted my holdings in Suzhou. I would have no place to go even if I were to take all the silver there. Thus I see no reason not to set up residence here, as Master Ma has suggested. Heaven destined me to discover the carapace and to make Master Ma's acquaintance, and I should continue now to pursue that destiny. Little do I care whether or not the shop and the properties are worth five thousand taels of silver, for all of these are a gift of providence." To his host, he announced, "Your advice seems to me most sound, and I shall accept it in every detail."

Ma then invited Wen to go with him to the pavilion in which the silver was stored. Turning to Zhang the First and Master Zhu, he said, "Come with us. The other guests need not accompany us, and I pray them to sit here until we are finished." That said, the four left the hall.

Those of the guests who remained in the hall stretched their necks and chatted among themselves. Some said, "A marvelous thing indeed! Such good fortune! Had I known this would happen, I too would have gone on the island. There may have been other objects of value there." Others differed, "That was sheer luck, entirely fortuitous. One does not meet with such luck by design."

As they gave vent in this manner to their admiration and envy, Wen reappeared with Zhang the First and Master Zhu. Asked what they had seen there, Zhang replied, "The inner pavilion is in reality a large repository for silver, all of which has been stored in coffers. We marked out ten large coffers containing four thousand taels each and five smaller ones of a thousand taels each, the total contents of which come to forty-five thousand taels. These coffers are now secured with strips of paper bearing Wen's seal and will become his property once he delivers the merchandise."

Ma now emerged and announced, "The titles for the property and the shop's inventory are ready. Now that the fifty thousand taels is all accounted for. Let us now betake ourselves to the ship for the merchandise."

On the way, Wen cautioned his companions, "There are many people on the ship. Hold your tongues regarding this transaction, and I shall reward you for your discretion." His companions nodded understandingly, for they were concerned that their colleagues on the ship might demand a share of the fees if they learned what had transpired. Wen went on board and removed his personal effects from the carapace. As he did so, he stroked the carapace and murmured, "What rare good fortune!"

Ma then directed two young clerks to carry the carapace back to his house. "Be most careful," he admonished. "Do not leave it outside."

The merchants who had remained on the ship remarked to Wen, "So you have disposed of this unsalable object after all. How much were you paid for it?" Offering no explanation, Wen took his bags and left the ship. Those who had accompanied him previously also went ashore. They closely examined the carapace inside and out, and having done so, looked at one another and asked, "What is so exceptional about it?"

Ma now invited the witnesses to the contract to return with him, saying, "Let us go together with Master Wen to inspect his future residence and the silk shop."

The party proceeded to a large building on one of the busiest streets. The front part of the building was a store. To one side, an alley turned into a pair of stone gates opening onto a spacious courtyard, inside of which stood a large hall adorned with a wooden tablet that bore the inscription "Hall of Incipient Wealth." Wings on both sides of the hall were installed with cupboards along three sides, all of them filled with silks, satins, and brocades. Behind these buildings were more courtyards and chambers.

Wen reflected, "Even princes and dukes possess no better residences than this. And there is in addition the silk shop, from which I can derive much profit. I may as well become a merchant here and think no more about returning to my hometown." To his host, he observed, "This is indeed a good place, but I am single and would require servants to look after my needs." Ma replied, "That poses no difficulty. I shall see to the matter."

Highly pleased, Wen went back to Ma's house with his companions. Having instructed that tea be served, Ma advised Wen, "You need not return to the ship tonight, for you can stay at your silk shop. As for servants, there are already a few at the shop, and you may hire more in time."

In the meantime, many of Wen's companions wished to satisfy their curiosity. One commented, "The transaction is concluded and nothing more needs to be said about it. But one thing puzzles us: What is so fine about that carapace, that it should command such a price? We wish to be enlightened." Wen heartily agreed to this request.

Ma smiled, "You have sailed the seas so often, I thought you would have known what it is. Have you not heard that dragons beget nine kinds of offspring? One kind is called the turtle dragon, and its skin can be made into drums, the sound of which can be heard at a distance of a hundred *li*. When the turtle dragon attains ten thousand years of age, it sheds its carapace and turns into a true dragon. The carapace contains twenty-four ribs, which correspond to the twenty-four periods of Heaven, and in each rib rests a single large pearl. The turtle dragon does not turn into a proper dragon if it fails to shed it carapace after attaining full maturity. Some have been captured, but these can only be used to make drums, for the ribs of their carapaces are empty. Only when all twenty-four ribs are fully grown and filled each with a pearl does the turtle dragon shed its carapace to become a real dragon. The carapace you discovered was of such size because it was naturally shed by a mature turtle dragon having a pearl in each rib. We have been aware that such a thing existed, but knew not when such carapaces are shed and where to find them. The carapaces themselves have little value, but the luminescent pearls in them are invaluable. This is indeed a windfall, one which I had never anticipated!"

Because his listeners still appeared somewhat doubtful, Ma went inside the house and came back after a while with a satchel sewn together of cotton cloth from the Occident. He smiled and said, "Please observe." He opened the satchel to reveal a wad of cotton wrapped around a pearl measuring more than an inch across. Ma set the pearl on a black lacquered platter and carried the platter to a dark corner. The pearl rolled restlessly here and there, casting a circle of light a foot wide.

Dumbfounded, the guests stared with their mouths agape. The host turn around and thanked them for their assistance in consummating the transaction. "In my country," he informed them, "this single pearl will fetch a price equal to all the monies I have just disbursed. The rest is your gift to me." The guests were taken aback, but there was no way now they could retract their given word.

Ma observed their vexation. He wrapped up the pearl and hastily returned with it to the back of the house. A chest filled with silk was brought out and Ma presented all his guests, with the exception of Wen, with two bolts of silk each, saying: "This small token of my appreciation for your efforts will allow you to make a pair of robes for yourselves." Then, drawing a dozen strands of fine pearls from his wide sleeves, he handed one strand to each of his guests with the words, "This paltry object will keep you in tea for the journey." To Wen he gave eight bolts of silk and four strands of larger pearls. "Use these, for the time being, to make a few robes," he said. Wen and his shipmates warmly thanked him.

The host and guests then accompanied Wen to the silk shop, where Ma introduced the clerks to the new proprietor. That done, Ma took his leave, declaring, "I must return to my humble house once more." And before long, dozens of porters with carrying poles arrived, bearing the ten large and five smaller coffers Wen had sealed. Wen directed the porters to take these to a secluded bedchamber in the inner recesses of the building.

Then Wen said to his shipmates, "It is thanks to your help that I now have this unexpected wealth." So speaking, he opened his bags and gave to each of those present ten of the silver coins he had gained by selling the tangerines. Zhang the First and those who had put together Wen's first tael of silver each received ten extra coins. These coins were now of little consequence to Wen, but sufficed nevertheless to make his friends quite happy, and they were most grateful. Wen then brought out more coins, which he entrusted to Zhang the First, saying, "Please see to it that these are distributed among our colleagues on the ship, so that each has one coin for tea on the journey. Tell them I shall reside in Fujian until I am familiar with the business, then I shall return to Suzhou for a visit. Thus I shall not travel with you, and must bid you farewell here."

Zhang the First reminded him, "The one thousand taels in contract fees still remain to be divided. How should we proceed with this matter? It is best that you decide how it should be apportioned, for that would keep people's tongues from wagging." Wen exclaimed, "I had forgotten about that!"

After some deliberation, it was decided that one hundred taels should be subtracted from the total for distribution among the people on the ship. The remaining nine hundred taels was divided into shares according to the number of those present, with two shares to spare. Each man received one share, while the extra shares went to their leader, Zhang the First, and to Master Zhu, who had drawn up the contract. All were most content with this arrangement.

One man, however, made the remark, "It irks me that this Muslim has made away with so much. Master Wen should drop a few remarks around and seek some restitution." But Wen replied, "I have no reason to be dissatisfied. For me, a luckless man who had lost money on every venture he ever embarked on, this is an unexpected blessing, and I am now wealthy beyond my wildest expectations. It is clear that a man's destiny is preordained and should be taken as it comes. Were it not for Master Ma's discerning eye, I would still be laboring under the misconception that the carapace is something of no value. And it is only because he saw fit to enlighten us that we now know its true worth. I would be going against my conscience if I were to take issue over the matter with him now." Whereupon the other conceded, "Well spoken, Master Wen. You are an honest and sincere man and rightly deserve the riches you have come by."

Then, with many expressions of gratitude, Wen's colleagues assembled the money and valuables they had acquired and returned to the ship to tend to their own merchandise.

Thereafter, Wen Chi became a rich merchant in central Fujian. He took a wife and set up a household. A few years later, he traveled to Suzhou to visit some of his old acquaintances, but soon returned to Fujian. His progeny have since multiplied, and his house is enjoying ever greater prosperity.

The Abbot and the Widow

西山觀設籙渡亡魂
開封府備棺追活命

There was once in the city of Kaifeng in Henan, in the days of the Song dynasty, a woman named Mistress Wu, who at the age of fifteen married a local man surnamed Liu. She gave birth to a son, who was named Liu Dasheng. When Liu Dasheng reached the age of twelve, his father fell ill and died. Thus his mother, Mistress Wu, a clever and comely woman, became a widow before she was thirty years of age, and there being no in-laws or other clansmen in the city, she had charge of the household and provided for herself and her son. She did not forget the kindness shown to her by her departed husband, however, so she decided to offer sacrifices to save her husband's soul from suffering in the next world.

There was a temple nearby called Western Hills, where Daoist priests sought the truths of life. In this temple was a handsome Daoist priest called Huang Miaoxiu who was so well versed in the Daoist canon that he had been appointed abbot of the temple. One day, as he was engaged in religious rituals with his colleagues, he observed a young woman enter the temple garbed in white mourning clothes and leading a young boy by the hand. As is often said, "Dress in mourning to look more charming." Endowed with much grace by nature, the woman only appeared the more attractive for her white robe and the white mourning band coiled in her hair.

She approached Abbot Huang and, with hands folded before her face, made obeisances to him. The Abbot, quite dazzled by her beauty, made haste to return her obeisances and inquired, "Who are you, and what brings you here?" The woman replied, "I am Mistress Wu of the Liu family. My husband passed away recently, and I wish to have rites conducted for him. Hence I have come with his son to ask you to exert your wondrous powers, that my husband may have safe passage through the nether world."

Abbot Huang, moved by considerations that can hardly be termed innocent, said, "Since your husband died recently, I would think you still have a shrine for him in your house. The rites must be conducted in that shrine if the desired results are to be achieved. Little will be gained by conducting a perfunctory service here in the temple. So what is your wish?" Mistress Wu replied, "Both my son and I would be most grateful if Your Eminence could come to our humble abode. I shall go home and put the shrine in order and await your arrival."

The abbot inquired, "When should I go to your house?" Mistress Wu replied, "Eight days hence will be the hundredth day of my husband's passing away. We should start tomorrow if the rites, which last seven days, are to completed in good time. The sooner Your Eminence comes, the better." The Abbot then said, "In that case no time should be wasted. I shall go to your house

25

tomorrow." Mistress Wu withdrew a tael of silver from her sleeve and gave it to the Abbot to purchase paper and wooden slips on which to write incantations. Then she went home to put things in order and prepare for the coming ceremony.

Mistress Wu was, at first, quite earnest in her desire to conduct rites for her husband and harbored no unseemly intentions. Little did she suspect Abbot Huang of being a lecherous fiend who had wanted nothing more than to possess her the moment he laid eyes on her. On the other hand, although Mistress Wu was innocent of any evil thoughts, she had admired the Abbot's rare good looks and hearty manner of speech, thinking, "How is it that such an attractive man should become a priest! His lack of affectation pleases me. And his willingness to come to my house the moment I asked him to do so shows he is a warm-hearted person as well."

The next morning, Abbot Huang, together with two young acolytes and an artisan priest, arrived at Mistress Wu's house. Because her son was still too young, Mistress Wu had to attend to all matters, so she received the visitors and led them to the hall where the shrine was erected. The Abbot and his company at once busied themselves hanging up images of the Daoist deities and laying out their religious paraphernalia, after which they performed rites to solicit the indulgence of the gods. Mistress Wu, too, joined in the burning of incense. The abbot took note of this and became increasingly flirtatious in his behavior.

When the abbot and the acolytes had chanted passages from the scriptures, he knelt before the images of the gods to offer prayers, calling on Mistress Wu to kneel beside him. She did so, and the distance between them was no more than a few inches. Attracted by the fragrance of incense that emanated from the abbot's clothing, Mistress Wu ventured a peek at him. The abbot sensed her action and cast back a sidelong glance. Thereafter they exchanged looks with such frequency one might well have thought they would fall into one another's arms right then and there.

After the prayers, both rose to their feet and Mistress Wu went to kowtow before each image, all the while looking surreptitiously around her. She observed the two young acolytes with their long black hair falling to their shoulders, their rosy lips and white teeth, and their clear and tender complexions, and she thought to herself, "How handsome these young priests will become when they are grown men!" Desire stirred within her and, in spite of herself, she stole glances at them from behind the curtains in the hall.

A circumstance most to be feared in life is an infatuation. Once a person is smitten, little matters whether the object of the infatuation is tall, short, fat or thin; any attribute becomes admirable and desirable. Moreover, as women are in general quite single-minded in their amours, they find it well-nigh impossible to put a man out of their heart once they become enamored of him. Being young and newly widowed and sensually in her prime, Mistress Wu paled and flushed by turns. She loitered behind the curtains, showing now half of her face, now portions of her person as though to communicate her feelings to the abbot. The latter was, of course, quite aware of her performance, since it fitted well with his own intentions. But he could hardly act on them at once, this being the first day of his arrival. So he limited his advances to sending veiled messages from the corners of his eyes.

Liu Dasheng, meanwhile, was entirely unaware of this by-play. He peered at the pictures of the gods and played with the abbot's bells and drums, suspecting nothing of his mother's wanton behavior.

When the lanterns had been lighted and everyone had dined, Mistress Wu prepared a wing room for the abbot and his companions. Abbot Huang sent the artisan priest back to the temple and then lay down to sleep, occupying the same bed as the acolytes.

Mistress Wu went back to her room with her son. She took to her bed, reflecting, "While I lie here alone, the abbot must now be disporting himself with those two pretty young boys." The more she thought of it, the more unbearably the fires burned in her loins. Shuddering and perspiring, she clenched her teeth until they made grinding noises.

As she dozed off, she suddenly heard footsteps by her bed and raised her head, only to see a man draw aside the canopy and slip lithely under the covers. Then she heard the abbot's voice saying, "I thank you for the messages your eyes conveyed to me. I could not but notice them. Now that the hour is late and all are asleep, I hope we may do the good thing together." As he spoke, he thrust out his jade stalk which was like a large cucumber. Mistress Wu did not protest and gladly drew it in.

Just as the two were enjoying themselves most heartily, one of the acolytes came in search of the abbot. He swept aside the canopy, and when he saw his master fully engaged he cried out, "Woman! You would seduce a man who has taken the vows? How could you do such a thing! However, if you let me have a go at you, I shall keep quiet about this!" So saying, he extended his hands and fumbled at Mistress Wu's waist. The abbot snapped, "I am here, so mind your manners!" Frightened, Mistress Wu, who had been brought close to consummation by the abbot's pleasurable ministrations, woke up with a start— and realized that all that had transpired was just a dream! She felt between her thighs and found them both to be wet with *yin* waters that had flowed even onto the mat of her bed. Wiping these up with a kerchief, she sighed and exclaimed,

"What a dream! If only I were so fortunate!" Some time passed before she fell into a restless sleep.

The next morning, she woke up to the sound of bells and drums and told the maidservant to carry water to the Abbot and tend to his needs. Meanwhile the acolytes, taking advantage of their youth, came to ask for food and drink. Mistress Wu called one of them to her side and asked his name. The acolyte responded, "My name is Taiqing." Mistress Wu continued, "And that of your older companion?" The acolyte replied, "His name is Taisu." Mistress Wu then inquired, "Did you sleep last night with your head on your Master's pillow?" The acolyte countered, "What difference would it make if I did?" To which Mistress Wu replied, "Your Master might do naughty things." The acolyte chuckled, "Mistress Wu must be joking!"

The acolyte left the room, and later, in private, told the Abbot about his conversation with Mistress Wu. His words set Abbot Huang's heart to throbbing. "She must surely be craving a liaison to be saying such things!" he thought. "We are divided by the rules of propriety, yet we stood but a few inches apart at the shrine. What can I do to further provoke her?" Then he had an idea.

After a while, Mistress Wu came to the shrine to light some incense. Abbot Huang hastened to position himself next to her and chanted the following ode:

> *Bowing to the highest heavens,*
> *You joined with him as man and woman.*
> *You were as a blooming flower.*
>
> *But now your bed is bleak and chill,*
> *And lonely is your single pillow.*
> *Alone you bear the endless torture.*
>
> *With pious heart you built a shrine,*
> *Saying prayers for his summoned spirit,*
> *To speed it through the nether world.*
>
> *Now join me by the sacred bridge,*
> *And let us slake our thirst together,*
> *Sharing like the gods our pleasure.*

Mistress Wu knew now that the abbot desired her. She repaired to her room where she peeled a bowlful of succulent fruit and made a pot of green tea. These she told the maidservant to take to the abbot, and instructed her to say, "My mistress wishes to slake your thirst."

The abbot was overjoyed by this explicit message and instructed his acolytes to spy out Mistress Wu's sleeping arrangements. He was sorely disappointed when he learned that she shared a room with her son and the maidservant, for he knew he could not break in on her under such circumstances.

As he lay in bed with his acolytes the same evening, his mind went back to Mistress Wu's behavior that day, and he vented his inflamed passions on acolyte Taiqing, causing the bed to creak from his exertions. With his arms wrapped around the boy's waist, he said, "My boy, I seek your advice. I have noticed that our hostess has taken a fancy to me, and if I succeed in possessing her, both you and Taisu are likely to benefit from her sweetness. But there is no place we can meet, since she sleeps with her son and maidservant. Nor is it convenient here with the two of you in this room. What should I do?" Taiqing replied, "We will be no hindrance to you." But the abbot disagreed, "This is her first affair, and she will wish to avoid the eyes of strangers." Taisu then proposed, "In the shrine there is a spirit bed with fresh and clean bedclothes. What better place could you want for a tryst?" To which the abbot exclaimed, "How right you are, my boy! Now I know what I will do tomorrow!" He then whispered instructions into the ears of the acolytes who clapped their hands in glee. By this time the abbot had done his business with Taiqing, and the boys, whose senses had been aroused, applied the five-finger funnel before dropping off to sleep.

When morning came, the abbot said to Mistress Wu, "Today is the third day of the ceremonies. I am able to cast a magic spell that may bring back your late husband's spirit for an encounter with you. Would that please you?" Mistress Wu replied, "That would be most wonderful! But how does Your Eminence propose to do such a thing? " The abbot explained, "White silk will be drawn across the hall like a bridge and I shall invoke the spirit, which will cross this bridge to meet you. But only one kinsman of the deceased may be present. More people will only strengthen the forces of *yang* which will prevent the spirit from appearing. And the door of the shrine hall should be kept shut so that no person may peer in and see the secret rites." Mistress Wu observed, "My husband has only two survivors, myself and the boy. And since the boy is too young and artless, he has nothing to say to his father. I, however, must meet my husband, and so I alone will be in the shrine with Your Eminence." The abbot nodded in approval, "That is best!"

Mistress Wu then returned to her room where she took a bolt of white silk from her chest. This she gave to the abbot, who took one end of the silk and asked Mistress Wu to hold the other end. He then took its measure, pulling the silk this way and that, and all the while casting tender glances at Mistress Wu. She said nothing, even when their hands crossed and he stroked her wrist with his fingers. The abbot then placed some tables in the form of a bridge, which in effect blocked the doorway and prevented any person outside from looking in.

The abbot then went out and instructed the acolytes, "I shall close the door to the shrine and call up the spirit of the deceased. You two will stand guard here. See to it that no one attempts to look in, for that will disrupt my magic." The boys assented and exchanged knowing looks. In the meantime, Mistress Wu spoke to her son and the maidservant. "The abbot will invoke the spirit of the deceased and requires that you remain silent. You shall stay in this chamber. Do not come out or make any noise." Hearing that his father's spirit would be called up, Dasheng cried, "I, too, wish to see my father!" Mistress Wu replied, "My son, the abbot said the power of *yang* will be too great if others are present, and the spirit may fail to appear. Hence, I alone will keep vigil. And if your father's spirit does indeed appear, I will allow you to see him the next time he comes." She prepared some sweetmeats for him, then locked him in her bedchamber together with the maidservant, after which she hurried to the shrine.

The abbot shut the doors and, picking up his tablets, proceeded to mumble incomprehensible words. He then turned to Mistress Wu and addressed her with a smirk. "Please sit down on the spirit bed. I must, however, forewarn you. Though I can summon up your husband's spirit, it will only be like a shadow in a dream and can serve you no good purpose." Mistress Wu replied, "I only wish to meet his spirit to tell him of my suffering. What do you mean, when you say he can serve me no good purpose?" The abbot elucidated, "I mean that you may speak with him, but will not be able to relive with him the delights of the connubial bed." Mistress Wu retorted, "There you go again! I ask no more than to see his spirit. So where does such talk come in?" But the abbot continued, "I also have the power to bring him back in such a way that you may enjoy each other once again." Mistress Wu asked in astonishment, "How is that possible?" The abbot explained, "His spirit may enter my body, and through me share his pleasures with you."

Mistress Wu said unbelievingly, "A spirit is a spirit, and an abbot is an abbot. How can one take the place of the other?" The abbot continued, "This is one of the magical powers invested in us Daoists, and many a spirit has entered our bodies to meet the living." Mistress Wu remonstrated, "But it is hardly proper to do what you propose!" To which Abbot Huang replied, "If I should be the least bit different from your husband, you may take me to task!"

Whereupon Mistress Wu chided him, saying, "What a honeyed tongue you have, you scoundrel!"

The abbot took her by the arm and led her to the bed, laughing, "Now just imagine that I am your husband!" By this time, Mistress Wu's passions were fully awakened, and the two rolled onto the bed.

When they had finished, both felt truly gratified. The abbot asked Mistress Wu, "Is my performance in any way inferior to that of your husband?" But she spat back at him, "You scoundrelly priest! Why do you embarrass me with such questions?" The abbot quickly changed his tack, saying, "I am truly beholden to you for honoring me with your favors." To which Mistress Wu replied, "Now that you have beguiled me, I only hope that our liaison will be a lasting one."

The abbot pondered a moment, then said, "The only way we will be able to meet one another without arousing suspicion is by claiming that we are relatives." Mistress Wu agreed, whereupon the abbot asked, "How old are you, my good woman?" Mistress Wu replied, "Twenty-six." The abbot said, "Then I am a year older than you. Ergo, I shall be your elder cousin. I know now what to do!"

He crawled out of the bed and, clapping his tablets together as though concluding a ceremony, opened the door. To the acolytes standing outside, he announced, "I have just summoned the spirit of the dead, and it would seem that our hostess, unbeknown to either of us, is actually my cousin. Or so the spirit has informed us. Hence, Mistress Wu and I are intimate kin." The acolytes sniggered and remarked, "Quite intimate, indeed!" In the meantime, Mistress Wu let her son out of her bedchamber and repeated to him what the abbot had said. "Your father has told us this," she declared, "so come and say 'Uncle' to the abbot." Dasheng, being young and innocent, did as his mother instructed him to do.

Thereafter, Mistress Wu and the priest came to the shrine every night, supposedly to call up the spirit of the deceased, and the spirit bed served them as the scene of their revels. Believing that the spirit of his father was being invoked, Dasheng insisted upon attending. But his mother dissuaded him, saying, "You are a *yang* person and may not see him." Dasheng had, perforce, to desist, but a suspicion was born in his mind and he thought, "Why should I alone be kept away?"

On the seventh day of the rites, the hundred days of mourning came to an end. Mistress Wu thanked the abbot and his acolytes and set about dismantling the shrine. The abbot, after setting a time for their next tryst, repaired with his acolytes to the temple, while Mistress Wu sent her son back to school.

In the days and weeks that followed, the young acolytes often came to deliver messages, and at night, after Dasheng had fallen asleep, Mistress Wu would open the front gate for the abbot. Only the maidservant knew of these assignations, and she was bribed and sworn to secrecy. Three years passed in this manner without incident.

In the meantime, as Liu Dasheng grew older, his mind gradually opened to matters of love and sex, and he began to understand what these goings-on meant. Being an intelligent and sensitive boy, Dasheng was greatly disturbed by his mother's escapades, though he could never bring himself to mention them. One day at school, however, a fellow student maliciously addressed him as "little Daoist priest." Dasheng flushed hotly in mortification, and when he went home he said to his mother, "I must speak of something with you, Mother. Do not let uncle come here any more. Someone has ridiculed me by calling me 'the little Daoist priest'."

Two spots of red spread from behind Mistress Wu's ears and suffused her cheeks. She rapped her son on the forehead and said: "Ignorant child! Uncle is your mother's elder brother. What business is it of anyone else that he visits me?" Dasheng protested, "The year before last, before the rites for my father, no one ever told me I had an uncle. And if indeed he were my uncle, and you behaved with him as sister and brother, why should tongues be wagging?"

Unable to refute the boy's logic, Mistress Wu flew into a fury, crying, "I have toiled to bring you up, and now, when you hear people slander me, you fling their words in my face. I have no need for such an ingrate!" She struck the tables and chairs and then broke into loud wails. Alarmed, Dasheng fell on his knees and muttered, "I was wrong, Mother. Forgive me!" After a while, seeing that Dasheng was seeking her pardon, Mistress Wu dried her tears and said, "From now on you shall pay no more attention to such rumors!"

Dasheng heard this in silence, not daring to reply. But he thought to himself, "My mother is not speaking the truth. Perhaps the only way to stop this affair is to catch them red-handed. From now on I shall keep my eyes open to her behavior."

One night as Dasheng was sleeping in his mother's bedchamber, he was awakened by the sound of someone going out of the door. His suspicions aroused, he quietly threw on some clothes and got out of bed to look around. The door of the bedchamber was open and he surmised that his mother had again gone out to engage in her nefarious pursuits. Turning around, he passed his hands over her bed and ascertained that she was not there. Instead of going out to search for her, however, he shut the door, bolted it, then pushed a table against it and went back to bed.

Mistress Wu had, of course, gone out to meet Abbot Huang. The shrine in the main hall was no longer in existence, but the bed had been retained especially for these trysts and was closely screened from prying eyes. The abbot had already installed himself on the bed before Mistress Wu emerged from her bedchamber, and after she arrived the two of them coupled for the remainder of the night. Just before daybreak, Mistress Wu rose and let the abbot out through the main gate, then returned to her bedchamber. She never expected anything untoward to arise, as such wanton behavior had become a habit with her. But this night, when she returned to the door of her bedchamber, she found it shut and could not push it open. Knowing now that her son was aware of what she had been doing, she felt sorely put out; she gnashed her teeth with inexpressible fury as she sat silently by the door and waited for the dawn.

Dasheng rose from his bed and opened the door when it was broad daylight. Seeing his mother there, he feigned surprise and asked, "Mother, why are you sitting at the door?" Unable to reply, Mistress Wu lied, saying, "I heard footsteps out here last night, so I got up to take a look. Why did you shut the door?" Dasheng replied, "I saw the door open, and fearing there might be thieves I closed it and propped the table against it. I thought you were sleeping in your bed and did not know you had gone out. But since you were outside, why didn't you call me to open the door? Why did you sit out here all night?" Mistress Wu remained silent, as she could find nothing to say. But she thought to herself, "I cannot keep this little wretch in my room any longer."

A few days later, Mistress Wu said to Dasheng, "You are reaching manhood and it is unseemly for you to sleep in my bedchamber anymore. The bed in the main hall is ready for use. Henceforth you willl sleep there." With her son out of the way, Mistress Wu intended to have the abbot come to her chamber, where they could fornicate in greater security. Dasheng, however, was not without guile and perceived his mother's intentions. He obeyed his mother's orders, reading books in the study in daytime and sleeping in the main hall at night, but he resolved to keep his eyes and ears open.

The next day, an acolyte came and Mistress Wu sent him back to tell the abbot how her son had locked her out of her bedchamber several nights before. She said, "I have therefore told him to sleep elsewhere. When your master comes tonight, he should enter through the small side gate and come straight to my bedchamber."

The abbot came again that night. As Dasheng lay awake in his bed, he heard some sounds by the side gate. Rising and standing in the shadows of the eaves, he saw the maidservant open the gate and then close it behind the abbot who made straight for his mother's room and shut the door behind him. Dasheng reflected, "Being my mother's son, it would not be proper for me to seize her in the act of fornication. I will merely give them no peace."

After a while, when all became still in his mother's room, he found a thick rope and securely fastened the door. He then thought to himself, "When the abbot finds he cannot open the door, he will certainly jump out the window. I shall give him a malodorous send-off!" He brought a slop bucket and a cracked jar filled with excrement and placed them under the window. This done, he went back to bed.

The abbot woke after his debaucheries when the cock crowed twice. Knowing that it would soon be light, he clothed himself and prepared to depart. But when he pushed the door, it would not open. He then woke up Mistress Wu and the two pushed on the door until it rattled, but to no avail. It had obviously been secured from the outside. Mistress Wu said, "This is most strange! Is this perhaps a prank played by that little brute? Go out through the window, and I shall deal with the matter in the morning. But hurry, for the sky is brightening."

With eyes still bleary with sleep, the abbot opened the window and jumped out. One foot landed with a splash in the bucket, and when he strove to maintain his balance, his other foot ended up in the jar of excrement. As he struggled to withdraw his foot from the bucket, he kicked it over and fell flat on the ground. Urine and excrement covered half of his body and even smothered his mouth, but he dared not call out. Bearing the pain in silence and holding his nose, he hurried to the side gate and made off as fast as his legs could carry him.

Meanwhile, Mistress Wu had been greatly annoyed when the door would not open. But the fracas outside, after the abbot had left by the window, filled her with misgivings. She tried to look out of the window but could see nothing since it was still quite dark. Moreover, her nostrils were assailed by a stench she could not account for. Filled with foreboding, she went back to her bed and lay down to sleep.

Dasheng waited for daylight before going to remove the rope from the door. When he saw the ground strewn with slops and turds and the bucket lying on its side, he was both angry and amused. Quietly, so as not to awaken his mother, he removed the bucket and jar.

Some time later, Mistress Wu rose and again tried the door. To her surprise it opened. Wondering why it had not opened when she and the abbot had tried it earlier, she concluded that they had perhaps been in too much of a hurry. Then she saw under the window a mess of excrement and a trail of footprints leading to the side gate. She called her son to ask him, "What is the reason for all this filth?" Dasheng replied, "I do not know. But these wet footprints would seem to have been made by a man's shoes. Perhaps this person was so anxious to leave he could no longer control his bowels." Mistress Wu flushed and paled by turns. She could find nothing to say, but boiled with wrath. From this moment she began to regard her son as a thorn to be pulled out of her flesh.

Meanwhile, after his misfortunes that night, Abbot Huang stayed in the temple, washing and tending to his no longer fragrant clothing, every item of which was smeared with filth. And because he had bruised his lips during his fall, he stayed away from Mistress Wu's house for several days.

One day, the abbot sent the acolyte Taisu to see how things stood. Mistress Wu said to him, "Your master must be angry, that he does not come any more." Taisu replied, "The truth is he fears your son and intends to stay away for a while." Mistress Wu said, "Dasheng is at school all day, so tell your master I would have him come during the daytime, as I wish to discuss a certain matter with him."

Taisu, being already eighteen years old and well aware of Mistress Wu's nature, now said to her suggestively, "Should my master be unable to come some day, I am fully capable of taking his place." Mistress Wu exclaimed, "You little rascal! Do you wish to seduce me, too? I will inform your master who will whip your backside!" Taisu laughed, saying, "My master would hardly do that, since he uses my backside like he does yours!" Mistress Wu scolded, "Shame on you for saying such things!"

Mistress Wu, however, had long wished to try out this handsome youngster and had only refrained from doing so because of his tender age. But now that he was grown and making flirtatious advances, desire overcame her. She put her arms around him and gave him a kiss. Then she lowered her hand and touched his member, which she found to be mightily erect. She was drawing Taisu toward her bed, when they heard someone call his name. It was Taiqing, whom Abbot Huang had sent when Taisu did not reappear at the temple. Fearing the displeasure of the abbot, Taisu hastily disengaged himself and returned to the temple with Taiqing.

The next day, the abbot did indeed come in the daytime. Mistress Wu shut the gate and had the abbot sit in the main hall, after which she inquired, "Why have I had no news from you after that night? And why is it that you sent your acolyte to me only yesterday?" The abbot replied, "Your son is a most tricky fellow. He is growing up to become a formidable adversary! It is no longer convenient for us to see one another, and it appears that our arrangement is no longer feasible."

Mistress Wu, who had been avidly looking forward to further pleasures with the abbot, and even to snaring his two handsome young acolytes, bridled at the abbot's words. She said heatedly, "I have no parents to constrain me and am only hindered by that little brute! I would be as free as the wind if I could devise a way to do him in. I can no longer put up with him!" The abbot replied doubtfully, "He is your son and you gave birth to him. How could you bring yourself to kill him?" Mistress Wu declared, "He is my son only if he truly cares for my well-being. But he is an obstinate trouble-maker, and I would be better off without him!" The abbot quickly said, "That is a decision you must make for yourself. No one else can urge you to do a thing that you may eventually regret." After a moment's reflection, Mistress Wu said, "I shall try to bear with him for a few more days. In any case, come tomorrow with your mind at ease, and we will enjoy ourselves. We will disregard him even though he may sense that something is happening. I'd like to see what he can do to me!" They spoke thus for a long time, after which the abbot left, promising to return the next day.

The following day, however, Dasheng did not go to school, as his teacher would be away on some personal matter for a few days. He sat before the main hall reading his books, now and then rising to walk back and forth. When he saw Taiqing come through the gate, he placed himself before the acolyte, barring his way, and inquired, "What brings you here today?" The acolyte replied, "I wish to see Mistress Wu." Dasheng said, "If you bring a message, I shall transmit it for you." However, Mistress Wu, who was in her room, heard their voices and recognized Taiqing's. She quickly ordered the maidservant to call him in. Dasheng also came in and made no move to depart. Not daring to say anything of a private nature in Dasheng's presence, Taiqing mumbled, "My master hopes that all is well with Mistress Wu and Master Dasheng." Dasheng at once replied, "We are all well, and he need not concern himself. You may go now." Having no other choice, Taiqing exchanged glances with Mistress Wu and left with obvious reluctance. During the next two weeks, Mistress Wu's hatred for her son grew more venomous as no more word was heard from the abbot.

One day, a schoolmate came to tell Dasheng that their teacher had returned. Dasheng took leave of his mother and went to school. Mistress Wu, feeling as though she had been given a heavenly reprieve, was preparing a message for the abbot when Taiqing came in.

It so happened that the two acolytes had been taking turns watching her house, not only to keep the abbot abreast of matters, but also in the hope of making some hay of their own. Thus, Mistress Wu had Taiqing tell his master to visit her that very night. He should come somewhat later than usual, and through the front gate, where Dasheng would least expect him to enter. Mistress Wu's previous discomfitures at the hands of Dasheng should have taught her greater circumspection but, driven by lust, she forgot all caution. And so the appointment was made.

Dasheng returned later than usual and supped with his mother. After the meal, Mistress Wu made much ado of lighting lanterns and going with the maidservant to secure the front and back gates. Then she enjoined Dasheng to retire for the night and went back to her own bedchamber. Dasheng, however, had become suspicious. He reflected, "There is likely to be some hanky-panky tonight since I was absent during the day. Why, then, should she close the gates? I shall stay awake and see what happens." He sat up until it was quite dark, then slipped out of his room to look around. He found the back gate fastened with a lock and the side gate securely bolted. He surmised: "He will doubtlessly enter by the main gate." Thereupon he went to the front courtyard and squatted down in the shadows.

Before long, he saw by the light of the stars his mother and the maidservant emerge from their room. Mistress Wu stopped by the main hall to guard against Dasheng, while the maidservant went to the main gate. There she stood listening, until she heard a few taps produced by a fingertip. Making no sound, she unbolted the gate and drew open one side of it to admit a man. When the gate had been closed again, the three stealthily returned to Mistress Wu's bedchamber.

Dasheng sprang from his place of concealment, threw the gates wide open and snatched a gong from its hook beside the gate. Striking it with all his might, he cried at the top of his voice, "Stop thief! Stop thief!"

Kaifeng being far from the capital city and plagued by thieves and robbers, the authorities had decreed that each household should provide itself with a gong, which was to be struck when a thief or robber was discovered. Ten households in the same street were charged with protecting each other and coming to each other's rescue, and in the event of a theft, all ten households were obliged to pay for the loss. Hence, the procedure was rigorously observed.

The abbot had just entered Mistress Wu's bedchamber when the gong began to sound at the gate. In great alarm, he hurried out of the door and made for the back gate. Finding it locked, he turned toward the front gate. Much to his relief, he saw it was open and scuttled from the courtyard, wishing he had another pair of legs to carry him. Dasheng had no intention of apprehending him, since he did not wish to make his mother lose face. So he merely picked up a stone and flung it with might and main at the fugitive, hitting him in the leg. The abbot stumbled and lost a shoe, but, being then of no mind to pick it up, he hobbled away with one foot unshod. By this time neighbors were gathering to inquire what had occurred. Dasheng told them the thief had gotten away, then picked up the shoe and shut the gate.

In the meantime, Mistress Wu, much affrighted by these events, had been cowering in her bedchamber together with the maidservant. When she heard the gate close, however, she surmised that the abbot had already departed and breathed a sigh of relief. Dasheng now entered, announcing, "I have just chased away a thief, mother. Were you greatly alarmed?" Mistress Wu replied, "Where is the thief? I fear there has been much fuss about nothing!" Dasheng produced the shoe, saying, "I failed to catch the thief, but I have his shoe. Mayhap someone will recognize it tomorrow." Knowing that Dasheng had done all this intentionally, Mistress Wu hated him all the more, although there was nothing she could say. The abbot no longer dared to come thereafter; nor did Mistress Wu ask him to do so for fear of her son. But she began to plot ways of getting Dasheng out of the way.

A few days later, when it was time again to commemorate the anniversary of the late husband's death, Mistress Wu had an idea. She said to Dasheng, "Take some joss-paper money and go first to your father's grave to sweep the ground. I shall come later by sedan chair after I have prepared some sacrificial food." Dasheng at once thought, "Why should the commemoration be held at the grave? And why should I go first? This is clearly a trick to divert me while she slips away to the temple." He said to his mother, "I will go and wait for you there." But after leaving the house, he made straight for the Western Hills Temple instead of proceeding to the gravesite.

The sight of Dasheng entering the temple was a nasty shock for Abbot Huang, who had yet to recover from the fright he had received the other night. Collecting his wits with an effort, he inquired, "What brings my good nephew here?" Dasheng answered, "My mother will be coming soon." The abbot heard this with skepticism. He thought to himself, "This is most odd. I have never known mother and son to go out together. And if she is coming, why should the son come first?" Precisely at this moment, however, a sedan chair arrived in the temple and Mistress Wu descended from it.

Mistress Wu gave a start of surprise when she saw Dasheng standing before her, and thought to herself, "What is this little devil doing here?" Aloud, she hastened to explain, "This being the anniversary of your father's passing, I felt we should have a powerful charm written for him. That is the reason I have come to see your uncle." Dasheng said, "I had the very same idea, for I believe there is no need for a ceremony at the grave. That is why I am here." The abbot, on his part, attempted to put on a good face as he served them tea and refreshments. He wrote out a talisman, which he then consecrated and ceremonially consigned to the flames. All this while, he found no opportunity to privately communicate with Mistress Wu. After the ceremony, Mistress Wu told Dasheng to go home ahead of her, but Dasheng refused, saying, "I will follow your sedan." Mistress Wu had no choice but to mount the sedan chair and depart. The farther she was borne away from the temple, the greater grew her hatred for Dasheng, and she made up her mind to rid herself of him once and for all.

On the way back, the bearers trotted along so swiftly that Dasheng was unable to keep up with them. He also felt an urge to relieve himself. Halting, he reflected, "Nothing is likely to happen now, since this road leads only to our home. I need not follow her anymore."

But as fortune would have it, Taisu was soon observed coming down the road. Mistress Wu hastily called to the bearers, "Is the young master following us?" To which the bearers replied, "He has fallen behind and is not within eyesight." Mistress Wu thereupon called the acolyte to the side of the sedan and whispered in his ear, "Tonight I shall find a way to distract that little brute of mine. I must confer with your master upon a matter of the utmost importance." Taisu demurred, "My master is too scared now to enter your house." Mistress Wu said, "If that is the case, then let him wait outside and cast a stone to signal his presence. I shall come to the gate and speak with him, and he shall enter only if the coast is clear. In this way there can be no risk."

Mistress Wu then smiled at Taisu so seductively that the young acolyte's eyes flamed with passion. Were it not for the presence of the bearers, he would have taken her forthwith among the bushes by the roadside. Mistress Wu spoke softly, saying, "Come with your master tonight. I promise you will not regret it." Bobbing his head up and down, Taisu took his leave.

By the time Mistress Wu had reached home and paid off the bearers, Dasheng had also arrived. Evening was approaching, and Mistress Wu had some food and wine prepared and brought to her chamber. She then invited Dasheng to eat with her and said to him with a show of kindness, "My son, now that your father has passed away, I have only you left. Why do you set yourself against me?" Dasheng replied, "Precisely because father has passed away, you should strive to keep up the family's appearances. But now people are saying things about you that I cannot tolerate." Feigning relief, Mistress Wu said, "To be frank with you, I committed some indiscretions when I was younger, which gave rise to the gossip you hear. But now that I am in my thirties, I regret my previous behavior and have resolved to spend the rest of my days with you, in abstinence." As Dasheng listened to his mother's expressions of contrition, he beamed with pleasure and said, "If what you say is true, I shall be eternally happy." Whereupon Mistress Wu filled a cup with wine and urged, "Drink this to the bottom to show that you have forgiven me!"

Taken aback, Dasheng asked himself, "Can it be that she means me ill and has poisoned the wine?" He took the cup but dared not drink. Mistress Wu read his doubts and inquired, "Would you suspect even your mother of harboring evil intentions?" She took the cup from his hand and emptied it with one gulp. Ashamed that he had wrongly suspected his mother, Dasheng took the wine pot and filled his cup again, announcing, "Let this be your son's penance!" And he drained his cup three times in succession. Mistress Wu then said, "I have told you all this because I have decided to mend my ways. If you care for me and forgive my past, let us together eat, drink, and be merry this night."

Much gladdened by these words, Dasheng drank again and again as his cup was repeatedly filled. Mistress Wu was capable of holding her wine, but not so Dasheng, who was still a callow youth. As Mistress Wu intentionally plied him with one drink after another, Dasheng yawned with increasing frequency. After emptying a few more cups, he felt as though heaven and earth were spinning around, and he could no longer hold himself upright. Mistress Wu told the maidservant·to take Dasheng to her bed, where he immediately fell asleep. As she locked the door of the room, Mistress Wu remarked, "Humph! Now it is your turn to succumb to my wiles!"

Mistress Wu went out into the courtyard, and had not long to wait before she heard a stone clatter on the tiles of the roof. She ordered the maidservant to open the back gate, and soon Taisu stood before her. He said, "My master is at the front gate and dares not enter. He is waiting for you to admit him." Mistress Wu enjoined the maidservant to keep watch at the door of her chamber, then went with Taisu to the front courtyard. As they advanced in the darkness, Taisu suddenly put his arms about her, and she, turning around, did the same. She whispered, "I have long desired you, you little scoundrel! The other day we missed our chance, so let us make up for it now." She led Taisu to her son's bed in the main hall and there they set to fornicating.

When they were done, they straightened their garments and together went to open the front gate. They found the abbot standing woodenly outside, and when Mistress Wu asked him to enter he was reluctant to do so. Mistress Wu stated, "The little brute is lying drunk in my bedchamber, and I wish to consult you on the possibility of ending his life right now. So come in quickly!"

As he entered, the abbot cried, "Impossible! How could you slay your own son!" Mistress Wu replied, "I shall be doing this for your sake. Besides, I can no longer endure his mischief-making!" The abbot asked, "Have you considered the consequences if you are found out?" Mistress Wu answered, "I gave birth to him, and it would not be regarded as a major crime if I took his life." The abbot continued, "People surely know about our affair. Should we be accused of slaying him, for you it would be counted as no more than terminating your own offspring. But I could be incriminated and accused of complicity in murder and made to pay with my life!" Mistress Wu countered, "But if we do not rid ourselves of him for fear of the consequences, we shall never have any peace!"

The abbot pondered the matter, then proposed, "We could find a wife for him, and then embroil her in a liaison as well. With his own manliness in question, Dasheng will have little time or inclination to meddle in your business." Mistress Wu protested, "That is out of the question! We would have no way of knowing in advance what manner of person the girl is. Should she and I fail to get along, there would only be another pair of eyes to spy on me. The best solution is to get rid of him. With him out of the way, I still could not marry you since you are of the cloth, but we could let it be known that we are as brother and sister and no one could tell us nay. We could then be together for all time."

The abbot said, "In that case, I have a plan. Let the authorities rid us of him." Mistress Wu inquired, "How so?" Abbot Huang explained, "The Magistrate of Kaifeng detests nothing more vehemently than unfilial sons, and anyone proven to be such is either beaten to death or imprisoned under charge of a grave crime. Should you bring a charge of unfilial behavior against Dasheng, he would hardly be able to defend himself. You are his real mother, not a step-mother, and your word would not be doubted."

Mistress Wu asked, "But what if, in his desperation, he tells the magistrate about our affair?" The abbot replied, "A son may not accuse his mother of adultery. But should he bring the matter up, you may say your son is slanderously attacking you, and the magistrate will take his utterances as further proof of his lack of filial piety. Moreover, a charge of adultery can only be sustained when both the accused have been apprehended in the act. Dasheng has no evidence and can prove nothing against us, and the authorities would not charge a mother with adultery when a son's behavior is being brought into question."

Mistress Wu agreed, saying, "Yes, and he also declined to sweep his father's grave today as I instructed him to do, but went instead to the temple. That, too, can be cited against him as proof of unfilial behavior. However, he must not know what we are preparing for him."

Abbot Huang continued, "You can take no action with the boy constantly at your side. But I have close friends at the yamen, and will have the accusation sent up and the case put on the docket. Dasheng will suspect nothing before the bailiffs come to arrest him. Then you may step forward and testify against him."

Mistress Wu said, "That would seem to be the best way to proceed. But after my son is dead, you must treat me with complete sincerity and accede to all my wishes. If not, my son will have died for nothing." The abbot asked, "And what is it that you wish?" Mistress Wu replied, "I wish that you keep me company every night and never let me sleep alone." But the abbot demurred, saying, "I have my duties to attend to at the temple and cannot come every night!" Mistress Wu then proposed, "If you are unable to spare the time, send me one of your acolytes. I cannot bear to spend the night alone." Abbot Huang agreed, saying, "That shall be done. I have full trust in my acolytes, both of whom are most prudent. And if it appeals to you, they could also come when I am here, and we could all disport ourselves together. Does that not sound delightful?"

Her lust aroused by these words, Mistress Wu led the abbot to the bed in the main hall, and there they copulated wildly and passionately. Mistress Wu whispered in the abbot's ear, "I am willing to sacrifice even my son for your love. Never desert me!" The abbot declared, "Should I ever be unworthy of your love, may I have no coffin when I die!"

After the encounter the abbot felt fatigued, but Mistress Wu's ardor had yet to be expended. So she said to the abbot, "Why not let Taisu have a go at it!" The abbot replied, "Excellent idea!" He rose and prodded the acolyte's shoulder, saying, "Mistress Wu calls for you." And when Taisu stood by the bed, the abbot urged, "Get in and keep the mistress company!" Though Taisu had fornicated once already, he was young and quite able to repeat the performance. Hopping into the bed, he resumed his exertions. Sitting on the edge of the bed, the abbot remarked, "This is the sort of benefit you will enjoy after that business is over." He, of course, was unaware that the acolyte was having his second turn.

At last, having disposed of two lovers in succession, Mistress Wu was satisfied. To the abbot she remarked, "When that little brute is no more, we shall be able to enjoy such pleasures frequently and without hindrance!"

Waking up the next morning, Dasheng was astonished to find himself in his mother's bed. "I must have been very drunk last night!" he thought. Then, reflecting on his mother's words the night before, he began to doubt their veracity. "Can it be that she took advantage of my state to do other things again?" When Mistress Wu saw him, however, she seemed bent on creating a scandal and scolded Dasheng, saying, "Have you no shame? You souse yourself in wine and then fall asleep on my bed, leaving me no place to sleep!" Dasheng was much embarrassed and dared not speak up.

Early the next day, Dasheng heard loud raps on the front gate and much shouting. Wondering what was going on, he opened the gate, only to admit two bailiffs who forthwith cast a rope around his neck. Greatly alarmed, Dasheng inquired, "What's the reason for this?" The bailiffs cursed him, saying, "You knave! Your mother has accused you of unfilial behavior, for which the magistrate will have you beaten to death. And you ask what the reason is!" Terrified, Dasheng began to weep. He pleaded, "Allow me at least to see my mother." The bailiffs replied, "Your mother, too, will come with us to the yamen!" With that, they took Dasheng into the courtyard.

Mistress Wu had heard the rapping and the voices in the courtyard and knew full well what was happening. As she hastened out of her chamber, Dasheng threw his arms about her, crying, "Mother! Though I am not a good son, it is you who gave birth to me! How could you do this thing to me?" Mistress Wu replied, "Why do you disobey me in all matters? Now you shall see that I am not to be trifled with!" Dasheng asked, "In what matters have I been disobedient?" Mistress Wu answered, "Two days ago, I enjoined you to sweep your father's grave, but you refused to do so." Dasheng protested, "But you did not go either. Why do you lay the blame on me?" The bailiffs, who knew not what had transpired previously, now interrupted, shouting, "It is a son's duty to sweep his father's grave, and you may not blame your mother. Enough has been said! Away to the magistrate!" And together with Mistress Wu, they dragged Dasheng to the yamen.

Magistrate Li had just ascended to his seat in the courtroom that day. A man of great integrity and ability, he had a strong aversion for people who disobeyed and rebelled against parental authority. And when he saw that the case before him concerned an accusation of unfilial behavior, his face darkened with anger. Yet he felt some perplexity when the prisoner brought before him turned out to be a young boy only fifteen or sixteen years of age. He wondered, "What can such a child have done to merit such an accusation from his mother?"

Striking the table with his gavel, he said, "Your mother has accused you of unfilial behavior. What have you to say for yourself?" Dasheng replied, "Though I am young in age, I have had some schooling and would never dare to show disrespect for my parents. But it is my misfortune to have lost my father as well as the favor of my mother, for which reason I now stand accused. Such being the nature of my crime, I am prepared to be beaten to death to appease my mother's ire. I have nothing else to say for myself." He then wept bitter tears.

This discourse aroused feelings of compassion in the magistrate. He thought, "How can a son who speaks such words be unfilial? There is more to this matter than meets the eye." But again he reflected, "Yet, who can tell? It may also be that the boy has a glib tongue!"

The magistrate then summoned Mistress Wu, who minced forward with a kerchief covering her head. When she removed the kerchief, the magistrate saw that she was a young woman of seductive appearance, which had the effect of putting him on his guard. He inquired, "In what way has your son been unfilial?" Mistress Wu replied, "Ever since my husband passed away, the boy has refused to obey me and has done exactly as he pleases. I have tried to reason with him, but he reviles me with obscene utterances. Thinking him to be but a child, I have avoided confrontations with him, but matters have only gone from bad to worse, and I am unable to control him any longer. That is why I must ask the law to deal with him."

The magistrate then asked Dasheng, "What argument do you offer against your mother's accusations?" To which Dasheng replied, "I cannot argue against my mother. It is as she says it is." The magistrate continued, "Does your mother favor another child over you?" Dasheng replied, "My mother is most loving and kind. And she favors no one else since I am her only child." The magistrate called on Dasheng to approach his table and said in confidence, "I suspect there are other aspects to this case. Tell me what they are, and I shall see to it that justice is done by you." Dasheng merely kowtowed and said, "There are no other aspects. I am in the wrong." The magistrate finally declared, "So be it. Since a child's parents are ever in the right, and your mother has accused you, I must punish you." Dasheng replied, "The punishment is deserved."

The foregoing exchange strengthened the magistrate's suspicions. Constrained to maintain appearances, however, he commanded, "Administer ten strokes to the culprit!" Dasheng was thrown to the ground and given ten strokes with a bamboo stave.

The magistrate, meanwhile, covertly watched Mistress Wu. She showed not the least sign of compassion for the boy, and, indeed, even approached the magistrate on her knees and urged, "If it please Your Honor, have him beaten to death right now!"

Greatly angered, the magistrate said, "Spiteful woman! The boy must necessarily be the issue of a previous wife or concubine of your husband's, that your heart is so hardened against him!" Mistress Wu replied, "I am indeed his own mother. You may ask him about this." The magistrate turned to Dasheng and asked, "Is she your true mother?" Weeping, Dasheng replied, "She is in truth my mother." The magistrate continued, "Then why does she hate you so?" Dasheng said, "I do not know, Your Honor. But fulfill her wish and have me beaten to death."

This confirmed the magistrate's suspicions, but he did not reveal his true thoughts and instead thundered, "You are indeed unfilial! And mark my words, you shall die for it."

On hearing the magistrate's stern pronouncement, Mistress Wu kowtowed again and said, "I beseech Your Honor to execute the sentence as soon as possible, so that my mind may be at rest." The magistrate asked, "Have you any sons by adoption?" Mistress Wu replied, "No, I do not." The magistrate then said, "Since he is your only son, I am of a mind to spare his life and let him off with an admonishment, so that he may support you in your old age." But Mistress Wu declared, "I would prefer to live alone, without my son." The magistrate reminded her, "Once he is dead, he cannot be brought back to life. Are you certain you will have no regrets?" Grimly, Mistress Wu replied, "I will have no regrets!" Whereupon the magistrate said, "Then come tomorrow with a coffin to retrieve the body." He had Dasheng put in prison, and then dismissed Mistress Wu.

Elation marking her features, Mistress Wu departed. The magistrate followed her with his eyes as she stepped out of the courtroom. He conjectured, "This woman's bearing is not that of a person of good character. She is surely hiding something. The boy was unwilling to divulge her secret, which shows that he is a filial son. I must get to the bottom of this matter."

Summoning a sharp-eyed and nimble minion, he commanded, "Follow that woman everywhere she goes. Some person will surely accost her. Take note of who this person is and what they say to one another regardless of the status of that person, and report to me all you see and hear. If your information is accurate, you will be rewarded. Otherwise you will pay with your life."

The minion made haste to follow Mistress Wu. He had only a few steps to go before he saw a Daoist priest approach her and inquire, "How did it go?" Mistress Wu laughed and said, "It is all done. I need you now to purchase a coffin for me, so that I may return tomorrow to get the corpse." The Daoist priest clapped his hands in joy and exclaimed, "Excellent! Excellent! Have no worries on that account. I shall have a coffin transported and deposited before the yamen early tomorrow." The two departed, chatting and laughing gaily.

The minion, meanwhile, had recognized the priest as the abbot of Western Hills Temple, and he reported to the magistrate all the details of the conversation he had overheard. Magistrate Li exclaimed, "It is as I surmised! Little wonder that she sought the death of her own son with such callous insistence! Despicable!" He wrote out a document, which he then sealed and handed to the minion with the words, "Tomorrow the woman will come and I shall order the coffin to be brought in. In that instant you shall open this document and do exactly as is written therein."

The next day, no sooner had the magistrate taken his seat in the courtroom than Mistress Wu entered and announced, "I have brought the coffin to collect the body of my unfilial son in accordance with Your Honor's instructions." The magistrate announced, "Your son was beaten to death last night." To which

Mistress Wu replied, "And I thank you, My Lord!" The magistrate then commanded, "Have the coffin brought in!" Whereupon the minion made haste to unseal the document. It turned out to be an urgent court injunction, and on it was written: "Detain Mistress Wu's accomplice in adultery, the Daoist priest who is bringing the coffin." The minion at once went outside to where the abbot was overseeing the coffin bearers. He showed the injunction to the abbot and placed him under arrest. Aware that resistance would be useless, the abbot followed the minion into the presence of the magistrate.

The magistrate asked, "As a Daoist priest, why did you purchase a coffin for this woman and then hire porters to bring it here?" The abbot responded, "She asked me to help her in this matter, which I did, since she is my cousin." The magistrate pursued, "As the boy's uncle, you would help to put him to death!" The abbot defended himself, saying, "Their family matters are no concern of mine." The magistrate said, "You claim to be a relative, and while you do nothing to mediate this dispute, you exhibit great zeal when asked to obtain a coffin. Yet you deny complicity and conspiracy? Even death would not expiate this villain's guilt!"

He ordered vises to be brought and applied to the abbot to compel him to speak the truth. Unable to bear the torture, the abbot soon made a full confession. The magistrate then had the culprit affix his mark to the deposition, on which it was recorded: "The abbot of the Western Hills Temple admits to being guilty of adultery leading to a plot to commit murder." All the while Mistress Wu watched the proceedings, speechless with terror.

Magistrate Li then ordered Dasheng to be brought to the courtroom. When Dasheng had been sent to prison the day before, he had reflected, "My life may not be in danger, since the magistrate spoke kindly today." But as he was led into the courtroom and saw a new coffin standing outside, fear struck him and he asked himself, "Will I be beaten to death today, after all?"

As he fell, trembling, to his knees, the magistrate asked, "Are you acquainted with Abbot Huang Miaoxiu of the Western Hills Temple?" Dasheng replied, "No, I am not." The magistrate pursued, "Though he is your enemy, you say you do not know him?" Dasheng looked around, and saw the abbot lying on the ground, groaning with pain from the injuries he had sustained from the vises. Aghast, he kowtowed to the magistrate and muttered, "Your Honor sees all with the clarity of cloudless skies! I dare not speak any more untruths!"

Magistrate Li continued, "I asked you many questions yesterday, which you did not reply to out of your sense of filial loyalty. Yet now I have all the answers!" He then ordered Mistress Wu to rise, saying, "I shall now give you back the coffin with a body in it." But as Mistress Wu came forward, expecting to see her son beaten, the magistrate commanded the sergeant-at-arms in loud tones, "Throw down Huang Miaoxiu, and use your stave with added force!" The abbot's flesh was soon reduced to bloody tatters. And, as Mistress Wu looked on with ashen face and chattering teeth, the magistrate had the body thrown in the coffin and the lid nailed fast even before the abbot had breathed his last.

The magistrate then turned to Mistress Wu, saying, "As for you, you hussy, you would have your own son slain in order to live with a man in adultery. I see no good reason for sparing your life. You would be better dead. Sergeant-at-arms! Seize this woman and beat her!"

The officer pounced on Mistress Wu and flung her down before the magistrate. But in this moment Dasheng sprang forward and lay across his mother's back, crying, "Beat me instead! Beat me instead!" Unable to apply his stave, the sergeant-at-arms called some of his fellows to try to pull Dasheng offby force. But Dasheng clung tightly to his mother and wept.

Satisfied that Dasheng was making no pretense, the magistrate ordered the sergeant-at-arms to desist. He then told Dasheng to rise, saying, "Your mother attempted to have you killed, so I was about to let her suffer a few blows to appease your anger. Why do you protect her in this manner?" Dasheng replied, "I cannot seek revenge against my own mother. And although Your Honor has not chastised me for unfilial behavior, I am nevertheless guilty of provoking my mother's ire. I hope Your Honor will take this circumstance into consideration."

The magistrate commanded Mistress Wu to rise and declared, "You deserve to die, but in view of your son's intercession I shall let you live. Henceforth you must mend your ways. Should you commit any further misdeeds, I shall not let you off so lightly again."

When Mistress Wu saw the abbot put to death, she believed that she, too, would die. Having seen now how her son shielded her with his own body and pleaded that she be pardoned, and hearing the magistrate's final words, she understood what a good son she had in Dasheng, and she shed tears of remorse. To the magistrate she said, "I have committed a heinous crime and am unworthy of my son. I pledge to care for him hereafter until he is a grown man, and never to misbehave again." And there and then in the courtroom, Dasheng and his mother threw their arms about each other and wept loud and long.

Soon afterward, a summons was sent to the Western Hills Temple for the abbot's disciples to come and retrieve his body. Taisu and Taiqing were chosen to fulfill that duty. When a bailiff brought them into the courtroom, the magistrate looked up to see two well-favored young boys, and he thought to himself, "The priests in the temple have surely enticed these young acolytes into performing lewd acts with them. And, with such fair countenances, there is little doubt they will in the future become embroiled with women in scandalous affairs." He called a bailiff and enjoined him to see that the acolytes had the coffin properly interred. Then he commanded the boys to go back to their families and never again to set foot in the temple.

Meanwhile, Mistress Wu went home with her son, and in her gratitude took good care of him thereafter. Dasheng, on his part, comported himself toward his mother with great consideration and obedience, and never spoke of his mother's escapades. And, indeed, with the abbot dead and his acolytes gone, Mistress Wu could do little else but restrain her fancies and live in modesty. Yet she could not overcome sensations of melancholy when her thoughts returned to previous events. These, and the shock and horror she had experienced, and from which she never fully recovered, sent her to an early grave.

Dasheng buried his parents side by side, and when the requisite period of mourning had elapsed, he took a wife. The couple treated one another with great dignity and became widely reputed for their respectability. And when Dasheng entered government service, he was given many favorable recommendations by Magistrate Li and eventually became an official of considerable rank and renown.

As for Taisu and Taiqing, the day they left the temple they discussed these events as they walked along. Taiqing said, "I had a dream the other night in which the venerable Lao Zi said to me, 'Your master is exceptionally well learned in the Way. I shall let him have an official position, and you too shall benefit from it.' As it turns out, the master was learned in no other ways but those of debauchery. And what official position was there for him? All he got from the magistrate was a coffin, which affords us no benefit." Taisu demurred, saying, "But the master did get much pleasure from what he did, and he did not die in vain. It is a pity that he is gone, for such pleasures are no longer open to us." Taiqing remarked, "Even if the master were alive, we could only swallow our saliva at the thought of those pleasures." Whereupon Taisu confessed, "I did more than swallow my saliva. Indeed, I had a taste of that pleasure, albeit quite fleetingly." He then related to Taiqing all that had transpired. Taiqing observed, "Though we were disciples of the same master, you made the most of it. Now that we are being sent back to secular life, however, we can each find ourselves a wife with whom to gratify our desires."

The two then discussed what they should do with the abbot's coffin and decided to bury it in his ancestors' cemetery. That done, they returned to secular life.

As time passed, however, Taisu kept recalling the pleasures he had shared with Mistress Wu and could not lay his cravings to rest. He returned to the Liu residence to inquire about her, and was deeply grieved when he learned that she had died. Thereafter, he went about as though in a trance. He had but to shut his eyes at night, than he would dream that Mistress Wu came to sleep with him and that the abbot sometimes came too to vie for her favors. He suffered from so many nocturnal emissions that he became sickly and consumptive, and soon died.

Meanwhile, Taiqing, who had already taken a wife, sighed when he heard of Taisu's demise and said to himself, "Now I know why followers of the Way must not break their vows in this manner. The Master died on account of his debauchery, and Taisu sickened and died because he dabbled in the same sort of thing. It is my fortune that I was not implicated; otherwise I too would would have died a futile death." And from then on he lived out his days as a good and decent subject.

Judge Bao Uses Guile to Right an Injustice

張員外義撫頌蛉子
包龍圖智賺合同文

The tale you will now hear took place during the Song dynasty. Just outside the West Gate of the Song capital city, Bianliang, in a town called Yidingfang, lived a man known as Liu the First but whose real name was Liu Tianxiang. His wife, being a woman of the Yang family, was therefore called Mistress Yang. His younger brother, Liu Tianrui, also known as Liu the Second, had married a woman from the Zhang family. The brothers and their families lived under one roof and had resolved not to divide up the family property.

Tianxiang, the older brother, had no children of his own, although his wife, Mistress Yang, a twice-married woman, had brought along a daughter from her first marriage—an "oil bottle," as a child from a previous marriage is called by the common folk. Tianrui, the younger brother, had begotten a son who was named Anzhu.

In the same town lived a certain Village Chief Li who had a daughter called Dingnu. She was the same age as Anzhu, and because Village Chief Li and the Liu family were close friends, Dingnu had been promised to Anzhu even before either of them was born, following the custom known as "marrying by pointing at the bellies." And when Anzhu was just two years old, his father had already formally betrothed him to the Li family's daughter.

Now, Mistress Yang, the wife of Liu the First, was a selfish woman of very little virtue. It was her secret ambition to bring a son-in-law into the family when her daughter came of age, thus appropriating to herself a large part of the family properties; for that reason there was frequent discord between the sisters-in-law. Fortunately, Tianxiang and his brother were on good terms with one another and Mistress Zhang was a fairly easy-going person, so that there were no serious rifts within the family and all lived together in relative peace.

Then one year a famine struck the region as harvests failed of all the six principal crops—rice, barley, wheat, soybeans, red beans, and sesame. The authorities issued an ordinance that residents should split up their households and have some of their members seek refuge in other townships and counties in order to diminish the local populace and thus lessen the ravages of starvation. Tianxiang told his younger brother that he intended to join the refugees, but Tianrui disagreed, saying, "Brother, you are no longer young and should not go far away. If anyone should go, let it be me and my wife."

Tianxiang agreed. He invited Village Chief Li to their house and told him, "Dear In-law, life will be very arduous all this year because of the dire crop failures. As you know, the authorities have ordered households to split up and send some of their members elsewhere to reduce the number of inhabitants here. My brother and his family have decided to go and will be choosing a date to depart. Now, my brother and I have never divided up our family's property and have no intention of doing so. Therefore we wish to draw up two copies of a covenant in which will be listed all our family's fields, tools, houses, and other belongings. My brother and I will each keep one copy in his possession. Should my brother return in a year or two, all will be well and the covenant will not be necessary. However, in the case that he is away for five or ten years and something untoward takes place during that time, the covenant will serve as an important testimonial. We have asked you to come and witness the writing of this agreement and to sign your name to both copies." Village Chief Li gladly consented:, "Of course, of course! That goes without saying."

Tianxiang then took two sheets of paper, raised his brush, and wrote on each as follows:

Resident Liu Tianxiang of Yidingfang Township outside the West Gate of East Capital, his younger brother Liu Tianrui, and his young nephew Anzhu will, as a consequence of failed harvests of the six crops and upon orders from the authorities, split up their household, certain members of which shall go to other places in order to reduce the number of inhabitants. The younger brother, Tianrui, is of his own accord taking his wife and son to some place far away. In spite of his departure, however, this household has not divided up its property, testimony to which are the two copies of the covenant written on this day, one copy of which shall remain in the safekeeping of each brother.

Year   moon   day   Writer of the covenant: Liu Tianxiang
His younger brother: Liu Tianrui
Witness: Village Chief Li

All three men made their marks, and the two brothers each took one of the copies. Village Chief Li was hospitably wined and dined, after which he went home.

Tianrui then chose a propitious date, packed some belongings, and took leave of his brother and sister-in-law. All in the family shed tears as he, Mistress Zhang, and Anzhu left on their uncertain wanderings—all except Mistress Yang, who was only too willing to see the three go and felt much malicious glee as they walked out the door.

Tianrui and his wife and son traveled many days, trudging along windswept roads and sleeping on riverbanks, until one day they arrived at Xiama Village in Gaoping County of Shanxi's Luzhou Prefecture. Learning that there had been good harvests here that year and that all kinds of commerce was thriving, they rented a room from a rich household and settled down to make a living. The master of this rich household was a certain Esquire Zhang. His given name was Bingyi, and his wife was called Mistress Guo. Husband and wife were a charitable and benevolent pair. They practiced philanthropy, made generous contributions to temples and monasteries, and possessed much farmland and many houses. Their one disappointment in life was that they had neither sons nor daughters, and they felt quite lonely. They observed that their tenants, the Lius, were congenial and amiable people, and so the two families got on famously with one another.

Liu Anzhu was three years old now, and Esquire Zhang took a great liking to the boy because of his fine features and quick wit. He conferred with his wife, saying that he wished to take the child as his adopted son, and found that his wife too had thought of doing just that. Thus they sought a go-between and asked him to say to Tianrui and Mistress Zhang: "Esquire Zhang is most fond of your young son and is of a mind to adopt him as his own son. In that way, our two families will become as one. What say you to that?"

Tianrui and Mistress Zhang were not at all displeased that this rich family wished to adopt their son, and they replied, "Our only concern is that because we are so poor people will accuse us of lusting after kinship with a family of higher social position. Nevertheless, should the esquire harbor such a felicitous desire, the two of us would feel greatly honored to make our home here."

The go-between brought these words back to Esquire Zhang, and both he and wife were much delighted. They forthwith chose a fortuitous date, adopted Liu Anzhu into their household, and changed his name to Zhang Anzhu. Then, since Mistress Zhang and Esquire Zhang shared the same surname, Mistress Zhang kowtowed to the esquire and formally acknowledged him as her elder brother, and Esquire Zhang thereafter called Liu Tianrui his brother-in-law. A profound friendship arose between the two families, and the esquire saw to all the Liu family's needs in such respects as housing, money, clothing and food.

Matters went on in this manner for half a year. The Lius had barely begun to enjoy their new-found happiness, however, when an unexpected calamity struck. Both husband and wife were laid low by a virulent contagious disease and became bed-ridden, never to rise again. Esquire Zhang, who now regarded them as his own flesh and blood, brought in physicians to give them the best treatment money could buy, but their illness only became more grave. The first to die was Mistress Zhang, which she did within a few days. Heartbroken, Tianrui wept, while Esquire Zhang purchased a coffin and had the body laid in it.

After a few more days, Liu Tianrui sensed that his condition was growing worse, and he knew his days were numbered. He asked Esquire Zhang to come to his bedside, and said, "My Benefactor, there is a matter of the utmost concern to me which I know not whether I should tell you." The esquire replied, "Brother-in-law, the bond of loyalty between us is like that between blood kin and I shall not betray your trust, no matter what it is you ask of me. So do not hesitate to tell me."

Therefore Tianrui said, "Of my living kinsmen, the only one who remains now is an elder brother. When I left my native place, my brother wrote out a paper, a covenant of which there are two copies. He retained one copy, whereas I took the other copy. This covenant was to serve as a testimonial in case something untoward should occur. My wife and I have had the good fortune to benefit from your favor, but fate has not been kind to us, and we are about to become homeless ghosts in a strange land. Anzhu is still young and unlearned, and since he has been adopted by you, our great benefactor, it is my hope that you will accumulate more merits for yourself in your afterlife by bringing up the boy. When he is a grown man, give him the covenant and instruct him to bury my bones and those of my wife in our ancestors' cemetery. I am unable to repay you in this life for your great kindness, but I shall do so in my next life, even if it means serving you as a beast of burden. However, I would request that you do not inform the boy of his provenance yet."

Having said these words, Tianrui shed copious tears. Esquire Zhang also wept. He assured Tianrui that everything would be done as he requested, and attempted to console him with kind words. Tianrui produced the covenant and entrusted it to Esquire Zhang. He lingered until evening, then closed his eyes and died.

Master Zhang procured another coffin and some burial clothing, laid the body in the coffin, then buried the couple in temporary graves to the side of the Zhang family cemetery. Thereafter he cared for Anzhu as he would his own son, yet kept the child ignorant of his antecedents, even as he grew older and went to school.

Anzhu, meanwhile, turned out to be a bright and clever youth who could recite any text after having cast his eyes on it just once. And by the time he was some ten years old, he was conversant with all the five principal classics and the works of the ancient historians. He had, in addition, a winning temperament and treated his adoptive parents with great respect, and both Esquire Zhang and his wife treasured him as they would a precious jewel. In spring and autumn every year, when they took him along to sweep their ancestors' graves, they would have him kowtow before his own parent's graves, although they never told him why he should do so.

Time indeed flies like an arrow as the sun and moon shuttle across the heavens. Fifteen years went by after the death of Tianrui and his wife. And when Anzhu reached eighteen years of age, Esquire Zhang conferred with his wife, and they knew the time had come to tell Anzhu about his past and have him bury his parents with their ancestors.

Meanwhile the Qingming Festival came around, and the husband and wife took Anzhu once more to sweep the ancestral graves. After this was done, Anzhu pointed at the two grave mounds off to one side and asked Esquire Zhang, "Father, you have told me every year to kowtow before these graves. I have never inquired what kinsfolk are buried in them. Could you tell me who they are?"

Esquire Zhang hesitated, then replied, "My son, your mother and I have been thinking of returning you to the place of your birth, but we fear that your affection for us who have raised you will pale once you learn who your real parents are. However, now is the time to tell you. Your true surname is not Zhang; nor were you born in these parts. Your original surname is Liu. You are the son of Liu Tianrui of Yidingfang Township outside the West Gate of the capital city, Bianliang, and your uncle's name is Liu Tianxiang. Your parents came here with you as refugees after the harvests there failed and households were forced to break up and scatter to reduce the populace. Thereafter, both your parents died and were buried here. Before your father passed away, he left with me a covenant in which is listed all of the Liu family's fields and property. He asked me to tell you this when you grew up. He said you should take this paper to prove your identity to your uncle and aunt, and to carry your parents' bones with you and bury them together with those of your ancestors. My son, I am telling you all this because it is my duty to do so. Although I and my wife did not share the ordeals of raising you during the first three years of your life, we have done our best by you for the next fifteen years and hope you will not forget the two of us."

Overwhelmed by the unexpectedness of what he had heard, Anzhu wept and fell down in a swoon. When the esquire and his wife had brought him back to his senses, he kowtowed before his true parents' graves and said with tears in his eyes, "Only now do I know that you are the parents who gave me my life."

He then turned to Esquire Zhang and Mistress Guo and said with feeling, "To you, my father and my mother, I respectfully submit that I cannot delay matters any longer, now that you have told me the truth. I beg father to give me the covenant and permit me to go to the capital with my parents' bones. After having buried these, I shall return to serve you and care for you for the rest of your lives. Father and Mother, do you agree to this?" The esquire replied, "I cannot hinder you, as you are going for the sake of fulfilling your filial duty. I only hope that you will go quickly and return soon, so as to spare us the anxiety of waiting for you."

They then went home, and Anzhu put together some of his belongings for the trip. The next day, when he went to kowtow his farewells to Esquire Zhang and Mistress Guo, the esquire took out the covenant and handed it to Anzhu. He also had the bones of Anzhu's parents disinterred for the young man to take along. Esquire Zhang once again enjoined him, "Do not tarry too long in your native place, or forget your adoptive parents!" And Anzhu replied, "I am not a person who repays benevolence with ingratitude. I shall return to serve you and care for you after this important matter has been dealt with." The three then parted with tears in their eyes.

Not for a moment did Anzhu tarry during his journey to Yidingfang outside the West Gate of Bianliang. Once there, he made inquiries until he found the Liu's residence. As he approached the house, he saw an elderly woman standing by the front gate and greeted her courteously, then said, "If it gives you no trouble, kindly announce my arrival. My name is Liu Anzhu, and I am the son of Liu Tianrui. I have learned that this is the residence of my uncle and aunt, and I am here to pay my respects to them and be reunited with my own clan."

As the elderly woman listened to his words, her countenance hardened, and she asked, "Where are Second Brother and my sister-in-law? You are a complete stranger to me. And since you claim to be Liu Anzhu, you must produce the covenant to prove who you are. Otherwise, how can I know that what you say is true?" Anzhu informed her, "Both my parents died fifteen years ago in Luzhou. I had the good fortune of being brought up by adoptive parents. The paper you ask for is in my bag."

The elderly woman reflected a moment, and then declared, "I am Liu the First's wife, and you must indeed be his nephew since you have the covenant. Let me have it, and stand out here while I go in and show it to your uncle. Then we shall invite you in." Anzhu hastily apologized, saying, "I was not aware that you are my aunt. Forgive me for being so discourteous." He opened his bag, extracted the covenant, and held it out with both hands. Mistress Yang took the paper and entered the gate while Anzhu stood outside. He waited a very long while, but his aunt failed to reappear.

It so happened that Mistress Yang's daughter had married some time ago and had brought her husband into her mother's house, as Mistress Yang's intention was to have the couple inherit the Liu family's property. Since then,

Mistress Yang had remained on guard day and night lest her brother-in-law, sister-in-law, and nephew return to Yidingfang. And now the nephew had indeed come back. However, because Mistress Yang had been apprised by him that his parents had both died, and since the uncle and the nephew did not know one another, it would not be difficult for her to delude her husband into believing the newcomer was not his nephew. Thus, when the covenant fell into her clutches, she hid it on her person, making certain it was well concealed. She would flatly deny having any knowledge of the covenant if Anzhu should enter the house and inquire about it. It was Anzhu's bad luck that he had encountered his aunt. Had he first seen his uncle, none of what happened subsequently would have taken place.

Anzhu, in the meantime, waited and waited, sighing and tormented with thirst, but saw no sign of his aunt. He thought of going in, yet felt he could not barge in so unceremoniously. As his puzzlement and doubts grew, an elderly man approached him and asked, not unkindly, "Young man, where do you hail from? And why do you stand so woodenly in front of my gate?" Anzhu inquired, "Are you my uncle? I am Anzhu who fifteen years ago went with my parents to seek refuge at Luzhou." The man exclaimed, "So you are indeed my nephew! Do you have your father's copy of the covenant I wrote?" Anzhu replied, "My aunt has taken it into the house."

All smiles, Liu Tianxiang took the young man by the hand and led him into the outer hall of the house. Anzhu fell on his knees and kowtowed to his uncle, who said, "My boy, this is not necessary. Besides, you must be exhausted after your long journey. Your aunt and I are both advancing in years and our lives are like candles in the wind. Ever since the three of you left us, fifteen years have gone by without any news of you. We two brothers have only you to look to, as there is no one else to inherit our considerable properties, and the worries this has caused me have dimmed my eyes and dulled my hearing. It truly gives me great joy that you have returned. But how are your parents? And why did they not come back together with you?"

Tears trickled from Anzhu's eyes as he recounted how both his parents had died and how he had been brought up by an adoptive father. Liu Tianxiang also shed tears. He then called out Mistress Yang and said to her, "Wife, our nephew is here to greet you."

Mistress Yang asked coldly, "What nephew?" Tianxiang replied, "Liu Anzhu who with his parents fled from the famine fifteen years ago." Mistress Yang snorted, "Is that Liu Anzhu? There are a great many tricksters these days. This one has, in all probability, seen that we have much property and pretends he is Liu Anzhu so as to lay claim to it. When Second Brother and his wife went away, they took a covenant with them. If this person has the covenant, he is your nephew. If he does not, he is an impostor. It is as simple as that!"

Tianxiang demurred, saying, "The boy tells me he has already given it to you." But Mistress Yang insisted, "I have not seen it." Anzhu cried, "But I gave it to you with my own hands! Why do you speak thus?" And Tianxiang added, "Woman, do not jest with me! The boy said you have taken it from him." But Mistress Yang kept shaking her head and would not admit that she had taken the covenant.

Tianxiang then asked Anzhu, "Where, precisely, is that covenant? Tell me the truth!" Anzhu protested, "I would not dare deceive you! The paper was in truth taken by my aunt. Why, before man's conscience and Heaven's reason, does my aunt deny it?" Whereupon Mistress Yang railed at him, "You lying young scoundrel! When did I ever see that covenant!"

Tianxiang turned to Mistress Yang and tried to placate her, "Woman, do not lose your temper! If you have taken it, why not let me see it? There can be no harm in doing so." But Mistress Yang flew into a towering rage and cried, "You doddering old fool! Rather than believe me, your own wife, you would place your trust in a complete stranger! What would I want with that covenant, other than to use it as window paper? If he were truly our nephew, I would welcome him with open arms! I would never attempt to suppress that piece of paper! But this young beggar is deliberately concocting a story so as to do us out of our property!"

Anzhu explained earnestly, "Uncle, I have no desire for our family property. All I wish to do is bury my parents' bones beside our ancestral tombs, after which I shall return to Luzhou. I have my own life and pursuits there." But Mistress Yang shrieked even more loudly, "Who wishes to hear your artful fabrications!" And with that, she snatched up a stick, rushed at Anzhu, and belabored his head and face with it so that the skin broke and blood flowed.

Tianxiang attempted to intervene, crying, "Let us first get to the bottom of the matter!" However, he was unable to determine whether Anzhu was his nephew or come to any decision, since he himself had seen his nephew only as a small child and his wife adamantly denied having taken the covenant. Finally, he could only let her have her way. Mistress Yang dragged Anzhu out on the road, and then bolted the gate.

Liu Anzhu lay unconscious for a long time before slowly regaining his senses. He then wept loud and long before his parents bones, and cried, "Aunt, what have I done that I deserve such cruel treatment?"

As he wept, a man came up to him and inquired, "Young man, who are you? And why do you grieve so?" Anzhu replied, "I am Liu Anzhu. My parents and I fled from the famine here fifteen years ago." Astonished, the man looked closely at Anzhu and then asked, "Who beat your head? Liu Tianxiang? " Anzhu hastened to say, "My uncle had nothing to do with this. It was my aunt. She refuses to acknowledge me. She took away my father's copy of the covenant, then flatly denied having done so and beat me over the head!"

The man then stated, "I am no outsider. In fact, I am Village Chief Li, and you are my son-in-law, as you were betrothed to my daughter when you were both very young. Now tell me in detail all that has transpired over the past fifteen years, and I shall see to it that justice is done ."

On learning that the man was his father-in-law, Anzhu made a respectful obeisance and said tearfully, "This is what has happened, Father-in-Law. After my parents and I fled as refugees from the famine, we went to Xiama Village in Gaoping County near Luzhou in Shanxi and rented a room in the house of Esquire Zhang Bingyi. I was adopted by Esquire Zhang and his wife and brought up by them after my parents both died of a contagious illness. Only this year, when I turned eighteen, did Esquire Zhang inform me about my origins. Thus I came here with my parents' bones to seek my uncle. For some unknown reason my aunt guilefully seized the covenant I brought with me, and then beat me over the head with a stick. Now I know not where I can seek redress for this wrong that I have suffered."

After Anzhu had given this account he shed more tears, and Village Chief Li's countenance turned purple with anger. He asked Anzhu, "This covenant that was seized from you, do you remember what was written in it?" Anzhu replied, "I do." And Village Chief Li commanded, "Recite the words to me!" Whereupon Anzhu recited every word without a single error.

Village Chief Li was satisfied and declared, "You are indeed my son-in-law, of that there can be no doubt. That harridan is wholly in the wrong. I shall go in and reason with her. Should I succeed in talking her around, so be it. If not, the current magistrate at Kaifeng Prefecture, Judge Bao, is a most able and astute official. I shall go with you to file a lawsuit, and there is no question that your property will be restored to you." Anzhu thanked him, saying, "I place this matter in your hands, Father-in-Law."

Village Chief Li rapped on the gate, and then entered the house with Anzhu. Coming straight to the point, he asked Liu Tianxiang and his wife, "What is the problem, my dear in-laws? Now that your own nephew has returned, why do you refuse to recognize him but break his head instead?"

Mistress Yang replied, "Village Chief Li, you are manifestly unaware that he is an imposter who is testing his luck here. Were he Liu Anzhu, he should have that covenant on which you, too, affixed your mark. If he does have it, then he is Liu Anzhu." Village Chief Li retorted, "He says you have seized the covenant by guile and hidden it away. Do you deny that?" Mistress Yang cried, "You, Village Chief Li, are a ridiculous fool! When did I ever see that bit of paper? Besides, this man is no more than a thief, and you have no call to poke your nose into other people's affairs!" With that, she brandished the stick again to strike Anzhu.

Fearing for his son-in-law's life, Village Chief Li hurriedly stepped between the two, and then led Anzhu out of the house. Wrathfully, he declared, "Never have I encountered such a vicious, evil-minded woman! It is not enough that she refuses to acknowledge you, but she must also attempt to do you in! But have no worry, my son-in-law. I suggest that you bring your parents' bones and your effects to my house and rest for the night. Tomorrow, we shall go to Kaifeng Prefecture to file a lawsuit."

Anzhu accepted this advice and went with Village Chief Li to his house. There, Anzhu paid his respects to his future mother-in-law while Village Chief Li saw to it that food and wine were prepared for him. Poultices were applied to Anzhu's wounds and a bandage was wrapped around his head.

Early the next morning, Village Chief Li wrote out a complaint, and then went with his son-in-law to Kaifeng Prefecture. Before long, a drum was beaten, bailiffs lined up on both sides of the yamen hall, and Judge Bao ascended to his bench. Thereupon Village Chief Li and Anzhu raised their voices and cried out for justice. Judge Bao took their complaint and perused it. He then called forward Village Chief Li and asked to be told the facts of the case, and the village chief did so.

Judge Bao inquired, "Are you, perchance, the author of this lawsuit? And have you instigated that young man to file these charges?" Village Chief Li replied, "That young man is this small person's son-in-law, and the covenant has my mark on it. I took pity on him for his youth and for the injustice he has sustained. Hence, I have come with him to file the complaint. I would not dare to deceive you, My Lord."

Judge Bao then asked, "Are you familiar with this person who claims to be your son-in-law?" Village Chief Li replied, "I am indeed not familiar with him, as he left these parts when he was three years old and has only just returned." Judge Bao went on, "Then why do you believe he is truly your son-in-law, since you are unfamiliar with him and he has lost the covenant, which is the only evidence for his claim?" The Village Chief explained, "No one else, apart from the Liu brothers and myself, has seen that covenant. Yet this young man is able to recite it from memory without a single error. That would appear to be very powerful evidence, would it not?"

Judge Bao then called forward Liu Anzhu and asked him about the facts, and Anzhu told the judge all that had happened. The judge examined his injuries, then, after a moment's reflection, said, "Tell me, why should I believe that you are indeed a son of the Liu family and that you have not come to defraud them?"

Anzhu replied, "My Lord, it is no easy matter to make false things look true, and I would be hard pressed to concoct such a fanciful scheme. Besides, my adoptive father, Zhang Bingyi, possesses so much farmland and so many houses that I could well live in ease and comfort for the rest of my life. I have already told my kinsfolk that I am willing to forgo my share of the family property, and that all I desire is to bury my parents' bones in the ancestral cemetery, after which I shall return to Luzhou to live with my adoptive father. I entreat My Lord to verify the truth of my words."

Having found that the statements made by both Village Chief Li and Liu Anzhu were plausible and reasonable, Judge Liu approved their complaint and forthwith summoned Liu Tianxiang and his wife to the yamen. When they arrived, he called forward Liu Tianxiang and asked him, "Why is it that you, as the head of the household, have no mind of your own and allow yourself be swayed by your wife? And tell me, is that young fellow your nephew or not?"

Liu Tianxiang argued, "My Lord, as I have not seen my nephew since he was a small child, the only evidence of his authenticity would be the covenant. This young man insists he had the covenant, and my wife just as adamantly disclaims ever having seen it. Since I have no eyes in the back of my head, I cannot determine who is telling the truth!"

Judge Bao then called forward Mistress Yang, but she denied having seen the covenant despite all the questions put to her by the judge.

After some thought, Judge Bao said to Anzhu: "Since your uncle and aunt are so hard of heart, I shall allow you to give both of them a sound drubbing, so that you may assuage your anger and resentment." But the judge's words merely distressed Anzhu, and he declared tearfully, "That I cannot do! Even my father, who was my uncle's younger brother, could not beat my uncle, so how could I, as a nephew, do such a thing? Doing so would run counter to all the rules of propriety. I have come to pay my respects to my uncle and bury my parents in fulfillment of my filial duty, not to vie for any properties. I would die rather than do a thing so unethical!"

Anzhu's protestations convinced Judge Bao, and he knew now what he should do. He called forward Mistress Yang and asked her a few more questions, and then announced, "This young fellow is a fraud, and what he has done cannot be countenanced. You, your husband, and Chief Li may all return to your homes now. I shall throw this fellow in jail and interrogate him under torture at some later date."

The three persons thus addressed kowtowed to the judge and left the yamen, while Anzhu was led off to prison. Mistress Yang secretly exulted. However, Village Chief Li and Anzhu were much bewildered, and both wondered, "Why has Judge Bao, who is famed for his wondrous perspicacity, thrown the plaintiff in this case in prison while letting off the defendants?"

In the meantime, Judge Bao sent secret orders to the prison guards that they should on no account mistreat Liu Anzhu. He then instructed the yamen staff to spread word that Anzhu had sickened with lockjaw as a consequence of his injuries and now lay on the verge of death. He also dispatched a messenger to Luzhou, asking Esquire Zhang Bingyi to come to the yamen, which the esquire did within a few days. Judge Bao thereupon plied him with questions to verify what Anzhu had said, and having satisfied himself, he instructed the esquire to meet Anzhu at the prison gate and say some comforting words to the young man.

The next day, Judge Bao signed a mandate slip for a hearing and instructed the prison warden in private that he should do thus and thus when called to the tribunal. Then he summoned all parties to the hearing.

First, he had Zhang Bingyi and Mistress Yang confront one another. Mistress Yang stood by her previous statements and ceded not an inch of ground, whereupon Judge Bao ordered that Anzhu be brought out of prison. After a while, the warden came to report, "The prisoner is gravely ill and about to die; he cannot be moved."

This was the first time that Village Chief Li and Esquire Zhang had met one another, and the two compared notes and confirmed their perceptions, after which Village Chief Li became embroiled in a heated argument with Mistress Yang. As they were thus engaged, the prison warden returned again and reported, "Liu Anzhu has died of his illness."

Upon hearing these words, Mistress Yang, who did not understand the gravity of the matter, remarked spitefully, "And a good thing it is if he is truly dead! That would remove a big burden from my family." Judge Bao inquired of the warden, "Of what illness did Liu Anzhu die? Have the coroner examine the body and report to me."

Soon, the coroner came in and announced, "My examination shows that the deceased, who was about eighteen years old, died of blows delivered with some hard object to his head. This is proved by the presence of black and blue marks around the temples."

Judge Bao turned to Mistress Yang, and said severely, "Now what is to be done? This matter has become more grave; it has turned into a case of homicide. Ignorant woman! Who was that young man? Was he related to you?" Mistress Yang quailed, but continued to insist, "No, My Lord, he was not related."

Judge Bao then declared, "Had you been relatives, you would pertain to the older generation and he to the younger generation. And if he died after a beating administered by you, it would have been counted as an accidental death of an offspring, and you would not be required to forfeit your life but could get off with a fine. However, you say he is not related to you. You are doubtless aware that murderers are required by law to pay with their lives and debtors must pay back in kind. He was a stranger to you, and you could well have simply disclaimed him and let things go at that. What made you break his head with a stick, causing him to sicken with lockjaw and die? 'He who does another man to death shall also die.' Such is the law. Bailiffs, bring a cangue, affix it around the woman's neck, and confine her in the death house. When autumn comes, she shall be executed to pay for the young man's life."

Like a pack of tigers, the bailiffs uttered ferocious shouts and brought forward the heavy wooden collar, so frightening Mistress Yang that her complexion turned the color of mud. Groveling before Judge Bao, she cried frantically, "My Lord, he was this insignificant woman's nephew!"

Judge Bao pursued, "What proof do you have that he is your nephew?" And Mistress Yang whined, "I have the covenant as evidence." She hastily drew the sheet of paper from within her garments and handed it to the judge. Having read it, Judge Bao told Mistress Yang, "Since you now admit that he was your nephew, I shall have the corpse brought here and you shall take it with you and bury it. You may not shirk this responsibility." And Mistress Yang bowed her head to the ground and mumbled, "I shall willingly conduct a funeral for my nephew and bury him!"

Judge Bao then ordered that Liu Anzhu be taken out of prison, and when Anzhu was brought into the yamen, Judge Bao told him, "Liu Anzhu, I have now, by guile, recovered the covenant for you!" Whereupon Anzhu kowtowed in gratitude and said, "Had it not been for you, My Lord, I would have been driven to my death by the wrong done to me!"

Greatly astonished to hear Anzhu's voice, Mistress Yang raised her head from the ground and saw that Anzhu was not only alive and well, but that even the injuries on his head had healed. Utter confusion and embarrassment suffused her countenance, and she had nothing more to say.

Judge Bao now raised his writing brush and wrote his judgments as follows:

Liu Anzhu's filial piety and Zhang Bingyi's philanthropy are rare indeed, and should be widely commended among the populace. Village Chief Li shall select a wedding date for his daughter and son-in-law. Permission is granted to bury the remains of Liu Tianrui and his wife alongside their ancestors' tombs. Liu Tianxiang has behaved in a foolish and benighted manner, but is excused in consideration of his age. Mistress Yang should, by rights, be severely punished. She may, however, be released upon the payment of a fine to compensate for her crimes. Mistress Yang's son-in-law, who is unrelated to the Liu household, shall be driven out at once and may not encroach upon the Liu family's properties.

That done, Judge Bao ordered the prisoner released and announced the hearing closed. All persons present kowtowed to him and left the yamen.

In the next few days Esquire Zhang wrote a self-introductory letter to his new relatives and paid his respects to the families of Liu Tianxiang and Village Chief Li; he then returned to Luzhou without waiting for Anzhu. Liu Tianxiang, after going home, sternly reproved Mistress Yang for her reprehensible behavior, and then went with Anzhu to bury the bones of his younger brother and sister-in-law in their ancestors' cemetery. Before long, Village Chief Li chose a propitious date and formally married his daughter to Liu Anzhu. After one month had passed, the young couple journeyed together to Luzhou where they made their obeisances to Esquire Zhang and Mistress Guo. From then on, Liu Anzhu excelled in his studies and eventually became an official of note. And since neither Liu Tianxiang nor Esquire Zhang had any male offspring of their own, Anzhu eventually inherited the property of both households.

So we see that gain and attainment are ordered by fate and must not be tampered with by force, especially among flesh-and-blood kin, where unconscionable behavior such as that just described is most deleterious to the family's vital spirit. This storyteller has told his tale to admonish all persons not to hurt the natural ties of affection among kinsmen merely for the sake of some paltry property.

How a Childless Philanthropist Honored a Blank Letter and Begat Sons

[The Chinese edition from which this book was translated
offered no illustration for this story]

This story is about certain events that took place during the reign of Emperor Zhenzong [993–1022] of the Song dynasty.

At that time there lived in Luoyang County of Xijing, the Western Capital, an official whose name was Liu Hongjing and whose style name was Yuanpu. He had once served as the regional prefect of Qingzhou and had retired at the age of sixty to return to his hometown, where he now lived with his second wife, Mistress Wang, who was not yet forty years old. He possessed vast properties but had no offspring. So he placed all his farmland and businesses under the charge of his wife's nephew, Wang Wenyong, while he devoted himself solely to works of philanthropy, donating his wealth to good causes and scattering about his gold as though it were of no greater value than dust. As time passed, even he lost count of the persons he had helped, and people everywhere knew his name. Yet he had no sons, and that weighed heavily on his heart, day and night.

One year, when everyone was honoring the dead during the Qingming Festival, Liu Yuanpu directed Wang Wenyong to prepare wine and offerings, then set out for the family cemetery to perform sacrifices and sweep the tombs of his ancestors. He and his wife each rode in a small sedan chair and were followed by a retinue of servants and retainers. In a short time they arrived at the cemetery, and when the sacrifices had been completed and the wine sprinkled over the graves, Yuanpu fell on his knees and spoke these words:

> *I am childless, even at this venerable age,*
> *Lack of filial piety is a sin less grave.*
> *Few men live past their seventieth summer,*
> *And soon I shall end my earthly tether.*
> *I am here now to sweep your tomb,*
> *But who will do so in the years to come?*
>
> *I grieve, not for the lack of sons at my knees,*
> *But for the offerings that will soon cease.*
> *Sitting on high, and in your percipience,*
> *Show some compassion for your kith and kin!*
> *I have voiced my plea and shed my tears.*
> *What have I done to displease my forbears?*

Having said these words, Liu Yuanpu sobbed out aloud, which filled everyone in his entourage with sorrow. However, Mistress Wang, a most virtuous and honest woman, dried her tears and said consolingly, "Do not worry, my good husband. You may be getting on in years, but your virility has not waned. And even though I may not be able to bear children, I shall find you a young concubine and we may still hope for a son. Grieving serves us no good purpose."

With an effort Liu Yuanpu stopped weeping. He then ordered the servants to take their Mistress back to the house in her sedan chair and, retaining only a boy servant to keep him company, walked home slowly, hoping thus to dispel his melancholy mood.

As he was approaching his home, he came upon a seer who was holding up a signboard inscribed with the words: "My Clairvoyance Gives Access to the Immortals." Yuanpu had long wanted to consult a fortuneteller about his chances of acquiring a son, so he invited the man into his house. After they had seated themselves and enjoyed a cup of tea, Yuanpu sat up straight in his chair and asked the seer to carefully examine his physiognomy in order to read his fortune.

The seer did as he was asked, and then declared with candor, "Having read your physiognomy, I regret to say that not only will you have no offspring, but your life may soon come to an end." Whereupon Master Liu said, "Death would cause me no regrets, for I am, after all, close to seventy years old. As for offspring, at my age I have as much chance of begetting a child as I would of plucking the moon's reflection from a lake. Yet when I look back on my life, although I have done few good deeds I have wholeheartedly attempted to assist the weak and give to the poor. I know not what sins I have committed that would prevent me from serving my ancestors."

The seer smiled and said, "You, sir, are mistaken. As the ancient saying goes, 'resentments accumulate with wealth.' You may possess vast properties, but are you able to oversee and manage them all? Those in charge of your businesses are only interested in fattening their own purses and have no regard for fairness and justice. For purchasing they use large measuring scoops, but for selling they employ scales that give little weight. Such is their rapaciousness that the little folk do nothing but complain. You have attempted to be charitable, but your merits barely outbalance the wrongs done in your name, and so you are unable to build up your store of good fortune. If you should halt the malfeasance committed by your managers and perform more deeds of benevolence, I believe that good luck, many sons, and longevity will be yours." Liu Yuanpu listened to these words in silence.

The seer then rose to his feet, bid Liu Yuanpu farewell and, declining all offers of payment, strode out with airy dignity. Liu Yuanpu realized now that this was an unusual person and believed all that he had said. He had all the ledgers and accounts books pertaining to his land and businesses brought to him and examined them one by one. He also made discreet excursions into the streets and villages where he conducted extensive inquiries and learned many truths. He then reprimanded each and every one of his managers and even severely berated his wife's nephew, Wang Wenyong. Thereafter, Liu Yuanpu put even greater efforts into his charitable works.

At this point, let me tell you about a scholar in the capital, Bianliang, whose personal name was Li Xun and who went by the style name Kerang.

He was thirty-six years old, and his wife, who was from the Zhang family, had borne him a son, now seventeen years old. They had named the boy Li Yanqing and given him the pet name Chunlang. The family had originally lived in western Guangdong, which was a great distance from the capital, and since they were very poor Li Kerang had not been able to defray the costs of a journey specially to take the imperial examinations. Thus he had moved to the capital a few years earlier, bringing along his wife and his son. As a consequence, he had had the good fortune to succeed in the highest imperial examinations and to achieve the status of *jinshi*, after which he had been appointed to the minor position of a district magistrate in Qiantang County. He and his wife then chose an auspicious date to leave for his new position.

When Li Kerang saw the charming lakes and mountains in Qiantang County—so charming one would think one had come to the land of the immortals—he felt greatly uplifted in spirit. Who would have imagined, however, that the poor scholar's luck would be so meager. Within a month of his arrival he was struck down by an incurable disease.

Mistress Zhang and Chunlan, their son, sent for physicians who tried innumerable prescriptions, but none had any effect and it was obvious that the end was near. One day, Li Kerang asked his wife and son to come before his sickbed and said, "Having studied hard all my life, I have successfully passed the imperial examinations and can now die without regrets. However, we have no family or clan here to whom you can look for shelter or support, and it breaks my heart to leave behind a widow and an orphan. If you but knew the pain and pity I feel for you!" As he said these words, tears rained from his eyes. His wife and son could only do their best to comfort him.

All at once Li Kerang thought of something, and he said to himself, "I have heard that Liu Yuanpu in Luoyang is a noble and generous person whose name is known far and wide. He is reputed to grant any person's request, whether or not that person is known to him, so long as the request is made in sincerity. This is the only man to whom I can entrust my wife and son."

Calling his wife, he said, "Help me sit up." Then he instructed his son to bring him ink, a writing brush, and paper. Just as he raised the brush to write, however, he hesitated and reflected, "I have never met this man, which makes it difficult for me to exchange any amenities with him. How am I to write this letter?"

Suddenly he had an idea. He sent his wife and son out of the room, saying that he wished to have some hot water, and when they returned he had already sealed his letter and inscribed the following words on the envelope: "For the personal attention of my kind elder brother Liu Yuanpu of Luoyang. Your younger brother, Li Xun." Enjoining his wife and son to take good care of the letter, he said, "I have an old friend with whom I have an eight-kowtow bond of brotherhood. Originally from Luoyang, he once served as the prefect of Qingzhou County. This man's loyalty to his friends is utterly beyond question and he will certainly assist the two of you. Go to him with this letter, and you will not be rejected. And when you see Uncle Liu, bow many times to him and say to him that I shall no longer see him in this life."

He then spoke to Mistress Zhang, saying, "We have cared for one another these twenty years, and now is the time for the long farewell. Should Uncle Liu take you under his wing, behave with caution, and make sure to instruct our son to strive for the renown that I have failed to achieve. You are now two months with child. If we should have another son, have him study like his father before him. Should the child be a daughter, see that she eventually marries a good man, and I shall be able to rest in peace."

He then spoke to Chunlang, saying, "You must treat your Uncle Liu like a father and Aunt Liu like a mother. You must also show filial respect to your own mother and pursue your studies assiduously to gain honor and renown. Though I die, I shall still live on in spirit, and I shall not be able to find peace by the Nine Fountains of the nether regions if you disobey my words."

As his wife and son listened tearfully to his final instructions, he continued, "After I die, place my coffin in Fuqiu Temple for safekeeping and hold the obsequies when you have joined Uncle Liu. All I wish is to be buried in a quiet plot of land. There is no need to send me back to western Guangdong." Choking with sobs, he cried aloud, "Heaven! Oh, Heaven! Although poor, I, Li Xun, have led a clean life, so why could I not live to become a full magistrate?" And with that, he fell back in his bed, and no calls or pleas could bring him back to life.

Mistress Zhang and Chunlang wept their hearts out, and Mistress Zhang wailed, "Alas, bitter is the fate that awaits you and me, now an orphan and a widow! What shall we do if Master Liu refuses to countenance us?" Chunlang said, "We have no choice other than to follow my father's last instructions. However, my father was a good judge of men, and it may be that this Uncle Liu is truly a good person."

Mistress Zhang then took stock of their possessions, but found not the least bit of money. Indigent to start with, Li Kerang had nevertheless been scrupulously honest. He had, moreover, held his official position for little more than a month, and the paltry salary he received had all been spent on physicians and medicine. Fortunately his colleagues pitched in to buy him a coffin, in which he was laid out, and then had the coffin placed in the magisterial residence. There, his widow and son wept and offered sacrifices day and night, and after the requisite seven-times-seven days of mourning they entrusted the body to the Fuqiu Temple for safekeeping in accordance with the last wishes of the deceased. Then they assembled their few personal belongings and some money for the road, took the deceased's last letter, and set forth. Eating when hungry, drinking when thirsty, sleeping at night, and walking when dawn broke, they wended their way along the road that led to Luoyang.

Now let us go back to Liu Yuanpu.

He was in his study one day, playing with his collection of antiques, when a gatekeeper reported, "There are, outside, a mother and son from western Guangdong who claim to be family members of one of the Master's very close acquaintances. They have brought a letter with them." Yuanpu wondered to himself, "Do I have acquaintances in such distant parts?" He ordered that they be brought in.

When mother and son had entered and made their obeisances, Yuanpu inquired of them, "Worthy mother and son, where has this old person met you before? I have truly forgotten and beg you to enlighten me."

Li Chunlang replied, "The truth is that neither my mother nor your nephew have ever met you, but my late father was Uncle's close friend." Yuanpu asked for the father's name, and Chunlang replied, "His name was Li Xun, and his scholar's name was Kerang. My mother comes from the Zhang family. Your nephew's name is Yanqing, though I am known by my pet name, Chunlang. Our family was originally from western Guangdong, and my late father took us to the capital city so he could attend the imperial examinations, in which he succeeded, whereupon he was subsequently appointed to the post of a district magistrate in Qiantang County. He passed away one month later, and just before he died, feeling concerned that my mother and I would be alone in the world, he told us that we had an Uncle Liu in Luoyang who had become his brother of eight kowtows when my father was still very young. He instructed us to come to you after he died, bringing you a letter written in his own hand. That is why my mother and I have presumed to intrude upon your abode, and we apologize for causing this disturbance."

Chunlang's account bewildered Yuanpu, and he was no less mystified when he saw the writing on the envelope Chunlang presented to him. When he opened the envelope, he was astonished to see that it contained only a blank sheet of paper. Falling silent, he pondered the matter for a while, and suddenly found the explanation. To himself, he said: "That is undoubtedly the reason! However, I shall not divulge it now, but shall first provide mother and son with a place to stay."

When mother and son saw him deep in thought they assumed he would turn them away. Little did they know that he would be bestowing great favors upon them.

Putting away the letter, Yuanpu said to them, "Yes, Brother Li was indeed my brother of eight kowtows. I had been looking forward to meeting him again. Who would have expected him to die so soon? How sad! And what a pity! However, the two of you are now like my own flesh and blood, and you shall make your home here."

He then asked his wife, Mistress Wang, to come out, explained to her who the visitors were and where they had come from, and asked the two women to treat one another like sisters-in-law. Chunlang, on his part, comported himself both as a son and a nephew. A banquet was forthwith held to welcome the mother and son. While wine was being served, it was mentioned that Li Xun's coffin was still being kept in a temple in the town where the deceased had served as an official. Yuanpu at once promised to take charge of the obsequies. Also, as the women conversed with one another, Mistress Wang learned that Mistress Zhang was expecting a child.

After the banquet, mother and son were taken to the South Building where they were to stay. The rooms were fully equipped with furniture, utensils, and vessels. Several maids and young servants were assigned to look after their needs, and the three meals served every day were as tasty as they were abundant. Mother and son, who felt that Liu Yuanpu's willingness to take them in already exceeded their expectations, were overwhelmed with gratitude by such hospitality. And as time went by, Yuanpu, on his part, was impressed with Mistress Zhang's virtue and gentleness and with Chunlang's intelligence as well as honesty and trustworthiness, and he felt great respect for mother and son.

With their consent, he dispatched people to bring Li Kerang's coffin from Qiantang County.

One day, as Liu Yuanpu was sitting and conversing with his wife, his eyes became moist with tears. His wife inquired if there was anything wrong, and Liu Yuanpu said, "I have observed the behavior and courage of Master Li's son and I know he will perform great deeds in the years to come. If only I had a son like him, I could die without regrets. But another year has gone by with still no sign of any offspring for me, and for that reason I cannot help but feel sad." His wife remonstrated, "I have time and again advised you to take a concubine, but you keep refusing. I insist on procuring one for you, and I guarantee you will have a son!"

But Yuanpu only replied, "My wife, do not talk about such things. Although I am getting along in years, you are still in the prime of life and would certainly become pregnant were Heaven not of a mind to terminate the house of Liu. Since fate has decided that should be so, nothing can be done, even if I were surrounded with concubines." So saying, he walked out of the room.

Nonetheless, Mistress Wang was determined to find a concubine for her husband. Yet she knew he would refuse outright if she attempted to discuss the matter with him again. So she asked a servant to bring Dame Xue, a matchmaker, in secret, and proceeded to tell her what she desired. She instructed the matchmaker: "You are not to let the Master know anything before we find the right person. And make sure to find a young woman who is both virtuous and beautiful, for only then might the Master perchance become fond of her." Dame Xue agreed to do so and departed.

In the next few days, Dame Xue brought a number of girls for Mistress Wang's inspection, but none of them met with the latter's approval. The matchmaker said, "These are the best I can find here. If you desire something better, I would have to go to the capital city Bianliang where people from all regions congregate and live together."

It so happened that Wang Wenyong, Mistress Wang's nephew, had some business to attend to in the capital. So Mistress Wang gave him in private one hundred taels of silver and asked Dame Xue to go with him. This suited Dame Xue just fine, for she had to see to another matchmaking affair in Bianliang, so the two left together for the capital.

Now let me address yet another side of this same story.

There lived in Xiangfu County of Bianliang's Kaifeng Prefecture a *jinshi* whose name was Pei Xi and whose style name was Anqing. He was fifty years old, and his wife, Mistress Zheng, had died long ago. They had had only one daughter, called Lansun, who was sixteen years of age and exceedingly beautiful.

Pei Anqing had been a minor official for a few years and was now being promoted to the position of prefect of Xiangyang. An acquaintance said to him, "You have always been poor, but now that you have landed this high position your only worries will be about being too rich rather than too poor."

Anqing laughed and replied, "Where will such riches come from? I see greedy, cruel, and small-minded officials who are interested solely in personal gain, who dominate the common folk, who cause people to sell their children and wives, all for the sake of fattening their own purses. The Son of Heaven enjoins us to be like fathers and mothers to the people. He has never told me to oppress his subjects. When I go to my post, all I shall accept from Xiangyang is a cup of clear water. It is my lot to be poor, and I shall be receiving from the imperial court a salary that will suffice to keep me from hunger and cold. So why should I seek riches?" Having made up his mind to be good official, Pei Anqing chose an auspicious date and, together with his daughter, set forth to assume his post. They arrived in Xiangyang in less than a day. Six months after Anqing took up his duties he turned the prefecture into a place of abundant merchandise, content inhabitants, few complaints, and uncomplicated lawsuits. There was a folksong that went:

> *The road before Xiangyang Prefecture,*
> *Leads straight to Lord Pei's work table.*
> *Clerks nod off in their offices,*
> *Bailiffs go out to chop firewood.*

Time flew by, and once again there came the hot, sultry weather of the sixth moon. One day, as Pei Anqing and Lansun were partaking of their midday meal, the heat became unbearable and, to alleviate his discomfort, Anqing asked for some cool well-water. When this was brought to him, he drank two cups of the water, then offered some to his daughter as well. Lansun took a few sips and said, "Father, this water is so insipid. How are you able to drink it?" Anqing replied, "Do not be so disparaging. We are most fortunate to have this water, and you should not complain that it is insipid." But Lansun argued, "Father, in what way have I been disparaging? In weather like this, many noble and rich people do not think it extravagant to enjoy ice-cooled lotus roots, melons, or plums. But you, a county official, consider it a treat to have a cup of plain water. Are you not being rather unrealistic?"

Anqing replied, "My child, you know little of the realities of this world. Let me enlighten you. Nobles and rich scions bask in the power and glory of their ancestors and support their lifestyle with money amassed by their forefathers. They know nothing about tilling and harvesting and have no vocation to speak of. Their sole objective in this life is to enjoy themselves and acquire whatever pleases them. Little do they know that overindulgence leads to ruin, and that the day will come when their horses will die and their money is exhausted. And even if this does not happen, it is only because they are born with a bit of luck. Your father cannot compare with these people, as I come from a poor family and, moreover, have been charged by the imperial court with responsibility for the country and the people. Think of the warriors defending the borders of the country in this sort of weather! Wearing heavy armor and bearing weapons, they get no respite either by day or by night and never know whether they are fated to live or die. And then there are the farmers with their hoes and the merchants who transport goods. They suffer all manner of hardships as they drudge and toil with rainwater and perspiration coursing down their backs or with the sun scorching their skin. Compared to these people, your father lives a life of bliss, does he not? There are also people of an even lower order who have committed errors and are convicted of crimes, imprisoned, whipped, beaten, shackled hand and foot, and confined in places where they see neither the sun nor the sky. These people do not even get enough filthy water to drink, to say nothing of cool water. They cannot choose either to live or to die. They, too, have been given flesh and blood by their parents, and they, too, know pain like everyone else, yet they are put to such suffering. Compared to them, do I not live the life of the immortals? There are today some one or two hundred felons incarcerated in our prison. I intend to allow them freedom of movement within the prison and give them cool water once a day until such time as summer turns into autumn."

Lansun protested, "Father, you should exercise caution. Imprisoned criminals are not good people, and if something untoward were to occur because you wish to make things easier for them, you could find yourself in serious trouble." Anqing reassured her, saying, "If I show them kindness, they will certainly not do anything to hurt me. Moreover, I shall instruct the guards to maintain a tighter watch at the prison gates."

So when Anqing held court the next day, he instructed the prison warden to give prisoners freedom of movement within the prison's walls and to issue them cool water every day, all the while keeping them under careful supervision. Having received this order, the prison turnkeys went forthwith to each cell to unshackle the prisoners and give them cool water.

The prison guards kept diligent watch at first, and there were no mishaps, but after ten or more days their vigilance slackened. Then came the first day of the seventh moon.

According to an old prison custom, offerings were made to the gods whenever the moon was new. And on that day, having burned paper money, the prison guards commenced to drink and carouse in the afternoon, and continued to do so until dusk, by which time all were sodden drunk.

Meanwhile the inmates had conceived the intention of breaking out of prison as soon as they found that the prison rules had been relaxed. The more seasoned among them told their companions to keep sharp objects secreted close at hand. And on that day, when all the guards were inebriated, they found the opportunity to carry out their plan.

At about the time of the second watch at night, a loud outcry arose in the prison and all the hundred or more prisoners rose up in unison. They first killed the keepers in the prison houses, then fought their way out of the gate, cutting down the warden and the guards and felling all persons they encountered with a single blow. Some guards who were able to conceal themselves in dark places heard the convicts shouting, "The Lord is a kind man, let none of us harm him!" The prisoners made straight for the yamen offices and slew several of the clerks there. Then with raucous yells they ran toward the town gates, which had not been shut, since those were peaceful times, and dashed out into the countryside.

Pei Anqing woke from his slumbers when he heard the commotion outside and quickly rose from his bed. By this time, reports were being sent in, and his soul well nigh flew out of his body when he heard what had transpired. He uttered cries of despair and remorse, and said, "Matters would not have come to such a pass had I listened to Lansun's advice. Never did I think that people would fail to repay me in kind when I treated them with compassion!"

Anqing recruited the able-bodied among the local residents and sent them out in pursuit, but it was like fishing for needles in a vast sea, and not one of the prisoners was found. The next day, he reported the matter to the higher authorities. As was only to be expected, the case was viewed with the utmost seriousness in Bianliang, the capital, and before two weeks went by it was brought to the attention of the imperial court where the emperor discussed the matter with his ministers.

Had Pei Anqing been a venal and obsequious person, there might have been people at the court who would speak in his favor, but he was a man of uncompromising integrity and had always refused to pander to the rich and powerful. Besides, as his conduct was as clear as water and he had no means other than his official salary, he lacked the wherewithal to bribe those in power. Hence, no one attempted to defend him, and all concurred in the following opinion:

"As the person in charge, the prefect cannot evade responsibility for connivance in the convicts' escape from prison. Moreover, it would seem suspicious that yamen clerks were put to death while the prefect himself was spared. He should thus be taken in for questioning."

A memorial was written to this effect, and the emperor, having expressed agreement with it, issued an edict that judiciary emissaries be sent to seize Pei Anqing and bring him to the capital.

As behooved a good and loyal official, Pei Anqing could not but bend his head and allow himself to be shackled. However, he believed that with the good name he enjoyed as an administrator, he might still be able to exonerate himself. He instructed Lansun to pack some belongings, and when that was done, father and daughter set out together with the escorts.

They arrived in the capital a few days later. However, they found they had no place to stay, as Pei Anqing's former residence had already been confiscated by imperial edict and the few servants that remained had taken to their heels. Fortunately, his wife, before she died, had befriended the priestesses at the Daoist Qingzhen Temple, and these now agreed to lend Anqing and his daughter a room.

The next day, Anqing, clad in the black garments and small cap of a commoner, went with his escorts to the imperial court to await orders. Then, by imperial decree, he was taken to the Court of Judicial Review for interrogation and forthwith put behind bars. Lansun had no recourse but to take some money from the little she possessed and distribute it high and low as bribes so that she might have messages or tea and food sent in from time to time to her father.

Anqing was getting on in years, and the shock and suffering he sustained further weakened him. He worried day and night, and could neither eat nor drink. Lansun tried but was unable to have any food sent in to him. Her bribe money had been spent in vain. One day, Anqing saw Lansun just as she arrived at the prison gates and, calling to her, said, "I have great difficulty breathing and may not live this day out. I attempted to show kindness, but have only invited disaster as well as implicated you, my child. Although my sins will not be visited upon my offspring, you will have no place to go after I die and cannot escape the fate of becoming a servant or a slave."

As Anqing uttered these words, he felt as though a thousand arrows were piercing his heart. He cried out several times, and then died. Yet he was fortunate in that he had not yet been interrogated and was thus spared the sufferings caused by instruments of torture.

Lansun wept like a woman possessed, stumbling and falling to the ground and beating her breast. When she regained some measure of calm, she asked to take away her father's body, but was told that she was not at liberty do so as he was designated a criminal by the imperial court. Casting all caution and consideration to the winds, Lansun burst through the doors of the Court of Judicial Review and, weeping, recounted why and how the prisoners had escaped, and her grief and distress touched all who heard her. Fortunately for her, the magistrate of the Court of Judicial Review was a just and fair man. He felt great pity after he heard Lansun's account and forthwith wrote a report as follows:

> *This Magistrate of the Court of Judicial Review has found that Pei Xi, the erstwhile prefect of Xiangyang, was a kind man of good heart who attempted to be a good administrator. While it is true he was guilty of gross negligence in the prison affair, he has already been punished by Heaven. There is, moreover, no evidence to show that he harbored seditious sentiments and was anything other than a loyal subject. Now that he has passed away in prison, I make bold to suggest that he be treated with leniency. On my knees, I plead that Your Imperial Majesty exercise benevolence and allow his body to be buried without delay, as a mark of the imperial court's consideration for its subjects. It is with trepidation that your subject submits this report.*

The Emperor Zhenzong was not an unkind ruler, and when he learned that Pei Xi had died he was of no mind to raise harsh demands and thus decided to approve the magistrate's report.

To Lansun, this news brought her a modicum of happiness amid her pain and sorrow. Using all that was left of her silver, she purchased a coffin, hired men to retrieve her father's corpse from the prison and encoffin it, had the bier placed in Qingzhen Temple, and made an offering of food for the deceased. Then she wept as though her heart would break. Pei Anqing had brought along little money to start with, and by now nothing remained of it. Though the coffin had been bought, there was no money with which to inter it. After much casting about in her mind, Lansun admitted to herself, "The only relative we have is an uncle named Zheng who is the military commissioner of Xichuan and lives there with his family. But the road to Xichuan is long and treacherous, and there is no way he can render me any assistance."

Unable to come up with any ideas and having no other recourse, she wrote on a large sheet of paper the words "Selling Self to Pay for Father's Funeral" and went before her father's coffin. There, she kowtowed four times and intoned a prayer, saying, "My father's spirit that has not yet gone far away. Bless me, and let me meet a good person as I go forth!" She then tearfully rose to her feet and, racked with mortification and shame, walked through the streets, holding up the sheet of paper and offering herself for sale.

Poor Pei Lansun! She who had been a delicate and sheltered virgin and who blushed at the mere sight of a stranger was now forced to wend her own way in the world! Pain wrenched at her bowels whenever she recalled her father's last words.

It is said that Heaven always leaves one a way out of difficulties. As Lansun was selling herself in the streets, an elderly woman approached her and, bowing a greeting, inquired, "Young lady, for what reason are you selling yourself? And why do you look so forlorn?" Then, as she looked closer, she exclaimed, "Why, is this not Miss Pei? What has brought you to such a pass?" It so happened that the elderly woman was Dame Xue from Luoyang. When Lansun's mother, Mistress Zheng, had still been alive, Dame Xue had visited her whenever she came to the capital, and now she had recognized the girl.

Lansun raised her head and, when she saw it was Dame Xue, she led the matchmaker to a secluded spot and tearfully recounted all that had transpired. The older woman, being a person who was easily moved to tears, also wept when the girl came to the most sorrowful points in her account. She exclaimed, "So, such a great tragedy has befallen the master of your household! But you are the daughter of an official and should not become a person of the lower orders. If indeed you intend to sell yourself, what with your grace and beauty you should at least aspire to become a concubine, rather than any servant or bondsmaid." Lansun replied, "As I am doing this for my father's sake, I do not mind even if I must lose my life. Nothing matters to me anymore."

Dame Xue thereupon declared, "If that is the case, then you, my young lady, need not worry. There is a certain Prefect Liu of Luoyang County who is old but has no son. His wife, Mistress Wang, wishes to obtain a concubine for him and has asked me to find one for her. I searched for a long time in the area where we live, but have not found anyone to Mistress Wang's liking. Lately, a prominent family in Luoyang asked me to arrange a match with a minister's household in the capital. So Mistress Wang entrusted the purchase money for a concubine to her own nephew, Wang Wenyong, and had him come along with me to seek a suitable candidate. It is indeed serendipitous that I should have met you. Mistress Wang wants a person who is both virtuous and attractive. Your beauty, my young lady, is unparalleled, and selling yourself to pay for your father's interment is an act of the greatest filial piety. So this match can in all probability be concluded. Prefect Liu is a generous man who performs charitable deeds, and Mistress Wang is a most worthy and virtuous woman. Although you will perforce take second place to Mistress Wang when you go to their home, you will be assured of happiness and security for the rest of your life. So, what do you think?"

Lansun replied, "I shall do whatever you suggest. However, by selling myself as a concubine I shall be sullying my family's name, so it is imperative that you do not divulge my true circumstances. Just say that I am the daughter of a commoner's family." Dame Xue nodded and promised, "That shall be done."

Dame Xue took Lansun to Wang Wenyong's lodgings and told him how she had found the girl. Even from a distance, Wang Wenyong had seen that the girl's beauty was such as could cause the downfall of cities and states. He said, "A girl of such unrivalled beauty will certainly meet with my aunt's approval!"

And so, with one party having fallen into adversity and the other being a family of considerable wealth, there were no arguments over the deal, and an agreement was readily reached. A full one hundred taels of the purest silver was handed over to Lansun, after which Wang Wenyong requested that she prepare for the journey home. But Lansun demurred and said, "The reason I sold myself was to bury my father. I can only leave after the funeral." Dame Xue reasoned with her, saying, "My young lady, you are all alone here, and it would be difficult for you to handle all matters pertaining to the funeral. Would it not be easier for you to go first to Luoyang and marry, and then ask Master Liu to send someone to attend to the funeral?" Lansun could only agree.

Wang Wenyong was a worldly-wise man and, knowing that this girl was to become his uncle's concubine, he dared not commit any breach of propriety. He asked Dame Xue to accompany Lansun on the trip back home while he himself either preceded them or followed behind. The distance from Bianliang to Luoyang was a mere four hundred *li*, so the party arrived at the Liu's residence within a few days.

Once there, Wang Wenyong went to oversee his own business, while Dame Xue secretly took Lansun into the house to meet Mistress Wang. As Lansun greeted and kowtowed to her, the mistress of the house looked at her and saw a maiden with a natural beauty that required no makeup, a carriage of great poise and elegance, and a voice that was at the same time subdued and stirring. Highly pleased, she asked Lansun what her name and family name was, then prepared a room for her to stay in and assigned a maidservant to tend to her needs.

The next day, Mistress Wang said to Liu Yuanpu, "There is something I wish to tell my Lord, and I hope you will not take exception." Liu Yuanpu replied, "Madam, since you have something to say, say it. Why such hesitation?"

Mistress Wang continued, "My Lord, you have surely heard the adage 'few are the men since ancient times who have lived past seventy years of age.' You are now approaching that age and the road ahead of you may not be too long, yet you still do not have any offspring. As the saying goes, 'to be healthy is a blessing, and having sons is the supreme satisfaction.' I have long wanted to find a concubine for you but have hesitated to broach the matter, partly because My Lord is most prudent about such matters, and partly because I had not yet found the right person, and so I kept it to myself. However, I have now obtained from Bianliang the daughter of a family named Pei. She is in the best years of her life and of exceptional talent and beauty. It is my desire that my Lord will accept her as your concubine. Should she bear for you sons or daughters, these will be descendants of the Liu family."

After a moment's thought, Liu Yuanpu said, "I have never taken a concubine, as I have always feared that I am destined to remain childless, and it was not my desire to spoil the life of any young woman. However, since you have shown such concern and consideration in this matter, let the woman come out and meet me."

Lansun thereupon came out of her room, knelt before Liu Yuanpu, and kowtowed. Struck by her appearance, Liu Yuanpu thought to himself, "Judging from this girl's countenance and behavior, she is not from an ordinary family." He asked aloud, "What is your name? What kind of family do you come from? And why are you selling yourself?" Lansun replied, "This humble woman is the daughter of a commoner named Pei in Bianliang, and my name is Lansun. I am selling myself because my father died penniless and I needed the money to bury him." As she spoke these words, she averted her face to conceal the tears in her eyes.

Liu Yuanpu looked at her thoughtfully, then said, "Do not try to deceive me. You are assuredly not the daughter of a commoner. And it is clear you are deeply distressed and hiding something. Tell me frankly what it is, and I may be able to do something to help you in your sorrow."

Lansun tried once more to conceal the truth, but as Liu Yuanpu continued to question her, she finally recounted from beginning to end, in full detail, how her father had transgressed by slackening supervision over prison inmates. And all the while tears streamed down her face.

Deeply shocked by what he heard and shedding tears of sympathy, Liu Yuanpu exclaimed, "I knew that you did not look like someone from a commoner's family! My wife almost led me into error! And what a pity that such a good official came to such an unjust end!" He apologized repeatedly to Lansun, then said, "Since Miss Pei has no place to go, you may live here in our house. I shall also look for a suitable site to bury your father." To which Lansun replied, "Only Heaven can recompense you for your benevolence and consideration! But first, will My Lord accept an obeisance from this humble girl." Liu Yuanpu hastened to raise her to her feet, then ordered the maidservant: "See to it that Miss Pei is well attended to. And make sure that my order is obeyed!"

Liu Yuanpu then proceeded to the front hall of the house and dispatched one of his attendants to Bianliang to bring back Prefect Pei's coffin, which arrived within a few days. The coffin of District Magistrate Li of Qiantang County also arrived at about the same time. Liu Yuanpu had both coffins placed in the main hall of one of his houses and installed two sacrificial altars for the funeral ceremony. Mistress Zhang, together with her son, kowtowed to her late husband, while Liu Yuanpu accompanied Lansun in kowtowing to her late father. Liu Yuanpu also hired a well-known geomancer to select two good sites for the obsequies, which were set to take place on an auspicious day in the twelfth moon.

One day, Mistress Wang said to Yuanpu, "Although Miss Pei is from a noble family, she was rescued by my Lord when she met with misfortune, and there is no knowing to what depths she would have fallen had she ended up anywhere else. My Lord has also chosen a site to bury her father, which, too, is a no small act of benevolence. So I believe she will be willing to become your concubine. And who knows? Being the daughter of a prominent family and possibly sharing their good fortune, she might well produce offspring for you. Should that happen, not only will you have heirs, but she too will be guaranteed a secure life. I believe this is the sensible thing to do, and hope my Lord will think about it."

No sooner had these words left her mouth than anger suffused Liu Yuanpu's countenance and he said, "Woman, what are you saying! There are plenty of pretty women in the world and I can easily find someone else, should I wish to take a concubine. How dare I defile the daughter of Prefect Pei! If I, Liu Hongjing, were to have any thought of doing such a thing, may the gods in heaven punish me!" Hearing this, his wife knew that she had spoken indiscreetly, and she said no more.

Liu Yuanpu was displeased, but after giving the matter some thought he told himself, "What a dullard I am! Since I have no children of my own, I could very well adopt her as my daughter! That would forestall any more flights of fantasy on my wife's part!"

He instructed a servant girl to invite Lansun out of her room, and when she came, he said, "I am many years older than your father, and he and I both served as prefects. Furthermore, old as I am, I have no children. So if you do not think poorly of me, I would wish to take you as my daughter. What is your opinion?" Lansun replied, "This humble person is grateful to you and your wife for taking me under your care, and I am willing to serve you morning and night as your slave and servant. But how can I accept such generosity from you?" Liu Yuanpu quickly said, "Nonsense! You are from an official's family and the setback you have encountered is merely a temporary matter. Why should you relegate yourself to such a lowly position? I disagree with you. You should not be overly humble."

Lansun said, "My Lord and Lady have given me my second life, and I could not repay you even though my bones were to be ground to dust. Since you do not despise me for my sorry circumstances and desire to adopt me as your daughter, I cannot but comply with your wishes! Allow me to formally acknowledge you as my father and mother here and now."

Liu Yuanpu was much pleased, and he told his wife, "I have adopted Lansun as our daughter. We should let her perform the full ritual today." Lansun thereupon kowtowed, rose to her feet, then kowtowed again, altogether eight times in succession, and thereafter addressed Lord Liu and his wife as "Father" and "Mother" and treated them with the utmost respect and affection.

Mistress Wang now said to Liu Yuanpu, "Since you have adopted Lansun as our daughter, we should choose a husband for her. My nephew has lost his wife and is still a young man. He has managed our businesses for many years and is quite talented and clever and would not disgrace our daughter. My Lord could well fulfill the match with him." Liu Yuanpu smiled and said, "I shall of course see to your nephew's second marriage. But I have my own ideas about this matter, and all you need do is prepare the trousseau."

Mistress Wang did what she was asked to do, while Liu Yuanpu chose an auspicious date for the wedding. When that day came, he had pigs and goats slaughtered for a grand banquet to which all his kinsmen and friends in the county were invited. Mistress Zhang, her son, and Wang Wenyong also attended the wedding banquet. Many of the guests assumed that Liu Yuanpu was taking a concubine, whereas Mistress Wang thought that her nephew was to be married. However, no one could say for certain whom the legendary Goddess of the Moon would favor that night.

When the auspicious hour arrived, Liu Yuanpu gave instructions that a brand new suit of bridegroom's clothes be brought out and placed in the center of the hall. Liu Yuanpu then clasped his hands and said to all present, "I, Hongjing, wish to say something to all my respected relatives and friends here today. I have heard there is no righteousness in taking possession of another's beauty, and no morality in taking advantage of another's adversities. Master Pei, the prefect of Xiangyang who was unjustly treated and died in prison, had a daughter, Lansun, who has now come of age. My wife desired that I take the girl as my concubine. However, I would rather be without offspring than taint the moral integrity of a prefect. My wife's nephew, Wang Wenyong, has a talent for managing businesses, but he himself is not the issue of an official's household, and it is therefore inappropriate to match him to the daughter of an official. Now, Yanqing, the only son of my late friend, County Magistrate Li, springs from a prominent family. Young in age, his appearance rivals that of the most handsome men, and his talents surpass those of many a famous scholar. He is truly what is called 'a gentleman and a good mate for a virtuous maiden.' I am hosting this banquet today in the hope of fulfilling this excellent match. What do my respected guests think of this?"

People present at the banquet one and all praised Master Liu's boundless integrity. Young Master Li, for his part, was taken completely by surprise and attempted to decline the honor accorded to him, but Liu Yuanpu would accept no excuses and personally helped him don the bridegroom's attire. The music of flutes and pipes and singing arose in the hall, which was brightly lit by many lanterns. Then the tinkling of bracelets and jade pendants was heard in the distance as Dame Xue, in the role of the bride's companion, and several handmaidens escorted Lansun out of her chambers. The bride and groom then took their places on a flowered carpet and exchanged kowtows to become husband and wife. It was a scene of unsurpassed magnificence.

Mistress Zhang and her son Chunlang had never dreamed they would be given such Heaven-sent happiness. And Lansun, too, rejoiced as she saw by the light of the lanterns how uncommonly handsome the groom was. For she had fully expected to marry a fine old man, but was now wedded instead to a fine young scholar!

After the ceremony, the newlyweds were assisted into sedan chairs. Liu Yuanpu personally conducted them to the South Building, together with the bride's trousseau, which was worth a thousand taels of silver. Then he returned to the hall and, as the orchestra played with great verve and vigor, he entertained his guests who drank until dawn before returning to their homes.

In the wedding chamber, the union of the newlyweds was truly the ideal conjoining of a beautiful woman and a scholar, and thanks to the joyful love they shared that night, they became as closely attached to one another as fish are to water. Resting afterward on their pillows, they talked about Master Liu's great philanthropy, and their very bones were filled with gratitude.

They rose early the next morning to greet their mother, Mistress Zhang, who in turn took them to Master Liu, to whom they kowtowed and gave their thanks. Mistress Zhang then prepared some offerings and they went together before the coffins. At Mistress Zhang's behest, Lansun and Chunlang bowed to their respective fathers-in-law. Weeping, Mistress Zhang placed her hands on her husband's coffin and said, "My husband, you were an honest man in life, and your spirit surely enjoys high esteem in death. Master Liu has not only helped your widow and your orphaned son, but has additionally given us the daughter of a family of note to be your daughter-in-law. His benevolence is vaster than the sky. I hope that from where you are in the nether world you will see to it that Master Liu is blessed with sons and live to be a hundred years old." Chunlang and his wife, too, uttered silent prayers. From then on, their little family lived in harmony, and they kept incense burning day and night to ensure that Master Liu would enjoy the blessings of the nether world.

Time passed quickly, and the date of the burials, set for the middle of the twelfth moon, arrived. Master Liu assembled a crew of craftsmen and laborers and had the two coffins transported from their present resting place to the burial ground. Mistress Zhang and Chunlang and his wife wore attire of deep mourning to send off the deceased. After the coffins were interred, a tombstone was erected before each grave, one with the inscription "Tomb of Pei Anqing, Prefect of Xiangyang of the Song Dynasty ," and the other, "Tomb of Li Kerang, Magistrate of Qiantang County of the Song Dynasty." Situated amid pine and birch trees and encircled by mountains and water, the two graves stood together, symbols of the joining of the two families. Liu Yuanpu personally officiated over the sacrifices and the funeral rites, while Mistress Zhang and her family uttered loud wails of mourning. Then, turning their eyes to Master Liu, they prostrated themselves on the grass before him. Liu Yuanpu kowtowed in return and repeatedly insisted that he had done little to deserve such gratitude. Then all went home to attend to their own affairs.

That same night, Liu Yuanpu slept until around midnight, when he saw the shadowy figures of two men, both of whom were coiffed with the caps of officials, held ceremonial ivory tablets, and wore purple robes with gold belts. The men fell on their knees before Liu Yuanpu and kowtowed, calling him their Great Benefactor. Astonished, Liu Yuanpu hastily raised them to their feet, saying, "Why have you, respected gods, come to this world? Is it to take the life of this old man?"

The man on the left said, "I am Pei Xi, Prefect of Xiangyang, and this person is Li Kerang, Magistrate of Qiantang County. The God of Heaven, knowing us for our honesty and loyalty during our previous lives, has appointed me to the position of God of All Cities Under Heaven, and Master Li to the post of Assistant at the Heavenly Court of Appeals. After I died in prison, and when my daughter had no one to turn to, you, in your great benevolence, found her a good husband and gave my body a good resting place. Li Kerang and I have thus become in-laws in the nether world. There is little we can do to repay you for your boundless magnanimity, so we have submitted a joint memorial to the Heavenly Court. In recognition of your great virtue, the God of Heaven has advanced your official rank by one grade and conferred on you another three decades of life plus two sons. Although you are separated from us by the boundaries of light and shadow, we deemed that we should inform you of this decision."

The figure to his right added, "I never met you in life. That made it difficult for me to appeal to you at the time, which is why I implied my sentiments in that blank letter. However, you understood at once what I wished to say and, in your exceptional generosity, acknowledged the pretended relationship, provided a living for my wife and son, and interred my body. Still more, you found for my son a fair maiden to carry on my family line. Thus, even prolonging your life and giving you sons is insufficient to repay you a ten thousandth part of your boundless magnanimity. My daughter, Fengming, with whom my wife was pregnant when I died, will be born tomorrow morning, and I make so bold as to offer her as wife to the first son that will be born to you. Since you have given me a daughter-in-law, I give you a daughter-in-law in return as a token of my gratitude."

The two men then raised their folded hands in farewell. Liu Yuanpu rose to see them off, but the two pushed him back—and he woke up, to find himself lying in bed with his wife, Mistress Wang. He told her what he had seen in his dream, and she said, "I, too, admire your great generosity, the likes of which has seldom been seen and should, of course, be handsomely recompensed. I believe that what the gods said to you is true."

Liu Yuanpu said meditatively, "Pei Xi and Li Kerang were honest and upright men when they lived, so it is only natural that they became gods after they died. And it is also natural that they should be grateful to me for marrying off their children and come to tell me in my dreams. However, they told me I will have three more decades of life. Yet has anyone ever lived to be a hundred years old? They also said I shall be given two sons. I am seventy this year, and although my virility has not receded, rarely do men have children at such an age. I doubt this will happen."

The next morning, still pondering over the last night's dream, Liu Yuanpu put on cap and robe and walked toward the South Building. He was considering whether to relate his dream to its three occupants when Chunlang and his wife came out to meet him. Chunlang said, "My mother has just given birth to my younger sister and is presently resting. Last night, all three of us had strange dreams. We were about to go to Uncle's place to report the good news, but you have come to us first."

When Liu Yuanpu heard that Mistress Zhang had given birth to a daughter, he recalled Li Kerang's words in his dream and saw that these had, in part, been verified. Yet he did not wish to say so, as he himself did not have a son as yet. So he first inquired about Mistress Zhang's health, and then asked, "What else did you dream of last night?" Li Chunlang replied, "We dreamed that my father and father-in-law had both become gods. They said Uncle's great philanthropy had touched the God of Heaven and that your life would be prolonged and that you would have sons."

Thus the three had dreamed the same dream! Marveling, Liu Yuanpu recounted to them what he had seen in his dream, after which Chunlang declared, "All this should be ascribed to the virtue you have accumulated. This is a manifestation of Heaven's justice, and not a mere fantasy."

Liu Yuanpu went home and told his wife what he had learned, and she expressed wonder and amazement. She also dispatched a servant to the Li family to convey her congratulations. After a month had passed, Mistress Zhang, bearing her infant girl in her arms, came to visit the Liu family, and Yuanpu asked, "What is your little darling's name?" Mistress Zhang replied, "Her pet name is Fengming, for that is what my late husband instructed me, in my dream, to call her." Liu Yuanpu marveled even more, as this, too, accorded with his own dream.

Now, to make a long story short, Mistress Wang, who was already forty years old, suddenly conceived a taste for salty and tart foods and frequently vomited what she ate. Liu Yuanpu, believing her to have contracted an illness of middle-aged women, called in physicians to feel her pulse, but none could furnish an explanation. Only a few of the more experienced surmised, "Such a pulse is like that of a pregnant woman." But none dared to prescribe any medicaments for morning sickness, for they knew that Liu Yuanpu was seventy years old and Mistress Wang over forty and the two had never had any children. So they said, "Mistress Wang does not require any medicine, as the disorder will go away on its own." Liu Yuanpu, too, believed her malaise to be of little consequence, so he set his mind at ease and dismissed the physicians. After some time, Mistress Wang indeed began to feel better, but her body and limbs grew heavier, the drawstrings of her skirts seemed shorter, her eyes became more languid, and her bosom and belly began to swell. Uncertain as to what to believe, Liu Yuanpu asked himself, "Have the things I heard in my dream really come true?" As the days and months passed, the lying-in time approached and Liu Yuanpu had to prepare for the delivery, whether he believed in it or not. He called for a midwife and engaged a wet nurse.

One night, Mistress Wang had just fallen asleep when she smelled an unfamiliar fragrance and heard divine music. Feeling pains in her belly, she called for assistance, and in less than an hour gave birth to a son.

After the infant was bathed in warm scented water, one saw that he had well-formed eyebrows, clear eyes, a straight nose and square mouth, and a fine, strong body. His parents were happy beyond words. Liu Yuanpu declared, "Everything in that dream has turned out to be as lords Pei and Li predicted, and all has been bestowed on us by Heaven." He thereupon named the child Tianyou, which means Blessed by Heaven, and gave him the style name Mengzhen, or Propitious Dream.

Before long, the infant was one month old, an event that is never celebrated without a "soup-and-unleavened-bread" banquet for friends and relatives. The house was filled from door to door with guests who came to offer their congratulations, and the banqueting went on for five days. Chunlang and Lansun, it goes without saying, also dipped into their savings to give a dinner of congratulations for the Lius.

Now that he was married and his father properly buried, Li Chunlang applied himself assiduously to the study of the classics, so that he might advance himself and repay Liu Yuanpu for his great generosity. Through Liu Yuanpu's good offices, he was enrolled in the National Academy, and just as he was conferring with his uncle, aunt and wife about the best time for him to go to the capital in anticipation of taking the imperial examinations, an official messenger arrived from Bianliang. The messenger said he had been sent by the household of Minister Zheng of the Bureau of Military Affairs, and that he was to accompany Lansun's family back to Bianliang.

It so happened that Lord Zheng, Lansun's maternal uncle, had returned a few months earlier from his post as military commissioner in Xichuan and had been assigned by the imperial court to the position of associate commissioner of the Bureau of Military Affairs. The day he returned to the capital, he learned that his brother-in-law, Pei Xi, had died a tragic death. He went forthwith to Qingzhen Temple to inquire about his niece, and was told she had been sold to a family in Luoyang. He then sent someone to Luoyang to seek information and had found out that Master Liu had arranged a felicitous marriage for the girl, for which act of generosity Minister Zheng felt profoundly grateful. As Lord Zheng missed his niece very much, he had decided to bring her, together with her husband and mother-in-law, to the capital for a reunion.

Chunlang welcomed this arrangement, as it fitted in with his own plans. Lansun, on her part, was delighted that her uncle had come back to the capital.

Having reported the matter to the Lius, they chose an auspicious date for leaving together with Mistress Zhang and her baby daughter Fengming.

When the day drew near, Liu Yuanpu gave a farewell dinner for the family, during which he mentioned the dream he had had. To Mistress Zhang, he said, "In that dream last year, I met your late husband, and he said your daughter and my son would be joined in marriage. I dared not speak of the matter at the time, as my son was not yet born. But now, if you do not think poorly of my wife and me, we would be pleased to become your in-laws."

Bowing, Mistress Zhang replied, "My late husband said the same thing to me in my dream. I am glad Uncle does not consider us unworthy and, as we have not yet repaid you for your great generosity, we would hardly begrudge you this girl. But we are still as penurious as ever and dare not let her marry above her station. Should my son achieve renown, we should of course give the girl in marriage to your son."

As the dinner ended, Master Liu told Lansun, "You and your husband will be leaving to build yourselves a great future. You need not be concerned about me and my wife, as we shall be secure and happy at home." All wept, reluctant to part from one another. Before leaving, Mistress Zhang, her son, and her daughter-in-law once more kowtowed repeatedly to Master Liu and his wife to thank them for their generosity and, with tears in their eyes, set out on their journey. The two families corresponded frequently thereafter since there is no great distance between Luoyang and Bianliang.

Now about the young master, Liu Tianyou. The days and months went by until he was past his first birthday. One day, his wet nurse took him in her arms and, accompanied by a nanny who went by the name Chaoyun, went out for a walk. Chaoyun was eighteen years old and quite comely. After they had strolled around a while, the wet nurse said to Chaoyun, "Little Sister, take the boy in your arms for a while. It is too windy and I shall get some more clothes to put on him." Chaoyun took the child while the wet nurse went into the house.

When the wet nurse came out again, however, she heard the boy crying. Anxiously, she hurried forward, only to see Chaoyun cradling the boy with one hand and rubbing his head with the other. Scurrying up to them, she found that the young master had a large bump on his forehead. Flying into a rage, she scolded, "I have but to turn my back for an instant, than you let him fall! Do you not know that he is the life's love of the Master and Mistress? Should they learn what happened, I shall be blamed and made to suffer. I intend to tell the Master and Mistress, and we shall see whether you can escape punishment!" Angrily snatching the boy into her arms, she turned to leave.

Knowing that matters boded ill for her, Chaoyun lost her temper and retorted, "You old pig-dog! So you count on the Young Master's position to bully and scold me! Who do you think you are? No more than a wet nurse! As for the Young Master, I have never heard of a first-born from a seventy-year-old man! Who knows, he may have been picked up somewhere, or adopted! And you would insult me simply because he has taken a fall!"

Although Chaoyun spoke strong words, she was nervous and afraid and dared not follow the wet nurse into the house. Meanwhile, the wet nurse told Master Liu, word for word, everything that Chaoyun had said. Having heard her out, however, Master Liu was merely amused. He said, "She cannot be blamed, for rarely does a seventy-year-old man beget a child. Her words were spoken in the heat of anger and should not be taken seriously." The wet nurse had hoped that by telling on Chaoyun, the girl would at least be beaten half to death. Never had she expected Yuanpu to be so tolerant. Her fury cooled and, bearing the Young Master, she repaired to the inner chambers.

That night, after sharing an evening meal with his wife, Liu Yuanpu went alone to his study and told a servant-girl, "Have Chaoyun come to my study." All the servant-girls in the house, believing that the Master would be taking Chaoyun to task for what had happened earlier that day, felt anxious for her. Nonetheless they quickly laid hold of her, like hawks swooping on a sparrow, and delivered her to the Master. Poor Chaoyun! Guilt-stricken, she stood quaking with fear before Liu Yuanpu, preparing herself to be punished. Yuanpu ordered his servants, "You may all withdraw now, but leave Chaoyun here." The servants departed as ordered.

Liu Yuanpu asked Chaoyun to shut the door, which she did, wondering what the Master intended to do. Liu Yuanpu told her to approach, then said, "If men are unable to beget sons, it is because of a lack of virility during intercourse. Their efforts are shallow and flaccid, for which reason they have difficulty planting their seed. If they are healthy and vigorous, although old, they perform just as well as younger men. Now, you have said that old men cannot beget children, is that not so? And you have cast doubts on my capabilities, hinting that I have adopted my son or borrowed another man's seed. I shall keep you here tonight to test my virility and dispel your doubts."

The fact is that Liu Yuanpu had previously been disinclined to take a younger woman as he believed himself to be incapable of begetting children. Now that he had his firstborn he was more confident. Besides, he had been told in his dream that he would have another son, so he availed himself of this opportunity. Chaoyun, on her part, had not expected that her indiscreet remarks would lead to such a thing, but she dared not disobey. She had no choice but to help the Master disrobe and then get into bed with him.

Although LiuYuanpu was no longer young, his vigor remained undiminished. And Chaoyun was constrained to endure the discomfort up to the time the Master discharged his seed after engaging her for nearly two hours.

Liu Yuanpu slept with Chaoyun that night, and the girl returned to her quarters at daybreak. Liu Yuanpu then rose and told his wife what had taken place, and she merely laughed. All the maidservants and the wet nurse commented that the Master had always comported himself with the utmost rectitude, so why was he behaving in such a wayward manner in his old age?

Quite to everyone's surprise, Chaoyun became pregnant during that one night with the Master. Liu Yuanpu himself had not expected that he would be so efficacious, since he had only slept with the girl to disprove her doubts and show off his capabilities. His wife now had a servant's room refurbished and advised her husband to formally take Chaoyun as his concubine. Liu agreed, and Chaoyun had her hair done up as befits a married woman and became his concubine; after that Liu Yuanpu frequently went to her room to spend the night. Once, when Chaoyun observed that she owed her happy position to an impulsive remark, Liu Yuanpu teased her, saying, "So, are you now convinced that my son was not picked up somewhere or adopted?" Chaoyun flushed to her ears, and had nothing to say.

Time flew by, and another ten months passed. One day, Chaoyun felt sharp pains in her belly and also smelled a strange fragrance in her room, and then gave birth to a son. Just as the infant came into the world, there was a loud hubbub outside the house. Liu Yuanpu went out to see what was happening, and saw that a messenger had come to report that Li Chunlang had gained the title of *zhuangyuan* at the imperial examinations. On learning of his nephew's outstanding success, Liu Yuanpu felt he had been well recompensed for taking the Li family under his wing. He also felt that the news, coming as it did just when a son had been born to him, constituted a most favorable omen, and he felt most happy.

The messenger who brought the good news also presented him with a personal letter from Li Chunlang. Opening the letter, Liu Yuanpu read the following:

> *That your nephew and my widowed mother have lived to see this day is due entirely to Uncle's abiding protection. The renown I have now gained must also be attributed to your benevolence. I trust that my respected Uncle and Aunt have been well these days. I had intended to ask for leave to visit you, but I have been appointed tutor to the crown prince and must remain at his side day and night, and so I cannot fulfill*

my wish. For the moment, I am sending you two bottles of imperial wine for Uncle's enjoyment in your old age, and two palace flowers as portents of your worthy son's future scholarly attainments. I send this letter with expressions of my most humble respect.

Having read the letter, Liu Yuanpu took the wine and the flowers and went in to inform his wife. Just at this moment, their son, Tianyou, walked up. Liu Yuanpu called the boy to his side and gave him the palace flowers, saying, "Your elder brother has succeeded at the imperial examinations in the capital and sends you these palace flowers. He wishes you may one day be invited to the imperial banquet for successful candidates, as he was this year." The boy happily took the flowers and stuck them at random in his hair. Then he folded his hands and bowed deeply to his father and mother, to their great amusement.

Liu Yuanpu wrote a letter of congratulations, in which he also informed Chunlang about his second son, and sent a messenger to the capital with the letter. He then made a sacrificial offering of imperial wine to Lord Pei and Lord Li, after which he drank some of the wine together with his wife. From then on, his second son was called Tianxi, which means Bestowed by Heaven, and went by the scholarly name Mengfu, or Dream's Fulfillment. As the years passed, the two brothers displayed much intelligence, and Liu Yuanpu engaged teachers to guide them as they grew up. Grateful to Heaven for the blessings he had received, he built bridges and constructed roads and performed many other deeds that would bring him credit in the next world. Needless to say, the tombs of lords Pei and Li were sacrificed to and swept every spring and autumn.

Now let us see how Li Chunlang was faring in the capital. Lansun's uncle, Minister of Military Affairs Zheng, and his wife, Mistress Wei, had only one infant girl who was still in swaddling clothes and whose name was Sujuan. The uncle, distressed that his sister and brother-in-law had both died so young, showed great affection for his niece, and the entire Li family lived in his mansion and were very well treated.

Now, Li Chunlang, since achieving fame and becoming tutor to the crown prince, had won the prince's heart. Ten or more years later, when the Emperor Zhenzong passed away and the crown prince acceded to the throne as Emperor Renzong, he was especially gracious toward his tutor and, waiving normal protocol, appointed the latter to the position of minister of rites with a one-grade promotion in official rank. While still crown prince, Emperor Renzong had also frequently heard reports about the philanthropic deeds performed by Liu Yuanpu. So when Li Chunlang sent in a petition asking to be given leave to go home and sweep his father's tomb and pleading that his father be accorded a posthumous title, Renzong issued the following edict:

> *Li Xun, the late magistrate of Qiantang County, is posthumously conferred the title of Minister of Rites, whereas Pei Xi, the late prefect of Xiangyang, is restored to his original position, and both shall be accorded one imperial sacrificial feast. Liu Yuanpu, prefect of Qingzhou, shall be promoted by three grades. Minister of Rites Li Chunlang shall be granted leave for half a year, after which he is to return to the Imperial Palace to resume his duties.*

Upon receiving the edict, Minister Li, together with old Mistress Zhang, his wife Mistress Pei, and his young sister Fengming, took leave of Minister Zheng and set out in carriages for Luoyang. The horses, carriages, banners, and flags of their cavalcade stretched out several *li*, and officials of the prefectures and counties they passed through came out to welcome them. Li Chunlang had been very young when he left for the capital, having just undergone the capping ceremony for boys who come of age. Now, though only thirty years old, he was returning as a full-fledged government minister. Elders and residents of Luoyang crowded the streets to see him, and all praised Liu Yuanpu for his virtue and his ability to discern men of worth.

Minister Li and his family dismounted at Liu Yuanpu's house, and the master and his wife, having heard of their arrival, hastily prepared a table with incense and kowtowed thrice as prescribed by ritual to receive the imperial edict. Then, the old Mistress Zhang, Minister Li, and his wife, all clad in red robes with jade belts as befitted family members of a grade one official, together with the young Fengming knelt before the Lius to thank them for all they had done for their family. Liu Yuanpu raised the minister to his feet and Mistress Wang did the same for the womenfolk; then they called out their two sons to meet their aunt, elder brother, and his wife, and all expressed admiration when they saw how sturdy and handsome the brothers were, and how much they resembled Liu Yuanpu. All exclaimed, "It is because of the virtue accumulated by our big benefactor that he has begotten these precious sons."

Then the two imperial sacrifices were prepared, and all went to the tombs of lords Pei and Li where they burned paper money and offered libations of wine. And after Mistress Zhang and her family had a good cry, the sacrifices were put away and all returned to the house.

Liu Yuanpu then threw a banquet of celebration, which consisted of three different kinds of cuisine and many rounds of wine. During the banquet, Liu Yuanpu rose to his feet and, addressing the minister and his mother, said, "I have something to say—something that I have concealed in my heart for more than ten years and about which I can no longer remain silent. The truth is that your late husband and father and I had never seen one another when he was alive. I was completely bewildered when the two of you, mother and son, came to me, and was even more mystified when I opened the letter and saw no writing on it. I did not understand the meaning of this at first. Then, having given it some careful thought, I realized he had heard about my undeserved reputation and wished to place you under my care, but could not bring himself to say so because we had never met. That was why he sent such an enigmatic letter. I decided then to go along with the subterfuge and did not even tell my wife the truth. What he claimed as our brotherhood of eight kowtows never did exist. However, now that my worthy nephew has achieved such great success and brought such honor to his ancestors, I would be guilty— if I continued to keep this secret—of concealing the extraordinary pains to which his father went before passing away."

Yuanpu then produced the original letter and handed it to the mother and son for their perusal, and the two wept in gratitude, for none had known that Liu Yuanpu's acknowledgment of brotherhood had been based on a blank sheet of paper!

Then Liu Yuanpu once more brought up the matter of betrothing his son and Minister Li's young sister, and this time old Mistress Zhang happily accepted the offer. Then Lansun rose to her feet, and said, "I have yet to repay my adopted father one ten-thousandth part of the kindness you have shown me. Now, my Uncle Zheng has a daughter, who is also my cousin and whose name is Sujuan. She and my youngest brother were born in the same year, and I would gladly serve as intermediary to bring them together as man and wife." Master Liu thanked her, and after that all retired for the day.

Subsequently, Master Liu made out a formal request of betrothal between Tianyou and Fengming, and Minister Li composed a memorial to the emperor, in which he related how Liu Yuanpu had taken in his mother and himself on the strength of a blank letter. He also wrote a letter to Lord Zheng about the match between Sujuan and Liu Yuanpu's younger son. Upon reading the missive, the emperor was greatly pleased and moved by Liu Yuanpu's philanthropy. He issued a decree that, as a special honor, a memorial arch should be erected for Liu Yuanpu and that he be accorded the same rank as Minister Li.

Lord Zheng, on his part, had always admired Liu Yuanpu's integrity, and he, of course, agreed to the match. So Minister Li became both Tianyou's brother-in-law and Tianxi's cousin-in-law, a double relationship that was most felicitous. In later years, Tianyou became a *zhuangyuan* and Tianxi a *jinshi*, the two brothers passing the examinations in the same year. Liu Yuanpu lived to see both his sons marry and beget their own sons.

Then, one night, Liu Yuanpu had a dream in which Lord Pei came to greet him and said, "My tenure as City God has ended, and I entreat you to proceed to the position assigned to you, as the God of Heaven has given orders to that effect." And the next day, Liu Yuanpu died even though he was not ailing in any way. He was exactly one hundred years old.

Mistress Wang lived to be more than eighty years old. And after both had passed away, Minister Li and his wife were doubly grieved and, while not wearing mourning garb, they observed a mourning period of six years. Although the Lius now had their own sons and grandsons, Minister Li continued to make sacrifices to them every year. As for Lord Pei, who had no male progeny, his tomb was cared for, generation after generation, by offspring of the Li family.

From then on, the Li family lived in Luoyang to tend to the tombs of their ancestors and did not return to western Guangdong. Lansun, Minister Li's wife, gave birth to sons who gained high scholarly and official ranks. Li Yuanpu's eldest son, Tianyou, eventually rose to the position of joint manager of affairs in the Secretariat-Chancellery, and Tianxi, to head of the Imperial Censorate.

Thus Liu Yuanpu won honor upon honor, and had many sons and grandsons, and all of this was because of his great philanthropy.

The Fox Sprite's Three Sheaves of Herbs

贈芝麻識破假形
擷草藥巧諧真偶

It so happened that during the Qiandao reign [1165–1174] of the Song dynasty, an official from Jiangxi went to the capital, Lin'an, to received a posting, and on the way stopped over at West Lake to enjoy the scenery. He strolled around by himself for a quite some time and, feeling tired, sat down to rest on a rock under some tall trees growing beside a house. He looked toward the house and saw in it a girl with her hair braided up in two loops, and her appearance was so bewitching it set the official's heart all aflutter. The girl, too, cast glances in his direction, and it was evident that she took a fancy to him. Thereafter, the smitten official went frequently to that place to sit for a while.

The house was actually a wine shop, and the girl waited on its customers, so she was not one to hide herself away from people. She greeted the official with a smile whenever he appeared, and before long they struck up an acquaintance. And, indeed, a sentimental attachment soon arose between them. The girl would blush a little when the official flirted with her, but she was not in the least offended. However, the wine shop stood by the roadside in full view of passersby, and the girl's parents were constantly in the shop. Thus there was no opportunity for them to give rein to their desires, and they had to keep their mutual feelings pent up in their hearts.

The official soon had to depart from Lin'an, since he had already received his appointment. Being quite unwilling to leave the girl, he went to her house to bid farewell. Her parents were out at the time, so the girl was at home all by herself, and when she learned that the official was going away, tears welled up in her eyes and she said softly, "Ever since we met, sir, we have been attracted to one another. But my parents would certainly disagree to my marrying you, and if I ran away with you I would have to bear the stigma of having eloped for lewd reasons. Yet if we part like this, I will yearn and fret for you even in my dreams. What can we do?"

Deeply touched by her sincerity, the official begged a neighbor of hers to take handsome gifts to the parents and ask for her hand on his behalf. But her parents refused outright when they learned that he was from another part of the country, and the disappointed official had no choice but to pack up his belongings and leave. Thereafter, he had no more news about the girl.

Five years later, the same official went again to Lin'an to receive a new posting. On his arrival, he found an inn, set down his luggage, and proceeded at once to West Lake to visit his previous haunt. There he was told that a new family now lived in the former wine shop and that nobody knew about the one that had resided there five years earlier. Even neighbors who had been acquainted with the family had all moved away.

Desolated, the official walked back toward his inn, and on the way suddenly came upon the girl. She looked somewhat older, but was even more attractive than before. The official hastily clasped his hands in an obeisance which was immediately returned by the girl. "You have been gone for a long time," she said. "Do you still remember me?" The official replied, "I have just been to your former residence in search of you, but to no avail. I was quite put out, but am happy that we have met here on the road. Why did your family move away? And where do you live now?"

The girl replied, "I am married now, and we live in a small street in the city. My husband is engaged in storehouse affairs and is presently sitting in prison, which is why I have come out to seek assistance for him. I never expected to meet someone I knew five years ago. Would you be willing to come to my home for a cup of tea?" The official accepted with delight, declaring, "I had intended to visit you."

As the two walked along and conversed, they passed the inn at which the official had taken a room, and the official proposed, "Let us stop and talk here for a while, as this is where I am staying." In truth, the official was eager to sleep with her and satisfy his old desires, and he thought this a good place to do so since he could hardly wait until they arrived at her home. His invitation was accepted with alacrity. So they went in and shut the door and, having hugged one another briefly, fell on the bed and began to make clouds and rain.

The official's room, being the only one in the courtyard, was quite secluded, and the inn had no occupants other than the official himself. Observing this, the girl said, "No one knows we are at this inn, so let us stay here and enjoy one another. We need not go to my home, which is less convenient since other people also live there." The official agreed, saying, "If you are willing to stay here, it would indeed be most convenient for us."

So they lived at the inn for half a year. The girl would sometimes go out, but only for short periods of time. She never again mentioned her family's affairs; nor did she ever seem to miss anyone there. The official, on his part, was so deeply attached to her that he even forgot she was married.

When the official's transfer was eventually confirmed, he thought of going back to Jiangxi before proceeding to his new post, and he said to the girl, "Let us leave in secret and go to my home. Then we could be permanently together. What do you say?" But when the girl heard he intended to leave, she began to weep, and she said, "There is something I must tell you. But please do not be frightened." Mystified, the official asked, "And what is it you wish to tell me?"

The girl then said, "After we parted company five years ago, I longed for you so much that I fell ill and died a year later. This body of mine is not that of a human being, but because you and I had pledged our love to each other during my lifetime, my spirit did not dissipate and has stayed here to be with you. However, our days of happiness are limited and have reached the number allotted to me by the netherworld, and so I cannot go with you to that distant place. I also fear that your suspicions may be aroused in the future, so I have resolved to tell you the truth. Because of our encounters, you have been profoundly invaded by the *yin* energy and will have acute bowel discharges after I am gone. So you should promptly take some stomach-calming powder. It will nourish your substance and you will be cured."

This account filled the official with profound consternation. Then he remembered what the girl said about the stomach-calming power and asked apprehensively, "Is it truly so effective? I have read in history books that the ancient scholar Sun Jiuding also encountered a ghost and took the same medication. But it seems to me this is quite a commonplace kind of medicine." The girl assured him, "The medicine contains the magical atractylode root that drives away evil influences. So just do what I tell you."

After saying these things, the girl cried inconsolably, and the official, too, was sorely distressed. That night, the two slept together and gave each other the fullest pleasure. They wept bitterly as they took leave of one another the next morning. Then the girl walked out of the inn, vanishing in thin air after she had taken but a few steps.

The official did indeed have severe bowel discharges after the girl left, but recovered when he had taken the stomach-calming powder as the girl had instructed him to do. And he was moved to tears whenever he told people about his encounter with his ghostly lover.

This little story goes to show that when two people are truly in love, their attachment endures even after one of them dies. And if the one who remains alive should fall ill, a well-disposed ghost may even provide a prescription to cure the ailment!

I shall now tell you a strange tale about a supernatural being who not only became intimate with a man, but also left the man some medicinal herbs that cured him of an illness and procured him a life-long helpmate to boot.

*   *   *

During the Tianshun reign [1457–1465] of the current Ming dynasty, there lived a merchant who was of the Jiang family and conducted all of his commerce in the regions of Hunan, Guangdong, and Jiangxi. Still in his twenties, he was extraordinarily handsome and his features were quite exceptional in their perfection. Indeed, he was so handsome that his colleagues asserted that he could, because of his appearance alone, be chosen to marry a daughter of the imperial family, and they therefore jokingly called him "Prince Consort Jiang." He himself was aware of the attraction he held for others, but few were the young women he deemed worthy of his notice. He declared that none but the loveliest of beauties would be a match for him. And although he had traveled much among the rivers and lakes of the South over the past few years, he had yet to encounter a woman who captured his fancy. True, he had on occasion visited houses of pleasure with his friends, but only to dispel his boredom; in all truth, the women in these places derived more satisfaction from him than he did from them.

One day, he brought some merchandise to the Makou district of the Hanyang region and stayed at a place called the Ma Yuexi Inn. Ma Yuexi, the innkeeper, was a member of the household of a local dignitary, Vice-Minister Ma, and had obtained some capital from that official to open a large inn for traveling merchants. The inn provided quiet and secluded accommodations fit for the most discriminating guests and was therefore frequented by persons of culture and refinement. It stood just a few doors away from the residence of Vice-Minister Ma.

Now, Vice-Minister Ma had a daughter who went by the pet name Yunrong and who was of the rarest delicacy and charm. There was, in her residence, a small window in a pavilion that overlooked the inn, and when she had nothing better to do, Yunrong would ascend into the pavilion and divert herself by watching the comings and goings in the inn below.

As Yunrong stood by the window one day, Master Jiang caught sight of her from a distance, and his first sensation was that he had never seen such true beauty in all his life. He approached her step by step, and the closer he came, the more it seemed to him that everything he saw of her was the acme of perfection. Master Jiang felt as though his spirit had flown to the Ninth Heaven, and he fantasized, "Could I have but one night with such a beauty, I should not have been endowed in vain with such good looks. But can such a thing be brought to pass?"

As he gazed with uplifted eyes, enthralled, the young woman in the window became aware that someone was staring at her, and she concealed half of her face with her hand. However, as she peered from between her fingers, she saw that Master Jiang was a most handsome man, and she made no further attempt to escape his attentions. And when Master Jiang, on his part, saw that the she was observing him, he paraded his natural graces with the express intention of exciting her emotions. This he did until she descended from the pavilion, whereupon he returned to his chambers at the inn. As he shut the door, he thought to himself, "It is a pity that I am not skilled in the arts of the paint brush, for if I were, I would certainly paint a wonderful portrait of her!"

The next day, he questioned the innkeeper and learned that the young lady was the daughter of the inn's owner and that she had not yet been betrothed. Master Jiang was elated to hear this, but then he thought to himself, "Theirs is an official's family, and I am but a merchant, and an outsider at that. And although she is unbetrothed, it is not for me to yearn for her. Yet as far as our looks go, she and I fully deserve one another. If only there were some celestial matchmaker who would take this matter in hand!" As with most people whose passions are seldom stirred, Master Jiang had scant control over his feelings once they were unleashed, and from then on he kept thinking about the girl, whether he happened to be walking or sitting or lying down, and he could not put her out of his mind.

The goods Master Jiang dealt in consisted of silks, satins, brocades and all kinds of wares used and favored by women, so he asked a young servant at the inn to carry his boxes of merchandise to the Ma family's residence in the hope that he might encounter the young woman and feast his eyes on her. He did so twice, and each time the womenfolk of the Ma household asked to see first this and then that, rummaged through all his boxes themselves, and examined each article before bargaining over prices. Although the young lady also appeared amid the crowd of women, she did not make herself conspicuous but went about looking at the goods in an almost secretive manner. Now and then she glanced at Master Jiang, and their gazes would meet.

When Master Jiang returned to his chambers, he was hardly able to master his emotions. Sighing and breathing in gasps, he yearned for a pair of wings so that he might fly to the girl's chambers and be with her. Sensual fantasies filled his fitful nocturnal dreams, and visions of the girl preoccupied his thoughts day and night.

One evening, after Master Jiang had shut his door and prepared himself for a solitary night in bed, he heard footsteps outside and then a light tapping at the door. He had not yet blown out the lamp. Trimming it up, he opened the door a bit to see who was there, and a young woman slipped through the aperture. And when he took a closer look, he found it was the young beauty from the Ma household!

Stupefied with surprise, Master Jiang asked himself, "Am I dreaming again?" Once he had collected himself, however, he knew this was not a dream, that he was indeed facing that very young woman in the bright light of the lamp. But Master Jiang still could not believe this was true, and he knew not what he should do, or say.

The young beauty observed his discomfiture and spoke first, saying "Sir, do not be alarmed by my presence. I am Yunrong of the Ma family. I know you have favored me with your expectations, and I, too, have been enamored of you for some time already. Hence, during a lapse of vigilance at my home, I have slipped through the gates and, my unsightliness notwithstanding, I hope to relieve you of the loneliness from which you suffer as a visitor in these parts. It would give me happiness, sir, if you would not mock me for offering myself in this manner."

Master Jiang's feelings on hearing these words were like those of a man given food when starving and water when dying of thirst, or, more exactly, like those of an ordinary mortal who finds himself in the presence of a fairy maiden. Words fail to describe his joy and elation. He hastened to shut and bolt the door, and the two, hand in hand, went to his canopied bed where they lost no time soaring to heights of infinite pleasure.

After they had finished making clouds and rain, the young lady admonished Master Jiang, saying, "I was so attracted by your splendid elegance that I could not restrain myself from coming to your pillow and mat. However, my family's rules are strict and unforgiving, and should any gossip reach their ears, the consequences would be unthinkable. You must, in the future, stay away from the gates of my home and refrain from strolling about outside in such a way that would betray your intentions. And make sure that each night your door is shut but not bolted. I shall come to you after everyone has settled down to sleep. And if you keep a tight rein on your tongue, we shall enjoy a long and satisfying union."

Master Jiang replied, "I came as a lone visitor from afar, and the sight of your loveliness filled me with agonizing longings. Though I communed with you in my dreams, I knew in my waking hours that we were as far separated as mortals are from the gods. Never did I imagine that you would not despise me, or that you might come to my humble accommodations, share my pillow, and bring me the greatest bliss. Even if I should die this very day, I would die content. I shall always keep in mind the instructions that have come from your golden lips. Henceforth my feet will not take me out of these doors and my tongue will be carefully guarded. I shall remain here in patient anticipation of the night and your welcome arrival." The young lady rose from bed before daybreak and departed after repeatedly promising to return that same evening.

To Master Jiang it seemed as though he had truly encountered a celestial fairy, and his happiness knew no bounds. His only regret was that he could not share his elation with any other person. The young woman came in the evenings and left at dawn, and Master Jiang, in compliance with her instructions, never left his chambers without good reason for fear of giving himself away and betraying her trust.

Master Jiang, being a strong and virile young man, had always been able to indulge his sensual desires without tiring. But the young lady clearly reveled in their lovemaking. In bed, she gave and took like a seasoned boudoir warrior and frolicked like a wanton phoenix, never declining an encounter or showing signs of satiety. Master Jiang wished at times to desist, but the young woman seemed never to require any sleep and could disport herself all the night long without respite. Being greatly enamored of her, Master Jiang was gratified to see her enjoy herself so much. To his mind, she was a young woman long secluded in her chambers tasting a man for the first time, and who, having become deeply attached to him, placed no restraints on herself but gave full rein to her natural desires. This pleased him, for such complete abandon is seldom to be found, yet he feared lest she find his services unsatisfying. Thus he carried on for all he was worth, disregarding his own health and the possibility that excessive effluence of his *yang* essence could endanger his life.

As these nocturnal activities went on undiminished, therefore, feelings of fatigue gradually overtook Master Jiang, and his countenance became wan and sallow. As the ditty goes:

> *Sleek are the bodies of maidens sixteen,*
> *But down by their waists is a blade oh so keen!*
> *Tho' it may never make heads roll and bounce,*
> *It saps all the pith from their paramours' bones.*

In the meantime, Master Jiang's colleagues and acquaintances had observed that he slumbered deeply behind closed doors even in the daytime, and that he seldom left his chambers. And when he did emerge briefly, he would yawn unceasingly, like a man who has not slept a wink all night. They wondered what was ailing him, since he did not go out drinking with anyone in the evenings, or complain of sleeplessness, or carouse in houses of prostitution, or appear to have contracted a pox. Even when they succeeded in dragging him to a wine house or brothel, he would insist on repairing to the inn before night fell and refused to tarry an extra hour or two. All were suspicious, and, as one of them declared, "His conduct shows that he must have something on his mind, and he is perchance engaged in some clandestine activity behind people's backs." They agreed among themselves to spy on his movements that night, and were persuaded they could catch him red-handed.

That evening, just after dark, the young woman showed up as usual. Master Jiang hastily concealed her and, in order to allay his companions' suspicions, emerged from his chambers and joined them in chatting, joking and drinkng wine until all had dispersed and gone to their own quarters. Master Jiang then returned to his chambers, closed and bolted the door, and took the young lady to bed. There, they communed joyously and carried on with the wildest abandon, uttering many cries and moans, in reckless unconcern that others might overhear them. And they went on at such length and with so little respite that his eavesdropping colleagues outside the door exclaimed in wonderment: "Where did Prince Consort Jiang find such a woman to dally with him in his chambers? And how is it that they can do battle for so long?"

As the hours passed, however, all began to feel restless as well as inconvenienced by their upright members. And indeed, they were sorely tested, as many had been away from home for a long period of time. Thus they returned to their chambers, where some of them stoically bore out their discomfort while others applied the hand funnel before falling asleep.

The next morning, his colleagues came together and said, "Let us stand guard before Prince Consort Jiang's door and see who comes out." When they came to Master Jiang's chambers, however, they found the door slightly ajar. So they pushed it open and entered the room, only to see Master Jiang sleeping alone on the bed. "Where is she?" they inquired. Feigning bewilderment, Master Jiang asked in return, "Where is who?" His colleagues replied, "The one who fornicated with you last night!" Master Jiang parried, "Nobody was here." But his companions would not be put off, and said, "You cannot deny that someone was here. We all heard you."

Master Jiang continued to argue, saying, "Preposterous! You have been seeing ghosts!" His colleagues asserted, "We did not see any ghosts, but we fear you have been possessed by a ghost." Master Jiang asked, "And why should I have been possessed by a ghost?" His colleagues replied, "We heard you fornicating with someone last night, but no one was here when we came this morning. So that could only have been a ghost."

Master Jiang knew now that they had been listening at his door the night before, and he thanked his good fortune that the young lady was an early riser and had not been seen by them before she departed. Hastening to concoct an explanation, he said, "My brothers, I shall be candid with you. I have been away from home since I was young and have long led a life of celibacy. But I find it difficult to exercise restraint at night when I am in bed, so I mimic the sounds of intercourse to quench the fires of desire. The truth is that I alone, in my intemperance, acted out that scene, and I was not having intercourse with any other person. It embarrasses me greatly to tell you this, my brothers, but your suspicions are unfounded."

His companions' rejoinder was, "Many among us are intemperate persons, and if that is what transpired last night, there is no cause for embarrassment. Just so that you have not been possessed by some evil spirit. That would be no jesting matter!" Master Jiang assured them, saying, "No such thing has happened, my brothers. So set your minds at ease." His companions were only half convinced by his protestations, but they said no more.

However, Master Jiang's health was clearly failing, and his fatigue increased with each passing day, a circumstance that even Master Jiang could not but admit to himself.

Now, there was among Master Jiang's companions a man named Xia Liangce who was on the best of terms with Master Jiang, and who felt greatly concerned as he watched his friend's worsening condition. One day, he said to Master Jiang, "You and I both do much traveling together, and it is our greatest fortune if we can stay out of harm's way. However, I have observed of late that you have become thin and sallow, that your mind wanders, and that your speech is confused. I have also frequently heard the sound of whispering and secret murmurings issuing from your chambers, and I am persuaded that something strange and untoward is taking place. My brother, you may not be willing to confide in me at this time, but something serious will transpire one day, and I wager it will be no trivial matter. Your very life may be at stake. It would be a pity if you, who are so young, should die in this strange place, far away from your hometown. As you and I are the best of friends, you should tell me what is taking place so that we might together contrive a solution. I swear to you I shall not tell anyone else."

Convinced now of the sincerity of Xia Liangce's concern, Master Jiang resolved to tell him the truth. "You are a true friend," he said, "And there is indeed something that I should no longer conceal from you. The daughter of the inn's owner, Vice Minister Ma, and I have formed an attachment, and she comes every night to tryst with me. As we are both young, it may be that we have overindulged our desires and that I am becoming indisposed because I have overtaxed myself. However, my life is but a small matter. Should any rumor of our liaison leak out, even her life would be imperiled. She has enjoined me again and again to guard my tongue, and for that reason I have not dared to reveal the truth. Now that I have told you, my brother, you must on no account disclose this secret and disappoint the young lady's trust in me."

Xia Liangce laughed and declared, "That is where you are mistaken, my brother! The Ma family is the household of an important official. Their residence is one of deep courtyards enclosed behind multiple walls and tall gates. How could a girl come out of it every night? Besides, there are all manner of people living in this inn and, coming and going as she does, even though in the dark hours of the night, would she not be afraid to run into someone? It is quite certain that she is not that household's young lady."

Master Jiang protested, "I have seen the young lady from the Ma family, and there is no doubt that she is the one." But Xia Liangce continued, "I have heard that this region abounds in fox sprites who are adept at assuming different forms and seducing unsuspecting men. You, my brother, must have encountered one of these creatures. You should take precautions and protect yourself."

Master Jiang refused to believe these admonitions. Indeed, Xia Liangce could see that his friend was so obsessed that no advice could bring him back to his good senses. After a sleepless night, Xia Liangce suddenly had an idea. Turning it about in his mind, he thought to himself, "In that way, I can present him with indisputable proof. He will then be willing to desist."

The next day, Xia Liangce attempted once more to talk Master Jiang around, and when it was clear that his friend would not listen to reason, he said, "I have a proposal that will in no way interfere with your affair. But you must promise to do that which I ask." Master Jiang asked, "And what is it you would have me do?"

Xia Liangce said, "I have an object that is most capable of distinguishing the false from the true. When that person comes tonight, I suggest that you present this object to her and have her take it away with her. If she is indeed Miss Ma, no harm will be done. But if she is not the Ma family's young lady, it will help to reveal who she truly is, without, however, hindering your affair. I advise you once more to look after your health and your life, and to be careful." And Master Jiang declared, "That I can do."

Xia Liangce then handed Master Jiang a coarsely woven linen satchel filled with something. As Master Jiang secreted it in his sleeve, Xia Liangce once more reminded him, "Be sure not to forget."

Master Jiang did not know what Xia Liangce had in mind, but by now he, too, was beginning to entertain certain doubts, and he decided to do as Xia Liangce had asked, since no harm could come of it.

That night the young lady came again, and the two spent a joyful time together. Just before daybreak, Master Jiang remembered what Xia Liangce had asked him to do, so he produced the linen satchel and presented it to the young lady with the words, "I have a small gift for you. Please take it, and examine its contents after you return to your chambers." Since it was a gift, the young lady gladly accepted the satchel without inquiring what was in it and soon left the inn.

Master Jiang slept until the sun was high in the sky and then rose and put on some clothes. As he did so, he noticed that a sprinkling of sesame seeds lay in front of his bed and led out of the door of his chambers.

All at once, Master Jiang understood. He said to himself, "Brother Xia told me the satchel could distinguish between the true and the false. It was obviously filled with sesame seeds, and he made the satchel out of linen cloth so coarse that the seeds would leak out and leave a trail showing where the young lady went. So that is what he meant by distinguishing between the true and the false! I shall follow the sesame seeds, for they will certainly take me to some residence and tell me what I wish to know."

Without informing any of his companions, Master Jiang set out to pursue the trail of sesame seeds, and when he saw they did not lead to the Ma's residence he knew that the girl was not from that family. Following the unbroken spoor of sesame seeds that meandered over hill and dale, Master Jiang eventually came to the foot of the Dabie Mountains, and there the trail vanished into the mouth of a cave.

Master Jiang sensed that he was about to behold something quite out of the ordinary. Mustering up his courage, he stepped into the cave, only to see a she-fox, with the satchel next to it, reposing on the floor of the cave in a deep slumber. Greatly shocked, Master Jiang cried out aloud, "So this is the evil spirit that has cast its spell over me!"

In spite of being asleep, the fox sprite was quite alert and, at the sound of a human voice, sprang to her feet and at once assumed human form. However Master Jiang cried, "What purpose does it serve you to change into human form now? I have already seen you for what you really are!" Whereupon the fox sprite approached him and took his hand, saying, "Do not reproach me, sir, for what I have done. In any case, our liaison must come to an end, now that you have seen through my disguise." Yet when Master Jiang saw the fox sprite in the form in which he had known her, his heart was filled with sadness at losing her.

The fox sprite said, "I, sir, should let you know that I have been cultivating my spirit here for more than a thousand years, chiefly by mating with human males and thus refining my inner essence. I saw how handsome you are and wished to partake of your original *yang* vitality, but could find no way of doing so. Then I learned that you were enamored of the Ma family's daughter and worshiped her. Hence I assumed her form and, in that disguise, came to you and coupled with you. I truly believed that both you and I would benefit from my ruse, since I could bring you great pleasure and at the same time attain my own purpose. But now that my true colors have been revealed, I can no longer keep you company, and the time has come for us to part. Having associated with you for so long a time, however, it is only to be expected that I should have formed tender sentiments for you. I am aware, too, that your body has become ill on my account, and I should thus see to it that you are restored to health. As concerns the Ma family's daughter, you are in love with her, and I have made use of her identity to secure your affections. As I feel beholden to you in both of these matters, I shall contrive to make her your wife, and thereby fulfill your heart's desire and make amends to you."

Having said this, the fox sprite went to the mouth of the cave and plucked some rare herbs. These she separated into three sheaves and told Master Jiang, "Boil the first sheaf and wash yourself with the water. That will restore your energy, and you will be as strong as you once were. Then go in secret and scatter the second sheaf in inconspicuous places around the gates of the Ma residence, and their daughter will be afflicted with sores. When that happens, have the third sheaf of herbs boiled into a brew for her to bathe in, and she will be cured and become yours. When the two of you enjoy the bliss of the connubial bed, however, do not forget the sentiments you once shared with me, your matchmaker."

The fox sprite then handed the herbs to Master Jiang and enjoined him, "Be careful! And do not tell anyone about this matter! I am leaving now, never to return." So saying, the fox sprite reverted to the shape of a fox, and with a few bounds was gone.

With feelings of amazement and relief, Master Jiang watched the fox sprite vanish in the distance, and then secreted the sheaves of herbs in the folds of his gown and returned to the inn. There, he ordered the innkeeper to heat a cauldron of water, and when no one was looking, threw in the first sheaf of herbs and boiled them into a brew. That evening, he washed himself with the brew and at once felt uplifted in body and spirit.

The next morning, after a sound night's sleep, he looked in the mirror and saw that the wanness and sallowness that had marked his countenance of late had vanished. He now knew the miraculous powers of the herbs, and resolved not to tell anyone about them. So when Xia Liangce came to ask what had transpired the night before, he said, "I followed the trail of sesame seeds to the banks of a river and could proceed no further. I now realize the girl was some sort of she-devil, and knowing this, I shall have nothing more to do with her." Observing that his friend's complexion had returned to its former state of healthiness, Xia remarked, "You no longer look ill, now that your heart has returned to its right place. That girl was manifestly an evil spirit, and it is good that you have escaped her wiles. We may set our minds at ease now."

Master Jiang thanked Xia Liangce for his concern, but continued to withhold the truth from him and secretly went about fulfilling the fox sprite's instructions. Waiting until dusk when most people had retired to their homes, he surreptitiously approached the Ma family residence with the second sheaf of herbs. These, he scattered about in dark crannies under the thresholds of its gates; then he returned to the inn to await further news.

Less than two days later, rumors began to fly about that Miss Yunrong of the Ma family was afflicted with the mange. Sores had first appeared on two or three spots on her arms and legs, and although unsightly, had not yet occasioned too much concern. But foul-smelling pustules soon broke forth all over her body, emitting an unbearable odor. Her jade-smooth body became wrinkled and scaly, her flowerlike complexion took on the appearance of worm-pocked wood, and bits of skin fell like snowflakes under her fingernails as she scratched herself to alleviate the constant itching. A girl of unique beauty was very quickly reduced to a creature of repulsive appearance. Her parents were at loss what to do, and she herself felt so miserable that she only hoped to die.

A physician of external medicine was engaged to tend to her. He made light of the sores and declared that a few poultices would cure them. But after the poultices were applied, they had to be hurriedly washed off, as the patient complained of excruciating pain—pain as though she were being pierced all over with needles or flayed alive!

The family then sought a physician of internal medicine who confidently stated, "Her illness will be cured by the internal administration of medicines that regulate the flow of blood and adjust the vital energy. The use of external medicaments merely cures the symptoms but not the disease." Upon his recommendation, medicines were brewed and the girl took two or three doses every day, but with no effect other than to ruin her appetite. The physician of external medicine then argued that her illness fell within his area of specialization and only medicinals for rubbing on and washing would be effective. The internal medicine physician, on the other hand, insisted that the patient's lungs had been exposed to a noxious wind, for which reason medicines to dispel wind and toxins should be taken orally. The patient continued to suffer as medicines and prescriptions were changed virtually from day to day and the physicians exchanged abuse and accusations of incompetence, which, of course, did nothing to resolve the matter.

In desperation, Vice-Minister Ma put up a large notice at the gates of his residence. It said, "One hundred taels of silver shall be awarded to anyone who is able to cure my daughter's illness," and the sight of it had all physicians drooling with desire. Yet even the best among them failed to come up with even a remotely effective remedy, though they applied all their skills and delved through all their books of secret prescriptions.

By this time, Miss Ma's health was rapidly failing and she lay close to death's door. At wits' end, Vice-Minister Ma conferred with his wife, saying: "Our daughter has been blighted by this incurable disease, and no one is able to cure her despite my offer of a rich reward. Perhaps we should resign ourselves to letting her marry any good physician who succeeds in healing her. We would furnish her dowry and allow the man to enter into our household. Our daughter was once famed for her beauty, and it is conceivable that some man may still desire her and be willing to contribute some miraculous cure that would save her. Of course, the marriage may not be a good match for us where social status is concerned, but that would be better than letting her die. And in any case, even if she does not die, few are the men who would be willing to take her as a wife, covered with sores as she is. By doing things this way, our child may still have a chance."

He thus wrote the following notice in big characters and pasted it up by the gate:

Our daughter Yunrong has sickened with the mange. Any man who is able to furnish a miraculous remedy that will save her shall have her hand in marriage, whether he be of high or low birth and whether he hails from near at hand or from afar, and he shall be married into our household. This notice bears witness to our good faith.

In the meantime, Master Jiang, in his chambers at the inn, had secretly rejoiced when he learned about the first notice, but had not ventured to take up the offer as no mention had been made of marriage. He feared lest, as a visiting merchant from afar, he would be rewarded merely with some money and objects of value if he cured the girl, but that her parents would be unwilling to give their daughter's hand to him. So he bided his time and waited to see how matters would progress. And when no cure was found and the family put up the new notice offering the girl in marriage to anyone who could heal her, Master Jiang rubbed his hands in glee and said to himself, "She is mine now!"

He proceeded to the Ma family's gate and, taking down the notice, announced that he was able to cure Miss Ma's illness. Upon hearing his words, the gatekeepers dared not delay but hurried at once to inform the master of the house. Vice-Minister Ma came out in person to greet his visitor, and even before they had spoken to one another he was pleased by Master Jiang's extraordinarily handsome features.

He inquired, "What is this wondrous prescription you have that will cure my daughter?" Master Jiang replied, "I am not a physician by calling, but have encountered an unusual person who gave me some miraculous herbs that are used especially for the mange. The illness will be gone after only one treatment. However, I do not desire money or wealth. The only thing I request for my services is that you do not go back on the promise you made in this notice."

Vice-Minister Ma at once declared, "I have only this one daughter, who is both talented and beautiful, and it is a great misfortune that she has been afflicted and blighted by this illness. Should you exercise some wondrous skills and bring her back from the verge of death, I shall certainly not go back on my word. I shall, without fail, give you my daughter to serve you for the rest of her days as a dutiful wife."

Master Jiang continued, "I hail from Zhejiang, which is far from this region, and I am a merchant, not a scholar, which, I fear, would blemish your family's name. You are willing now to offer your daughter in marriage because her beauty has been impaired by illness, but once she gets well and recovers her beauty, how do I know that you will not rue today's promise and cause my hopes to go up in smoke? You must declare yourself clearly and unmistakably."

Vice-Minister Ma said, "Jiangsu and Zhejiang are both regions of note that have close links with one another. Furthermore, commerce is a respectable calling and no base pursuit, and your bearing and demeanor show that you are not a man of lowly character. Besides, as I have already stated, anyone, irrespective of station or place of birth, shall have my daughter if only he cures her of her illness. I, as a man of honor, shall not go back on my word, for it is my own daughter that is ailing. I beg you to apply your medicaments and not to entertain any more doubts."

Reassured by these words, Master Jiang produced the third sheaf of herbs and instructed that they be boiled into a brew in which the young lady should bathe herself.

As the brew was being prepared, its fragrance alone brought relief to Miss Ma. And when it was poured into a bathtub and the young lady stepped in, to her amazement the pain and itching stopped wherever the brew touched her body, and an indescribably fresh and cool sensation penetrated her very bones. She scrubbed off all the foul-smelling pus, and when she emerged from the bathtub she felt her condition lighter by half. After a night's sleep, the scabs began to drop off and layers of coarsened skin peeled away. Within three days, she had fully recovered her health, and after she had taken another bath her skin became as clear as it had ever been and even more delicate.

Vice-Minister Ma was overjoyed. He asked where Master Jiang was staying, and when he learned that the merchant had taken lodgings at his own inn, he invited the latter to stay at his residence and had his servants sweep and clean a set of rooms for that purpose. All that was needed now was to choose a propitious date for the wedding. Happy beyond words, Master Jiang moved his belongings to the studio and settled down to wait for the happy event.

Miss Ma was quite willing to marry Master Jiang, as she was grateful to him for curing her illness; yet she wondered what sort of a person he was. She dispatched her handmaiden to make inquiries, and was gratified to learn that the groom-to-be was none other than the merchant who had come to her home to sell silks and satins and whom all the women had found to be so handsome.

When the propitious day came around, Vice-Minister Ma fulfilled his promise and wedded his daughter to Master Jiang. Both were young, and both were of highly personable appearance, and it goes without saying that they satisfied one another's passions and desires.

Master Jiang felt as though he knew his wife quite well already, as he had spent much time with her impersonator, the fox sprite, prior to their marriage. But Miss Ma, now Mistress Ma, wished to learn more about her husband, and one day she asked him, "You come from some other place, so what force is it that brought you to my home, that made me ill, and that joined us together in marriage? Who gave you those miraculous herbs that, in effect, served as the matchmaker between us? You should not forget these things."

Master Jiang laughed and replied, "There was indeed a matchmaker, but she is not here and I am unable to thank her today." But his wife would not be put off, and pursued, "Tell me, who is this matchmaker, and where is she now?" Master Jiang could not very well tell her it was a fox sprite, so he made up the following story.

"Once I had seen your beauty, I dreamed of you constantly in my dreams and was unable to swallow a bite of food or close my eyes in sleep. A fairy from heaven was touched by the depth of my feelings for you, so she impersonated you and kept me company for many days. I eventually saw through her disguise, and only then did she tell me she was not you. However, she knew that a calamity was awaiting you, so she gave me those herbs to cure you of your sickness, and she said that you and I were destined to be married, which has indeed turned out to be the case. In that sense, she was our matchmaker."

Mistress Ma remarked, not without a trace of pique, "No wonder you have treated me as though I were an old acquaintance. Someone came to you pretending to be me! But where is this person now?" Master Jiang replied, "She was a fairy from heaven, and once I saw through her disguise she stopped coming to me." Mistress Ma observed, "She could well have ruined my reputation. Yet she saved my life and thereby made it possible for us to become husband and wife. So in the end, she should be regarded as our benefactor."

Master Jiang said, "She is a fairy and, as such, has scant regard for the feelings of gratitude or resentment evinced by mere mortals. You and I were destined to become a couple, and were fortunate enough to have had her assistance in this matter, and for that we should be grateful. My only regret is that I am a person of little consequence and am therefore unworthy of you." Mistress Ma replied, "Such things need not be said between husband and wife. Besides, I am beholden to you for saving my life when I was about to die, and I should therefore serve you, without regrets, for the rest of my life."

From then on, the two were as inseparable as fish and water. Master Jiang had no thoughts of going back to his home region, and he stayed at the Ma residence where he and his wife lived to a happy old age. But that is another story.

When Master Jiang's fellow merchants learned that he had married into the Ma family, all wondered how such a thing had come to pass. Xia Liangce, too, was bewildered, as he had heard Master Jiang tell about his affair with Miss Ma and had insisted that the latter was a she-devil in disguise. But now his friend had somehow or other become the Ma family's son-in-law.

So when the merchants went to congratulate Master Jiang on this happy event, Xia Liangce took the opportunity to ask his friend how this had come about. Master Jiang related to him all that had transpired, omitting only the part where he had scattered the herbs that caused the young lady to sicken with the mange. He said Miss Ma's impersonator had been a fox sprite from the Dabie Mountains, and that thanks to Xia Liangce's artifice with the sesame seeds in the coarse linen satchel he had been able to track down and unmask the fox sprite. He told them that the latter had given him the herbs with which he had healed Miss Ma and then predicted that they would be married. He said in conclusion, "My happiness today is all the doing of the fox sprite."

His colleagues marveled at his story, and said, "We called you Prince Consort Jiang, yet never did we think that you would really become consort to the Ma family's daughter. It was heaven's will that the fox sprite should come to you and fulfill your union with Miss Ma. So it would seem that the nickname 'Prince Consort' was, after all, an augury that has now come true!"

South Boy Meets the Emperor

襄敏公元宵失子
十三郎五歲朝天

In the days of Emperor Shenzong of the Song dynasty there was a prime minister who went by the official title of Lord Xiangmin and whose personal name was Wang Shao. His entire household lived in the capital city, Bianliang, in a mansion for state ministers, which, needless to say, was the last word in grandeur and luxury.

This story begins on the fifteenth day of the first moon of the New Year, the day all people celebrate by making fancy paper lanterns and consuming sweet rice-flour dumplings. Wang Anshi, the draconian reformer, had yet to be engaged by the imperial court, so the New Laws were not yet in force. No invaders menaced the nation's frontiers, the populace lived and worked in tranquility and contentment, and peace reigned throughout the country. At this time, all families were hanging up colorful lanterns and, as the celebrations usually commenced on the thirteenth day of the month, the ten main streets and nine big markets bustled with activity both day and night.

On the official day of the celebrations—the fifteenth of the first moon, it was the custom, observed every year, for the emperor to come out in person to watch the night-long festivities, and all residents of the capital, both men and women, waited to behold his celestial countenance.

It was a time of rare beauty, with the rays of the full moon turning night almost into day, and the brilliance of all sorts of exquisite flower-lanterns blending in a scene of extraordinary enchantment. The women, young and old, of Lord Xiangmin's household, from the Lady of the house downward, had one and all attired themselves most attractively and now came out to admire the lanterns and amuse themselves, surrounded with curtains held up by servants and attendants.

Esteemed listeners, do you know why and how such curtains were employed? These were used because the womenfolk from the households of high officials were loath to be bumped and jostled by commoners in the streets, which would be beneath their dignity, and were therefore encircled with long, low curtains devised from lengths of silk or linen. They were thus separated from outsiders but could still walk along and enjoy the sights on all four sides. In the days of the Jin dynasty, this arrangement was known as a "walking enclosure," or variously, "purple silk walking enclosure" and "brocade walking enclosure," and was the usual practice among the families of the rich and powerful. But let us get back to our story.

Lord Xiangmin had a young son, the last of those produced by his latest concubine. The lad ranked thirteenth among his siblings, and his pet name was "South Boy." Having just turned five years of age and being already quite pert and clever and of unusually good looks, he was doted on by all members of the household, not to mention the Lord and the Lady therein.

Now, South Boy also wanted to go out and look at the lanterns and was handsomely dressed for the occasion, as behooved the scion of an important family. In addition, however, he wore a cap adorned with nonperforated imported pearls the size of soybeans, strung together to form two phoenixes disporting themselves among peony blossoms. A cat's-eye jewel glittered at the front of the cap, surrounded with precious stones of various exquisite colors. This cap alone was worth no less than a thousand strings of cash. Lord Xiangmin instructed one of his retainers, whose name was Wang Ji, to seat the boy on his shoulders and accompany the womenfolk on their lantern tour. Being a man, however, and conversant with the conventions of propriety, Wang Ji did not venture to walk within the curtained enclosure but followed along outside.

Just as this procession approached Xuande Gate, Emperor Shenzong made his august appearance on the gate tower. By imperial edict, all people were permitted at this time to look up and gaze upon him, and the imperial guardsmen were not to forbid them from doing so. A tortoise-shaped hill of lanterns bedecked the gate tower, their brightness dazzling to the eye, and the air was heavy with the fragrance of burning incense. The palace orchestra struck up clamorous refrains on flutes and drums, and theatrical performances were presented before the gate tower to regale the imperial entourage. So tightly squeezed together were the throngs of spectators below that not an interstice could be discerned among them.

Wang Ji stood among the spectators, yet felt greatly inconvenienced by the weight of the boy on his shoulders and was not enjoying himself as much as he might have done.

All at once, the load on his shoulders lightened, but he was so engrossed in the goings-on that he had completely forgotten himself and his charge. With a sense of relief, he straightened his back and raised his head and stared raptly at the spectacle before him. Suddenly, he thought to himself, "Where is the Young Master?" Hurriedly turning his head, he ascertained that the boy was not on his shoulders. He then peered around, only to see many strange faces but not a sign of the Young Master. He attempted to go in search of the boy but, hemmed in as he was by the press of people, his feet could not move.

Alarmed now, he pushed with all his might to make his way out, straining so hard that his bones ached and his muscles grew numb by the time he reached a less crowded spot. There he came upon a group of colleagues from the household and asked, "Have you seen the Young Master?" To which his colleagues replied, "You were carrying the Young Master, so why do you ask us?" Wang Ji explained, "Amid the noise and commotion, someone unbeknown to me took the Young Master from my shoulders. I surmised that a friend of mine in the household saw that I was tired and took over my load to give me some respite, but that may not be so. In any event, being too intent on my own ease and comfort, I failed to pay sufficient attention, and when I looked for the boy he was nowhere to be seen. Have you not come across him?"

On hearing this account, all the retainers became most anxious and scolded Wang Ji, saying, "Now look what you have done! This is no matter to be taken lightly! How could you have so negligent? You lose the boy in a crowd of thousands of people and then stand here asking us? You are simply wasting time! Let us separate and each go to make inquiries in the busy market places!"

So Wang Ji and the other retainers, some ten persons in all, sallied in and out of the crowds, shouting and calling out the boy's name. But to whom, among the teeming multitudes, could they address their inquiries? They peered around till their eyesight became blurred and they shouted their voices hoarse, but all to no avail. After searching for a while, they came together again to ask one another if they had found the boy, and when none had anything to declare they flew into a panic. One asked, "Can someone have taken him home?" But another replied, "We are all here, so who could have done that?" An elderly retainer opined, "I'll wager the boy is not at home. The things on his head are too eye-catching and some villain must have made off with them, together with the boy. Let us not alarm the Lady yet, but report the matter to the Lord and have a notice put up for the arrest of the culprit."

On hearing that the Lord was to be told, Wang Ji lost his nerve and objected, saying "How can we report this to the Lord? Let us take our time and search some more. Do not be in such a hurry." The other retainers, however, were too distraught to give any heed to Wang Ji's proposals, and all rushed back to the house.

After returning to the mansion, the retainers made discreet inquiries, but as no one had seen the Young Master they had no choice but go to the Lord. Once before the latter, however, they whispered and mumbled among themselves and none had the courage to directly broach the loss of the Young Master. Observing their unease and agitation, the Lord remarked, "It is but a short time since you went out, so why have you all come back? And all of you appear to be frightened out of your wits. There must be some reason." Only then did the retainers recount how Wang Ji had lost the Young Master in the crowd, while Wang Ji himself fell to his knees, knocked his head on the ground, and asked to be put to death for his negligence.

Lord Xiangmin, however, was not in the least concerned. Laughing, he said, "If he is gone, he will of course come back. There is no need for anxiety." The retainers protested, "He has surely been abducted by some villain and will not be able to come back. To be on the safe side, Your Excellency had best notify Kaifeng Prefecture to mount search-and-arrest procedures." But Lord Xiangmin merely shook his head and said, "That will not be necessary." And no matter how the retainers sought to persuade the Lord that the matter was of the utmost magnitude and urgency, he treated it lightly and remained as unperturbed as though the affair was of no greater consequence than a cup of melting snow.

As the retainers could not comprehend what was on the Lord's mind, they proceeded to the family's curtained enclosure to inform the Lady of the house about the boy's disappearance. Greatly perturbed, the Lady at once hurried back to the house and conferred with her husband with tears in her eyes. However, Lord Xiangmin assured her: "If another of our sons was lost, I would of course search for him in all haste. But since it is Thirteenth Son, I have no doubt that he will return on his own. You need not worry." The Lady protested, "He may be clever, but he is too young, a mere five-year-old child. Lost among tens of thousands of people, how can such a small child find his way home?" And the boy's nanny asserted, "I have heard that evil men abduct other people's children, put out their eyes or chop off their feet or cripple them in other ways, and then use them as beggars to solicit alms on the streets. If these men are not apprehended at once, the Young Master will assuredly suffer violence at their hands." Everyone began to weep.

A retainer proposed, "If My Lord is unwilling to seek assistance from Kaifeng Prefecture, we could at the very least put up some notices or large posters, so that persons who desire the reward offered will tell us what they know about the Young Master's whereabouts." A bedlam of voices ensued as everyone proffered his or her own ideas. Lord Xiangmin, however, maintained his cheerful nonchalance, declaring, "You may come up with a hundred proposals, but all of them will be unnecessary, as the boy will return on his own in a few days."

The lady remonstrated, "How can you bear to lose this child who is as adorable as a clay doll? How can you have the heart to make such pointless and dispiriting statements?" Whereupon Lord Xiangmin attempted to placate her, saying, "I will take it upon myself to return the boy to you in perfect condition. Will that do? Now calm yourself." But the Lady could not set her mind at ease and even the retainers and nannies were not persuaded by the Minister's assurances. So the Lady instructed the retainers to go forth and search every corner of the city.

Now let us return to the time that evening when South Boy was perched on Wang Ji's shoulders. Amid the jostling and the general hubbub, some person suddenly sidled up to Wang Ji and, with a swift and dexterous motion, lifted South Boy and placed the child on his own shoulders. Absorbed in and dazzled as he was by the sights around him, South Boy at first failed to notice the change. But when the man on whose shoulders he was riding began to push and squeeze his way out of the crowd, he said sharply, "Wang Ji, where are you going in such haste?" Then he looked down and saw that it was not Wang Ji. The cap and clothing were of a different appearance. Though still very young, South Boy had a quick mind and knew at once that this was a bad man who had taken advantage of the confusion to abduct him. He thought of crying out, but on looking around saw no familiar faces. He reflected, "He must have been attracted by my jeweled cap, and if he makes off with it I may never see it again. I had better hide the cap, for I do not think he will harm me personally."

With such thoughts in mind, South Boy removed the cap from his head and concealed it within one of his sleeves. He uttered not a word; nor did he succumb to panic, but allowed the man to carry him along as though he had not noticed what was happening.

As they approached Donghua Gate, South Boy saw four or five sedan chairs advancing toward the gate in close succession. He thought, "Either officials or noblemen must be riding in those sedan chairs. This the best time for me to call for help." Waiting until the sedan chairs came closer, he reached out, grasped the curtain of one of the sedan chairs and cried, "A thief, a thief! Help! Help!" The thief who was carrying him was taken quite unawares. Alarmed by the sudden outcry from above his shoulders and fearful lest someone seize him, he hurriedly put the boy down and vanished into the surrounding crowds of people.

The person riding the sedan chair had heard the boy's cries for help. He flipped open the curtain and saw, to his delight, a fair-skinned, dark-haired child with a countenance like a doll's. Ordering the bearers to stop the sedan chair, he drew the boy to himself and asked, "Where do you come from?" South Boy replied, "I was stolen and brought here by a thief." The man in the sedan chair then asked, "And where is the thief now?" South Boy replied, "He slipped away in the crowd when I called out for help." Pleased by the boy's lucid statements, the man patted his head and said, "Good lad, do not be alarmed. Come with me and we shall see what can be done." With both hands the man lifted South Boy and placed the child on his lap. The sedan chair then made straight for Donghua Gate and entered the imperial palace.

Can you guess who was in the sedan chair? He was the Imperial Grand Chamberlain, a high-ranking eunuch who had unrestricted access to all the sanctums of the imperial palace. After the Emperor had finished watching the lanterns, the Grand Chamberlain and four or five other eunuchs were returning ahead of the imperial entourage to oversee arrangements for a festive banquet. And it was then that the Chamberlain had heard South Boy's cries and decided to take him in his sedan chair into the palace. There, in the palace, the Chamberlain ordered his attendants to take the boy to his own chambers, bring him fruits and confections, and prepare a warm bed for him. He enjoined the attendants again and again not to frighten the boy. The eunuch had a soft spot in his heart for children, which is only to be expected!

The next morning, the Grand Chamberlain and four or five of his colleagues went directly to an audience with Emperor Shenzong. Kowtowing, he reported, "We wish to bring it to Your Imperial Majesty's attention that as we were returning from the viewing of the lanterns last night we picked up a lost child outside Donghua Gate and brought him to the palace. We see this as an omen that Your Imperial Majesty is soon to beget a son, for which reason we are happy beyond words. It is not known to whose family the boy belongs, and we have not presumed to take any action without first obtaining your Imperial instructions. Hence, this report."

At this time, Shenzong had no successor yet and was most anxious to acquire a son. When he learned that a boy had been found, he too thought this a good omen. Pleasure lit up his celestial countenance, and he cried, "Bring him here at once!" Thus instructed, the Chamberlain hurried back to his chambers and lifted up South Boy in his arms, saying, "You have received the imperial summons and are about to meet His Majesty. Do not be afraid!"

Hearing the words "meet His Majesty," South Boy knew that he would be seeing the Emperor. Calmly and without haste, he took out his bejeweled cap and donned it as he had the night before, then followed the Chamberlain into the Imperial presence. Still a young child, he had not yet learned the rituals of court behavior, but he knew how to fold his hands and bend his knees, and he proceeded to kowtow repeatedly.

Emperor Shenzong stamped his foot in delight, and asked, "Whose son are you? Do you know your family name?" South Boy replied respectfully, "My family name is Wang, and I am your subject Wang Zhao's youngest son." Emperor Shenzong was amazed by the clarity and well-ordered manner of the boy's speech, and he asked further, "How do you happen to be here?" South Boy replied, "Yesterday was the Lantern Festival and my whole family came out to admire the lanterns and to gaze with reverence on your imperial countenance.

Amid the confusion, a thief placed me on his back and ran off. I saw the sedan chairs of some court officials and called out for help. The thief ran away, after which I was brought to this place by those officials. It is now my ten thousand-fold fortune to see your imperial countenance."

Emperor Shenzong then inquired, "How old are you?" South Boy replied, "This subject of yours is five years old." Emperor Shenzong exclaimed, "How eloquently you speak at such a young age! Wang Zhao is indeed fortunate to have a son like you. We can well imagine your family's consternation at losing you last night, and We shall return you to your father at once. However, it is a pity that the thief has not been apprehended and punished."

But South Boy declared: "Should Your Majesty wish to catch the thief, that would not be so difficult." Surprised, the Emperor asked, "And what good ideas have you for catching the thief?"

South Boy proceeded to explain, "When your subject was riding on the thief's back, I suddenly realized that this person was not one of my family's retainers, so I took off my jeweled cap and hid it. On the crown of the cap was a needle with a silken thread, stuck there by my mother to avert ill fortune. As I sat on the thief's shoulders, it occurred to me that there would be no way to identify him later. So I removed the needle and thread from my cap, then secretly sewed the thread to the back of the man's collar and hid the needle in his gown to serve as a marker. Should Your Majesty send people to make inquiries and a man is found with a needle and thread in his collar, he would be last night's thief. So there should be no difficulty."

Astonished, Emperor Shenzong exclaimed, "What a miraculous child! So young and with such presence of mind! If We do not apprehend this thief, We shall be less than this child!" To South Boy he promised, "We shall send you home as soon as We have caught and punished the thief." Then, he lauded the boy to his close attendants, saying, "Everyone inside the palace must meet this amazing child. Make haste and ask Empress Qinsheng to come here."

An attendant with authority to enter the palace's inner sanctums delivered the imperial summons, and soon the Empress made her appearance. Once she had performed the ritual greetings, Emperor Shenzong said to her, "Someone's good son is in the outer chamber and will remain here for the time being. Take care of him for Us for a few days, as he is an augury that we shall soon beget a son." Although the Empress expressed compliance with this imperial order, she appeared to be somewhat hesitant, for she did not know what had previously taken place. Seeing her uncertainty, Shenzong said, "If you wish to learn all the details, take the boy to the inner palace and ask him. He will explain everything." Empress Qinsheng thereupon led the boy into the palace.

Emperor Shenzong now wrote out a secret edict and had a high official deliver it posthaste to the high commissioner of Kaifeng Prefecture. Also given were the full details of the matter and a time limit for apprehending the thief. On receiving the edict, the high commissioner understood that this was no ordinary request to catch a thief, and consequently dared not procrastinate for a single moment. He called in the superintendent of the day, Inspector Ho, and announced, "I have received a secret imperial edict today. You are ordered to apprehend within three days a band of persons who committed offenses on the night of the Lantern Festival."

Inspector Ho replied, "With neither booty nor any evidence of the crime, on what grounds am I to conduct this investigation?" The High Commissioner asked the inspector to approach, and then whispered in his ear all that the court official had said about the mark left on the culprit's collar. Inspector Ho conceded, "Since that is the case, I guarantee to resolve the matter within three days. But no word of this must be allowed to spread about." The High Commissioner enjoined him, "See to it that you do a good job, for the order comes straight from the emperor and this is no ordinary case of robbery or theft. Be very circumspect!" The inspector agreed and then left.

Proceeding straight to the duty room, Inspector Ho assembled a group of sharp-eyed, nimble-witted agents and discussed with them his dispositions. "More than one person committed evil deeds during the excitement of that night," he said, "and more than one family suffered loss. The thieves did not succeed in stealing this boy, but they are certain to have taken many other things. As these incidents took place only a day or two ago, it is quite possible that the scoundrels are still celebrating and disporting themselves in the brothels, wine houses, and eateries and have not yet dispersed. We may not know yet who they are or where they come from, but that should not put us off, as we have been apprised about the secret mark. We shall find them no matter how they try to cover up their tracks. With several tens of us spread out all over the city searching for them, we are certain to uncover something."

He then sent off the agents in different directions, each to his own accustomed haunt, whether a teahouse or a wine shop, to keep a close watch on groups of people of unfamiliar or suspicious-looking demeanor. And so the agents went on their way.

The band of thieves who had come out on the night of the Lantern Festival bore the sobriquet "Vulture's Claws." There were ten or more of them, and they sallied forth during public celebrations to ply their nefarious trade among the crowds. The thief who abducted South Boy had been skulking around the Wang household's gate and keeping an eye on the family's movements, when he spied the Young Master, sumptuously dressed, being borne out on the retainer's shoulders. Making up his mind, he followed them closely, and when the procession approached Xuande Gate, where the crowds were thickest and most noisy, he stole up to the retainer, slipped his hands under the boy, hitched him onto his own shoulders, and then walked away. The thief dared do this thing because his victim was still very young, and even if the boy realized he was being taken away by a stranger, he would at most begin to sniffle and sob, which was of no consequence. So the thief was not at all concerned. He had never expected the child to shout "Thief! Thief!" as the palace sedan chairs passed by! Caught completely unawares, and conscious of the danger of his circumstances, the thief promptly fled. Little did he suspect, however, that the boy had not remained idle while on his shoulders but had left a secret mark. Not even a god would have guessed such a thing!

Once the thief had made good his escape, he came together with his fellow thieves, who each showed off the things they had stolen, such as hairpins studded with precious stones, gold and silver jewelry, mink ear muffs, foxtail stoles, and all sorts of valuables. He alone had returned empty-handed. After he had recounted his misadventure, the others asked, "Why did you not simply take his cap?" The thief objected, saying, "His entire suit of clothes was adorned with pearls and precious stones, and he wore bracelets on his wrists and ankles. The boy alone, who was four or five years old, would have brought me several strings of cash. That bit of business was too good for me to pass up." But the other thieves derided him, saying, "So, where is the boy now? It would appear that you took on more than you could handle!" The thief protested, "He began to cry out just as the sedan chairs of some palace eunuchs were going past. They had hordes of attendants and servants, all as ferocious as tigers and wolves! I was fortunate enough not to get caught and had no time to think of securing any goods!" The other thieves conceded, "You indeed had a narrow escape! You are lucky to be safe and sound. Now let all of us chip in and treat you to a few drinks to help you get over the fright you had." And so the thieves all took turns playing host, frequenting only out-of-the-way wine houses, and they proceeded to soak themselves in liquor.

That day, they were all drinking and reveling at a small tavern near the Jade Ferry Crossing Garden. An agent named Li Yun happened to pass by and heard rowdy shouting inside, as when finger games are played and the losers are urged to empty their cups. Alerted, he walked in to take a look, and saw a group of men whose appearance and behavior at once aroused his suspicions. So he sat down at a small table to one side and called out, "Bring me wine and food!" A waiter laid out a cup and chopsticks and then went to the back of the tavern to fill in the order.

At this time, Li Yun stood up and strolled back and forth with his hands clasped behind his back, covertly scrutinizing each of the men from the corners of his eyes. One of the men indeed had an inch-long strand of colored thread hanging from his collar. Li Yun knew now that he had found his man.

Calling to the tavern-keeper, he said, "Do not warm up the wine just yet. I am going out to meet a guest who will dine with me." He then strode quickly out of the door and gave a whistle. Seven or eight agents gathered around him asking, "What have you found, Big Li?" Pointing at the tavern, Li Yun announced, "They are in there. I have seen the evidence. We shall stand guard here while one of us goes to assemble another ten or more of our men. Then we shall all take action together."

The swiftest runner among them sped off like the wind and soon returned with a dozen more agents. Then the command was given and all charged into the tavern, shouting, "By Imperial edict, we are here to arrest thieves who committed crimes during the Lantern Festival! All tavern staff should render assistance and not allow them to escape!" On hearing the words "Imperial edict," the tavern keeper realized the gravity of the matter. He called together the waiters, cooks and scullions, who armed themselves with various weapons and came out to help. Not one of the dozen or so thieves managed to elude capture. All were trussed up and thrown to the ground.

As the saying goes:

A man with a quiet conscience by day,
Fears not a knock on the door at night.

Thieves and robbers are as wary of police agents as mice are of cats, while police agents recognize thieves as readily as cranes sniff out snakes in their holes. That is why surreptitious arrangements are usually struck between these two sets of people whereby the thieves pay the agents a gratuity called "money to remain in business." When a thief is apprehended but the theft is of no great import, the offender may be let off for a small payment. This time, however, no such indulgence was possible since the thieves were wanted by imperial edict, and the evidence of the needle and thread left no room for maneuver. The thieves were tied up with ropes, and the outer clothing was removed from the thief in question. Although all the thieves insisted on their innocence, every one of them was quivering and quaking, and their faces were the color of dirt. A search of their persons revealed that each was in possession of miscellaneous stolen goods.

The thieves were taken straight to Kaifeng Prefecture and their arrest was reported to the High Commissioner, who forthwith held court, examined the evidence of the needle and thread in the collar, and ascertained that the arrests were fully justified. He then ordered, "Torture them to make them confess!" The thieves, stripped, suspended with ropes, and beaten, suffered considerably. However, their knavish flesh withstood the torments and not one of them owned up.

The High Commissioner then produced the collar with the needle and thread and asked the thief, "How did these things come to be on your person?" Not knowing the implications of this piece of evidence, the thief made up some lame excuse. The High Commissioner laughed, saying, "To think that a seasoned thief like you has been outwitted by a child! This is truly Heaven's justice! Do you recall the boy who cried out for help beside the eunuch's sedan chair on the night of the Lantern Festival? He left a secret mark on you! So how much do you believe your denials of guilt will avail you?"

Knowing now that the boy had gotten the best of him, the thief had nothing more to say, and he confessed. He also acknowledged that over many years, he and his colleagues, as well as coming out during festive events to steal and rob, had also kidnapped young children and taken people's lives.

Their crimes, so legion as to defy enumeration, had never been exposed to the light of day. The incident during the Lantern Festival was the first time they had ever been caught. And they had only been brought to this pass because a little boy had outsmarted them and caught the attention of the Emperor. It was Heaven's will that they should pay for their crimes, and now they could not escape death.

The High Commissioner took their confessions and had these written up for his files. As he did so, he was suddenly reminded of another case that had taken place a year ago, also during the Lantern Festival, and that had been investigated but never resolved. Can you guess which case that was? Let us leave the present case for the time being, esteemed listeners, and allow this humble person to tell you about that other case.

It also had to do with watching the lanterns at Xuande Gate. Curtained enclosures had been marked off on both sides of the gate for the womenfolk of aristocratic families, many of whom had come already during the daytime to wait for the evening's spectacle. On the eastern side of the gate was the enclosure of a prince of the imperial clan. The family had a daughter called True Pearl, and since the family's name was Zhao, like that of the imperial clan, everyone referred to the girl as "True Pearl, the Belle of the Imperial Clan." And indeed, seventeen years old and as yet unbetrothed, the girl was a dazzling beauty, with her exquisite countenance and gorgeous raiment.

The enclosure of the prince's sister-in-law was on the western side of the gate, and having learned that her niece, Lady True Pearl, was waiting in the Zhao family enclosure to see the lanterns, she dispatched a maidservant to ask her niece to come over to her own enclosure. As instructed, the maidservant said, "If you are indeed willing to come, I shall send a sedan chair to pick you up." Thrilled, True Pearl said to her mother, "I have been hoping to see my aunt, and now that she has invited me, I must go." Her mother readily gave her permission. So the maidservant went back to report to her mistress, while the Zhao family waited for the sedan chair to come for True Pearl.

Not long afterward, a covered sedan chair came from the west and approached the Zhao family's curtained enclosure. True Pearl was just like a child in her eagerness to go and play at her aunt's place. She asked her nannies to inquire whether the sedan chair was for her, and when the bearers said that was so, she quickly clambered in and, too impatient to wait, told her attendants to follow later. A little while after she had departed, the aunt's maidservant arrived with another covered sedan chair and said, "My mistress is waiting to meet Lady True Pearl. Would she please mount the sedan chair without delay." To which retainers of the Zhao family replied, "Lady True Pearl has already departed in a sedan chair. Why are you coming to fetch her again?" The maidservant insisted, "The sedan chair I came with is the only one. What other sedan chair are you talking about?"

The retainers knew now that something was seriously amiss and began to worry. They informed the Prince, who sent servants to make inquiries with the party at the western side of the gate. The latter affirmed that Lady True Pearl had not arrived. The Prince then hurriedly ordered all his servants and retainers to search the surrounding area, but to no avail. The case was then hastily filed with Kaifeng Prefecture and, since the matter had to do with the imperial family, the prefecture dared not delay the investigation but immediately dispatched detectives and agents to seek clues to the girl's disappearance. The prince's household also offered a reward of two thousand strings of cash to any person who could provide information. Nonetheless, no trace of True Pearl was found.

After True Pearl had seated herself in the sedan chair, the two bearers picked up their feet and ran like the wind. Curious, True Pearl thought to herself, "Why are they in such a hurry? It is but a short distance!" However, assuming that these bearers were accustomed to such a breakneck pace, she gave the matter no more thought. Some time later she looked up and observed that the sedan chair had turned off the main street and was entering some narrow alleys.

As the bearers still did not slow down and the sky was beginning to darken, True Pearl began to feel uneasy. All at once, the sedan chair came to a halt and the bearers quickly departed. No one came to meet True Pearl, so she lifted the curtain herself and stepped out of the chair.

Looking around, she saw to her shock and dismay that she was in an ancient temple. Lined up on both sides were ten or more ghostly warriors, each brandishing weapons in their hands. In the center sat a god-like figure with a broad, bewhiskered countenance, flashing eyes, and arms and shoulders that shook as though the god were alive. Filled with dread, True Pearl fell on her knees and kowtowed. The god then opened its mouth and spoke, saying, "Do not be afraid! I have transported you here with my magical powers because you and I were fated in our past lives to be together." But the sight of the god speaking only increased the girl's terror, and she began to weep aloud. Two of the ghostly warriors stepped forward and raised her to her feet, and the god said, "Bring wine to allay her fears." Another warrior poured out a cup of warmed wine and raised it to True Pearl's lips. She wished to decline but was too frightened to do so and, as she reluctantly parted her lips, the warrior forced her to drain the cup.

True Pearl's senses began to reel, and she soon fell to the ground in a faint. The god then stepped down from his throne. He guffawed, saying, "We have her now!" The ghostly warriors gathered around and, together with the "god," divested themselves of their costumes and masks. The truth is that all of them were real men—a band of unholy thieves and brigands in disguise. Having administered a somniferous potion to True Pearl and rendered her unconscious, they now carried her to the back of the temple. An old woman came out and helped them stretch True Pearl out on a bed. Then, as she lay in a swoon, the thieves took turns raping her. And thus was a delicate maiden of noble birth ravished by a band of scoundrels and ruffians. When these had slaked their lust, they told the old woman to take charge of the girl. This done, each went his way to commit other deeds of evil.

True Pearl slept in a stupor until dawn. When she opened her eyes she knew not where she was, and the only person she saw was an old woman seated beside her. Then she became aware of a pain in her private parts, and when she touched herself there she found the flesh tender and inflamed and knew that she had been molested.

She asked the old woman, "What is this place, and how is it that I am here?" The woman told her, "You were brought here by a band of bravos who often send me young girls at night. But do not fear, I guarantee you will end up in a good place." True Pearl expostulated, "I am the daughter of a prince of the

Imperial clan. How dare you evil people commit such a dastardly act!" The old woman merely replied, "What good does it do you now to say that you are of a prince's family? However, I can see that you are of aristocratic birth and promise not to put a paltry price on you." Having no idea what the old woman was talking about, True Pearl could only cover her face with her hands and weep.

The truth was that the old woman was a trafficker in human beings who specialized in selling boys and girls to rich families. The scoundrels would bring the persons they kidnapped to her house, and the old woman would keep the victims for a few days until a deal was struck with a buyer. The old woman held True Pearl for the time being in order to lull the girl, which she did with sweet words and blandishments; then two or three days later a sedan chair came and bore the girl away. She had been sold to a rich man who lived outside the city to serve as his concubine.

On the night the master of the house wedded True Pearl and took her to bed, he found out that she was no longer a virgin. He did not take exception to this, however, as he was highly pleased with her beauty. Nor did he ask her about her antecedents. True Pearl, on her part, felt so ashamed and humiliated that she was unwilling to volunteer any explanations. However, there were several other concubines in the house, and they grew jealous when the master bestowed all his favors on True Pearl. They said, "Her origins are unclear. She is most likely a maid servant who has been booted out of someone else's house for sexual misbehavior." Day in and day out so much malicious gossip was dinned in the master's ears that he finally lost patience and asked True Pearl where she had come from. Touched to the quick by this question, True Pearl sobbed loudly and recounted to him the whole course of events. The master was aghast to learn that a daughter of the imperial clan had been kidnapped and sold to his household. He had seen the notices offering a reward for the girl. Fearing now that the matter would be laid bare and he himself would get into trouble, he dispatched a servant to seek out the old woman, but that trafficker in human beings had vanished without a trace.

The master ruminated, "Such evildoers will sooner or later be uncovered, if not now then certainly at some later time. The girl is presently concealed in my house, yet if a thorough search is undertaken, there is no way I can continue to hide her. In that case, I will be held answerable for this enormity. Besides, womenfolk of the imperial clan are not to be trifled with, and the authorities will not rest until they get to the bottom of her disappearance. Those who did this evil deed have now left me holding the bag. Am I to pay for their crimes with my life?"

All at once he had an idea. Summoning two of his servants, he had them bring an old bamboo sedan chair from his house and patch it up. Then he asked True Pearl to come out of her chambers and, falling on his knees and kowtowing, said to her, "I was blind not to have recognized Your Highness, and even to have treated you in such an uncouth manner. But you should know that the abuse you have suffered is the work of some evil persons, and I knew not what I was doing. I shall now send you back to your residence, even if it means forgoing the price I paid for you. My only hope is that you will show mercy to me and not divulge my role in this affair, so that I will not be implicated."

To True Pearl, the news that she was to be sent home was like being given a reprieve by the Ninth Heaven. She also recognized that the master of the house had treated her well and, when she saw him apologize so abjectly, she even felt sorry for him. She replied, "If only I see my parents again, I promise you I shall never mention your name." The master then invited her to mount the sedan chair, and when she had done so, the two servants picked up the shafts and sped away, not even affording True Pearl a chance to bid the master farewell. They bore the sedan chair a few miles to a desolate and uninhabited spot. There, they set the chair down and departed with the utmost speed.

When True Pearl observed that the sedan chair had come to a stop, she peered out from behind the curtains and saw that no one was around. Stepping out, she looked in all directions. Even the bearers were nowhere to be seen. Panic-stricken, she thought, "Alas and alack! Why have they abandoned me here? What will I do if I meet more bad people?" Not knowing what to do, she mounted the sedan chair again and started to cry. In her grief and despair, she rocked back and forth, weeping, until her hair fell into disarray.

All this happened in the third moon in spring when city dwellers were in the habit of coming out for walks in the countryside to enjoy the fresh greenery. Some people heard with great astonishment the laments issuing from the unattended sedan chair, and they gradually gathered about it. At first, there were only a few persons, but a sizable crowd was soon attracted. As first one and then another shouted questions, a loud hubbub arose. Frightened out of her wits by the noise, True Pearl could not offer any articulate explanations. Then a man of greater maturity waved his hands to silence the clamor; he asked in a loud and clear voice, "Girl, to which household do you belong? And why have you been left here alone in your sedan chair?" Only then was True Pearl able to still her sobbing. She responded, "I am a princess of the imperial clan. I was kidnapped by some evil men and have now been left here. Any person who reports my presence to my family will surely be richly recompensed." Everyone in the assemblage was, of course, aware of the reward offered by the Prince's household and the notices posted up by Kaifeng Prefecture. Thus even before

True Pearl had finished speaking, some people, eager to obtain the reward money, were already running like the wind to report the discovery.

Very soon, a number of the Prince's attendants and retainers arrived to identify the girl in the sedan chair and quickly confirmed that she was indeed Princess True Pearl. Her parents hastily dispatched a proper sedan chair to carry her back to their residence, and when they and the rest of family saw the girl's disheveled hair and tear-streaked face, they enfolded her in their arms and wept. True Pearl herself was overcome with paroxysms of grief, and her lamentations were as those one might hear when a Buddha goes to Heaven before the new Buddha comes to this world.

When her grief was finally exhausted, she recounted in full detail how she had been abducted and why she had been released on this day. The Imperial Prince inquired, "Do you know the name of the household that bought you? It would help us find your abductors." True Pearl still wished to protect the master of the house, so she replied, "Were I to see them, I would recognize their faces, but I do not know their full names; nor can I say where they live. I was brought a long distance from an unknown direction." The prince, too, was thinking, "This is a family scandal that should not be made public." He feared that his daughter would never be able to find a husband if the full circumstances were made known. The Imperial Prince finally decided to exercise restraint. So, instead of demanding a thorough investigation, he merely instructed Kaifeng Prefecture in private to keep an eye out for the culprits.

Now, exactly a year later and also during the Lantern Festival, the case of True Pearl's abduction was finally cleared up. For when the Commissioner apprehended the thieves who abducted South Boy, he was reminded of the case of Princess True Pearl's kidnapping and had the prisoners interrogated about that previous case. It turned out that the perpetrators of that crime were the same band of brigands. Grinding his teeth with rage and slapping his desk, the Commissioner cursed them roundly and concluded with the words, "You pack of scoundrels! Even death is too good for you!" He forthwith ordered that they be caned. All received sixty blows applied with extra force, and were then consigned to the cells of convicts awaiting execution. The commissioner thereupon wrote a report, asking the emperor to pass the final verdict. The gist of the report was as follows:

> This band of brigands committed no more than acts of thievery during the current Lantern Festival. However, their crimes over the years are not limited to those enumerated herein. It would seem that violent criminals of their ilk should no longer be permitted to sully the imperial domains, and that they should one and all be executed to cleanse Your Imperial Majesty's lands.

When Shenzong read the report and learned that Kaifeng Prefecture had made a clean sweep of the scoundrels, he laughed and said, "Everything has happened exactly as the child anticipated!" Greatly pleased, he endorsed the report and ordered that all the thieves be executed at once. He also enjoined Kaifeng Prefecture to provide him with a complete copy of their confessions for his perusal. With these orders, Kaifeng Prefecture had the thieves beheaded and then submitted a report on the executions to which was appended a detailed transcript of the confessions as written out by the prison scribe. When Shenzong received this report, he thrust it in one of his sleeves and returned, smiling, to the inner palace.

Now let us go back to the Imperial Consort, Empress Qinsheng. Having received the Emperor's injunction to take care of this young outsider, and learning that the latter was regarded as a propitious omen for her begetting a son, she thanked Shenzong and took the boy to the inner palace. She commenced by asking him about his provenance, and the little boy replied unhesitatingly in a loud and clear voice. He was not at all shy before strangers, since he had already been in the imperial presence. In fact, South Boy behaved as though he were in his own home, and he smiled and laughed in a most natural manner. Qinsheng was exceedingly pleased and her heart overflowed with joy. Placing South Boy on her knees, she showered him with all sorts of endearments. Then she had a maid-in-waiting bring out her box of toiletries and combed the boy's hair and washed his face, after which she mixed some rouge and painted a red dot on his forehead to make him look more cunning and adorable.

By this time, the concubines of the imperial harem had heard that the Emperor had bequeathed a child to Qinsheng, and all trouped in to offer the imperial consort their congratulations and to see the child. And indeed, he was quite a rarity since there had never been a boy of his age in the inner palace. What they saw was a doll-like little boy with clear features, bright eyes, rosy lips, and white teeth, gifted with a clever tongue and able to answer fluently all questions asked of him; everyone was thoroughly delighted with the child. Wishing to please the Empress, and also because they loved children, the imperial concubines lavished the boy with such gifts as precious antiques, gold, pearls, and all manner of bracelets and jewelry, thrusting these into his tiny sleeves until they could hold no more. Qinsheng had an old eunuch draw up a list of these objects and place them in safekeeping. She also instructed attendants to take the child to other courtyards in the palace to meet their occupants and be entertained by them. The imperial concubines, who regarded these visits as festive occasions, all vied for the honor of playing host, and most of them plied the boy with still more presents. The whole palace teemed with excitement.

Matters went on in this manner for more than ten days. At the height of the furor, the Emperor made an appearance at Qinsheng's chambers and requested to see the child. Qinsheng at once took South Boy to the emperor and, after she and the boy had paid their respects, Shenzong asked Qinsheng, "The child is not frightened, is he?" Qinsheng replied, "Thanks to Your Majesty's indulgence, I have had the pleasure of the boy's company for the last few days. He is exceptionally intelligent, and despite the awe that this Forbidden City inspires he displays the aplomb of a person of much greater maturity. Indeed, it is owing to Your Imperial Majesty's all-encompassing good fortune that the country has produced a child of such rare talent. I, as your consort and subject, am deeply gratified."

The Emperor stated, "We wish to apprise you and the child that the persons who committed that evil deed the other night have all been apprehended by Kaifeng Prefecture, thanks to the needle and thread that marked the culprit's collar. Not a single one has escaped. This child is truly astute! Now that the thieves have all been beheaded, however, We are concerned that his family, being still unaware of his whereabouts, may be feeling alarmed and bewildered. Let us send the boy home in proper fashion today."

The Empress and South Boy kowtowed their thanks. An Imperial Edict was issued forthwith to the effect that the Grand Chamberlain who had brought South Boy into the palace that night should escort the child back to his house. A casket full of golden ornaments would also be conferred on the boy to atone for any fright or alarm he might have sustained.

On receiving the edict, the Grand Chamberlain came and, in the presence of His Imperial Majesty, took charge of the child and had him bid farewell to Qinsheng before leaving the palace. Loath to part with the boy, the Empress gave him more gifts. These, together with the presents given him earlier at the various palace courts, were packed in a large hamper, which was then entrusted to the High Chamberlain for transportation to the boy's home. The High Chamberlain thereupon left the palace gates and ordered a carriage. Inserting the Imperial Edict into one of his sleeves, he had South Boy sit in his lap and they departed together for the Wang family residence.

Meanwhile, at Lord Xiangmin's house, the entire family had been utterly distraught over the disappearance of the Young Master. All members of the household, whether young or old, went about with worried expressions and tears in their eyes. Only Lord Xiangmin showed not the least concern and even refused to order a search. The servants and retainers dispatched by Lady Xiangmin and the house steward to look for the boy had come back empty-handed. Frustration and despondency reigned, and no one knew what to do.

On this day, however, a Guardian of the Imperial Gates came in great haste and reported that the Grand Chamberlain would be arriving in short order to read an Imperial Edict. Not knowing what to expect, Lord Xiangmin hurriedly ordered that a table with incense be set out to welcome the imperial envoy. He himself donned cap, gown and girdle, took in his hands a tablet reserved for imperial audiences, then knelt down to wait for the Imperial Edict. In a few moments, the Grand Chamberlain descended from his carriage with a young boy clasped in his arms. Household servants and retainers pushed forward to see who it was, and were astounded to see that it was the Young Master! All of those present danced and waved their arms in transports of joy.

At this time, the Grand Chamberlain commanded, "Hear ye the Imperial Edict!" and then proclaimed in a loud voice:

> *The child that was lost to you during the Lantern Festival has been found by Us, and is being restored to you today. We have bestowed on him a hamper full of diverse objects to atone for the fright the child has sustained and to reward him for his extraordinary astuteness.*
>
> *The Emperor.*

After the Grand Chamberlain had finished reading the Imperial Edict, Lord Xiangmin kowtowed his gratitude for the Emperor's benevolence and asked to be given the text of the edict. When this had been done, greetings were exchanged and Lord Xiangmin and the Grand Chamberlain seated themselves as befitted host and guest.

The Grand Chamberlain's first remark was, "Old friend, you have a very shrewd son." Lord Xiangmin was just about to inquire into the reason for this statement when the Grand Chamberlain extracted a sheaf of documents from his sleeve, saying, "You will understand how your son was lost and found after you read this file." Leafing through the documents, Lord Xiangmin found them to consist of the confessions wrung from the bandits apprehended by Kaifeng Prefecture. As he read the first page, which was the secret order to the prefecture to arrest the culprits, he said, "It anguishes me that that young scamp of mine distracted the court and even caused the Emperor to put himself out over the capture of these thieves. Never shall I be able to repay one ten thousandth part of His Imperial Majesty's kindness, even though my flesh and bones were ground to powder." Laughing, the Grand Chamberlain replied, "In truth, the thieves were caught in large measure by your own son. The remarkable thing about it is that the Emperor was not put to one whit of trouble."

South Boy then described the long and short of what had transpired that night. He also recounted how he saw the Emperor, and how he had met the Empress, and his entire account was clear and fluent and delivered without the least hesitation. Earlier, when members of the household had heard about the arrival of the Imperial Edict and gathered around to watch, they had been astonished and delighted to see South Boy emerge from the carriage but had not understood the ins and outs of the matter. Now, after the boy had related all the details, the questions in their minds were dispelled, and they praised South Boy for his great intelligence. It was only now, too, that they understood why Lord Xiangmin had shown no concern, declined to initiate a search, and declared that the boy would return by himself. One and all marveled at the lord's foresight.

Lord Xiangmin now ordered that a banquet be prepared to entertain the Grand Chamberlain. On his part, the Grand Chamberlain brought forth the golden ornaments awarded by the Emperor and laid out all the gifts presented to South Boy by Empress Qinsheng and the palace courtiers. The display of gold, pearls, and precious stones, the value of which was no less than ten thousand taels of silver, lit up the hall with a dazzling refulgence. Patting South Boy on the head, the Grand Chamberlain jested, "My lad, you have enough here to keep yourself amply supplied with fruit and sweets." Lord Xiangmin again kowtowed in the direction of the Emperor to thank him for his magnanimity. He then had one of his secretaries write out a letter of thanks for the Grand Chamberlain to take back to the palace, pending such time as he and his son would attend a morning audience to thank the Emperor in person.

The Grand Chamberlain said, "It was I who first met your son and brought him to the Emperor, and I too have a meager present as a remembrance of that occasion." So saying, he produced two gold ingots and eight bolts of silk. Lord Xiangmin attempted again and again to decline this gift, but finally had to accept it, not however without presenting the Grand Chamberlain with a lavish gift in return. The Grand Chamberlain then mounted his carriage and returned to the palace to report on his execution of the imperial edict.

After seeing off his visitor, Lord Xiangmin held a celebration for the entire household. He said, "I told you not to panic. Did I not say that Thirteenth Son would come home on his own? Now he has not only returned, but has also brought back a great many gifts. Moreover, the persons who stole him have been apprehended, owing in great part to his own cleverness. So you see, I was right in not worrying, was I not?" And everyone in the household acknowledged his perspicacity.

In subsequent years, South Boy was formally named Wang Cai, and during the Zhenghe reign achieved considerable renown for his merits, literary and otherwise. One has but to look back on his actions as a child to comprehend his accomplishments as a grown man.

What a Scholar Suffered Because of His Foul Temper

惡船家計賺假屍銀
狠僕人誤投真命狀

During the current Ming dynasty, there lived in Suzhou Prefecture a rich man by the name of Wang Jia, who was embroiled in a bitter feud with Li Yi, also of Suzhou. Wang Jia concocted a hundred schemes to kill Li Yi, but had never had the opportunity to do so. Then one night a big storm arose. Li Yi and his wife ate their supper and had been asleep for some time when, just after the drumbeat of the third watch, more than ten ruffians with red and black ink daubed over their faces burst into their house. Alarmed by the noise they made, Li Yi's wife, Mistress Jiang, contrived to hide under the bed. From there she saw a man with a big beard and broad face seize her husband by the hair and fell him with a broadsword. Then the band of ruffians at once departed without taking anything from the house.

After they were gone, Mistress Jiang crawled out from under the bed, shuddering with horror. She put on some clothes and then wept loudly over her husband's body. Neighbors who came to see what had happened were all grieved by Li Yi's death and attempted to console Mistress Jiang, who declared, "The killer was his enemy, Wang Jia." The neighbors asked, "How do you know that?" Whereupon Mistress Jiang said, "I observed everything from under the bed. Wang Jia has a beard and a broad face, and I knew him although he had smeared ink on his face. Moreover, if those were bandits, why did they not touch anything after they killed my husband? Who else could the killer be if not Wang Jia? I entreat all of you to help me."

The neighbors declared, "We all know he hated your husband. Such crimes must be reported to the authorities. Write up a plaint, and we shall go with you to submit it at the yamen tomorrow. Until then, let us each go our way." And the neighbors all returned to their homes.

Mistress Jiang closed her doors and then started sobbing again. Incapable of sleep, she nursed her sorrow until daylight, and then begged a neighbor to write out a plaint for her. When that was done, she set out for the Changzhou County seat. She arrived just as the county magistrate ascended to his bench and announced he was ready to hear complaints. Approaching his bench, Mistress Jiang cried out for justice. The magistrate read her plaint and then questioned her about the matter. Seeing that this was a grave case of housebreaking compounded by murder, he accepted the plaint. Then, on the basis of this plaint and the report submitted by the local authorities, the magistrate sent a coroner to examine the body and assigned bailiffs to apprehend the murderer.

After Wang Jia killed Li Yi, complacent in the belief that no one had recognized him since he had disguised his face, he had not taken any other precautions. Thus there was no escape for him when a group of bailiffs descended upon his house with the suddenness of a thunderbolt. He was shackled and at once taken to the county yamen.

There, the magistrate asked him, "Why did you kill Li Yi?" And Wang Jia replied, "I had nothing to do with his death. He was killed by robbers." The magistrate asked Mistress Jiang, "Why do you say Wang Jia was the murderer?" And Mistress Jiang replied, "This humble woman was hiding under the bed and recognized him." The magistrate asked, "This happened in the middle of the night, so how could you recognize him?" Mistress Jiang insisted, "Not only did I recognized his face, there is something else that proves it was him. If the men were robbers, why did they not take anything and only kill my husband? Who else besides an enemy would do such a thing?" The magistrate then summoned some of the neighbors and asked them, "Were Wang Jia and Li Yi enemies?" And the neighbors all nodded, "Yes, they were indeed enemies. And it is also true that only a murder was committed and nothing was taken."

The magistrate then commanded that vises be applied to Wang Jia. Being from a wealthy family, Wang Jia was incapable of enduring pain and he soon confessed: "There was enmity between Li Yi and myself, and it is true that I killed him under the pretence of being a robber." Now that the magistrate had this confession, he had Wang Jia consigned to the cell for prisoners condemned to death.

Although Wang Jia had confessed to the crime he still hoped to argue his innocence, but when he failed to conceive of any strategy he thought to himself, "There is that crafty counselor, Old Man Zou, with whom I am on excellent terms. A person may be guilty of the most heinous crime, but if only one consults him there is always a way out. I shall wait for my son to bring me my food and then ask him to speak to Old Man Zou."

When his son Wang the Second arrived with his food, Wang Jia explained in detail what he had in mind and concluded with, "Do not begrudge any money if the expense is justified, for my life hangs in the balance." Wang the Second promised to do all that he had been asked and went straight to Old Man Zou's house. He related what had happened to his father and then begged the counselor to devise some means of saving his father.

Old Man Zou declared, "Your father personally confessed to the killing, and the magistrate is new to his post and handled this case himself. No matter how you appeal, you will not be able to go beyond the county's jurisdiction; nor will the magistrate be willing to overturn the conviction. Best you give me two or three hundred taels of silver. I shall go to Nanjing to seek opportunities, and there I believe I can find some way to rescue your father." Wang the Second asked, "How do you intend to present this?" But Old Man Zuo replied, "That is my concern. Just give me the silver and wait for results. I cannot tell you anything beforehand."

Wang the Second went home and put together three hundred taels of silver. Returning to Old Man Zuo's house, he placed these in the counselor's hands and urged him to set out for Nanjing. Old Man Zou assured him, "With all this silver, there can be no fear that opportunities will be lacking. Wait here, and do not worry." Wang the Second thanked Old Man Zou; then he left.

That very night, Old Man Zou packed some things and left for Nanjing the next day. Arriving in that city a few days later, he made detailed inquiries at the Ministry of Justice and learned that there was a certain Judge Xu of the Zhejiang Department who was a most easygoing and sociable man. Old man Zuo prevailed on someone to write out a letter of introduction and, bearing the letter and a handsome gift, went to visit Judge Xu.

Judge Xu received Old Man Zuo and, finding his visitor to be garrulous and witty, soon took a liking to him. Thereafter Old Man Zuo went frequently to see the judge, and they became well acquainted.

One day, as Old Man Zuo was casting about for some means to fulfill his mission, more than twenty pirates were apprehended by the Office for the Suppression of Piracy and sent to the Ministry of Justice for sentencing. Old Man Zuo made inquiries and learned that two of the pirates were men from Suzhou. Nodding with satisfaction, he said to himself, "This is exactly what I need."

That same day, he made arrangements for a banquet and sent an invitation to Judge Xu to join him in drinking some wine. The judge arrived in his sedan chair at the appointed time, and Old Man Zou smilingly welcomed him. After seating themselves, they drank and made small talk until late in the evening. Then, having asked all other people to leave the banquet room, Old Man Zou produced one hundred taels of silver and proffered these to Judge Xu. Astonished, the judge asked why he was doing this. Old Man Xu replied, "I have a kinsman name Wang who has been thrown in prison in my home county. I am begging you for assistance."

Judge Xu declared, "I am quite willing to oblige you. However, this matter has taken place elsewhere and I do not see how I can help." Old Man Zuo assured him, "That presents no difficulty at all! Wang had an enemy called Li Yi, and when Li Yi was killed, the real culprit could not be found and Wang was wrongly convicted and imprisoned. Now, I hear that there are two men from Suzhou among the twenty-odd pirates your ministry has just brought here. These two pirates could be made to confess to killing Li Yi. Doing so would not add to their punishment since they are to die in any event, but my kinsman would have a new lease on life, thanks to your kindness."

Judge Xu agreed to this scheme. He quickly took the silver and thrust it in his carrying case, then called in his servants, thanked his host, and departed in his sedan chair.

Old Man Zou visited the families of the two pirates in secret and promised them large sums of money, first distributing one hundred taels of silver among them as an earnest. He then obtained the pirates' consent for the plan.

When the trial was held, Judge Xu summoned the two pirates and asked, "How many people have you killed?" The pirates replied that they had killed such-and-such people at such-and-such places on such-and-such days and that they had gone to Li Yi's home and killed the latter on such-and-such a night. Judge Xu wrote down their statements, sent the pirates back to prison, and set up a file of their confessions. Old Man Zou had a scribe make a copy of the file for Changzhou County. He took this with him when he bade farewell to Judge Xu and, returning to Suzhou Prefecture, submitted the copy to the Changzhou County court.

When the county magistrate opened the envelope and saw the pirates named as the murderers of Li Yi, he said to himself, "So Wang Jia's confession under torture was false after all!"

As he was about to order the prisoner to be released, Wang the Second appeared at the yamen to appeal for justice. Already convinced now of Wang Jia's innocence, the magistrate had the latter brought out of prison and set free. And when Mistress Jiang learned about the magistrate's decision, she could only say that she might have mistaken the murderer's identity in the darkness of the night.

Wang Jia went home after being released from prison. As he swaggered gleefully through the gate there was a sudden gust of cold wind and he cried in a loud voice, "Woe is me! Li Yi is here!" He fell to the ground and no entreaties could bring him back to his senses. He died then and there. As the ditty goes:

> The King of Yama is quite in earnest:
> He who kills another must pay with his life.
> Heaven was not fooled by that substitution,
> And laughed at the wiles of Old Man Zou!

Esteemed listeners, the story you have just heard is about a real murder presented in a false light. Next I shall tell you how a false murder was made to look real—how an evil man engineered a minor incident into a matter of such gravity that the victim would have died an untimely death had the ways of Heaven not prevailed.

*   *   *

The events in this story took place in the current Ming dynasty during the time of the Chenghua reign [1465–1488].

In Yongjia Country of the district of Wenzhou, Zhejiang, there lived a man named Wang Jie whose style name was Wenhao. His wife was of the Liu family, and they had a daughter who was two years old. They also had a few servants, but the family lived in no great luxury since Wang Jie, who considered himself a scholar, had yet to pass the imperial examinations. He whiled away much of his time at home studying the Classics, going out only from time to time to meet friends and discuss scholarly matters. His wife, Mistress Liu, managed the household with diligence and thrift. A sensible and virtuous woman, she and Wang Jie lived in harmony and peace.

Now one day in late spring, two or three of Wang Jie's friends insisted that he go out with them to the countryside to see the fresh green landscape. Always agreeable, Wen Jie went along. He was much pleased as they drank wine and enjoyed the scenery, and by the time he turned his steps homeward he had become somewhat tipsy.

When he arrived at the gate of his house, he saw two of his manservants shouting at someone. This man was a merchant from Huzhou by the name of Lu, who was selling ginger roots from a bamboo basket and had entered into an argument with Wang's servants when they had attempted to bargain down his price. Wang asked the reason for the altercation and then told the merchant, "The price offered you is reasonable, so why do you make such a fuss in front of my gate? I see you are quite ignorant about the ways of the world!" The merchant, an outspoken man, retorted, "I run but a small business, so why do you short-change me like this? You, a gentleman, should be more magnanimous and not behave in such a miserly fashion."

Wang Jie, being under the influence of the liquor he had drunk, flew into a rage and cried: "Where did this old donkey thief come from! He has the gall to talk back to me like this?" Wang Jie stepped forward and struck the man several times with his fist and then pushed him. How was he to know that this middle-aged man suffered from phlegm-fire! That one push made the man stagger and fall, senseless, to the ground.

The worst thing a man can do is to give rein to his passions. The more so in this case since the cause for Wang Jie's ire was but a minor transaction in which the merchant would make only one or two coins—a sum of no great consequence. We often see arrogant servants of rich households banking on the power and prestige of their masters to beat and bully the poor, and when trouble ensues it is the household that loses face. That is why decent people place strict curbs on themselves and their households. Scholar Wang should not have lost his temper, and he suffered as a result, as we shall hear later in this story.

Scholar Wang was greatly alarmed when he saw the merchant unconscious on the ground, and the shock cleared the fumes of liquor from his head. He hurriedly instructed his servants to take the merchant into the main room of his house and lay him on a couch. Tea and soup were poured down the man's gullet, and soon he came to his senses. Scholar Wang apologized to the merchant for his behavior, treated him to food and wine, and presented him with a bolt of white silk in order to assuage his ire. The merchant's anger thereupon gave way to pleasure, and after thanking his host he departed for the nearest ferry crossing. Had scholar Wang possessed the magical powers to foresee the future, he would have quickly detained the man, drawn him back and willingly cared for him for a few months or even half a year, and thus spared himself dire trouble.

Scholar Wang's heart was still thumping after the merchant left. Going to the inner chambers, he told his wife, "I almost caused some big trouble and am most fortunate nothing came of it!" Night was falling, and Mistress Liu instructed her maidservants to prepared a few dishes of food and warm some wine so as to help her husband get over the fright he had sustained.

Scholar Wang had downed a few cups of wine when he was startled by loud and urgent knocking at the front gate. Lighting his way with a lantern, he went out, only to see the local boatman Zhou the Fourth at the gate, holding in his hands some white silk and a bamboo basket and looking greatly perturbed. Zhou the Fourth announced, "Sir, you have brought disaster upon yourself. Do you know you have beaten a man to death?" Scholar Wang's face turned ashen from fear, and he asked the boatman what he was talking about. Zhou the Fourth asked, "Master Wang, do you recognize this length of white silk and this bamboo basket?" Having examined the objects, Scholar Wang replied, "A merchant from Huzhou selling ginger roots came to my house today. I gave him the white silk, and he used the basket to carry his ginger roots. How have they come into your possession?"

Zhou the Fourth replied, "This afternoon, a certain Merchant Lu from Huzhou asked me to ferry him across the river. After he came on board, he had a severe attack of phlegm-fire. As he lay on the verge of death, he told me that he owed his condition to a severe beating you had administered to him. He left the silk and the bamboo basket with me to serve as evidence and requested that I submit this case to the authorities on his behalf. He also asked me to report the matter to his family in Huzhou so that they might register a complaint and seek redress. Having said all this, he died. His body is still in my boat, which is now tied at the pier in front of your house. You had best come and see for yourself and decide what should be done."

Scholar Wang was so consternated that his eyes widened, his mouth fell agape, his hand and feet became weak and numb, and his heart leaped about in his breast like a frightened fawn. Yet he feigned bravado, saying, "That is nonsense!" At the same time he privately instructed a servant to go to the boat and take a look. The boat did indeed contain a corpse!

Scholar Wang, a man fainthearted by nature, fell into a panic. Hurrying into the inner chambers, he told his wife what had happened. Mistress Liu asked, "What can we do?" Scholar Wang replied, "Circumstances being as they are, there is little else I can think of but to pay the boatman to discard the body under the cover of darkness. That may resolve the matter."

He placed a packet of pieces of silver amounting to some twenty taels in his sleeve and went out to speak with the boatman. He said, "Do not bruit this matter about, and let us come to an understanding. I know that I am at fault in this affair, but it was not intentional. You and I are both natives of Wenzhou and as fellow townsmen we should share some sentiments. Why do something to avenge a stranger? Besides, even if you did avenge him, what good would it do you? Better we keep this matter between ourselves, and I shall recompense you in some way for disposing of the body somewhere else. As the night is dark, no one will be the wiser."

The boatman protested, "Where can I dispose of it? Should someone recognize the body tomorrow and search for reasons, even I would be implicated Scholar Wang reassured him, saying, "Not many *li* from here is the grave of my late father. It is in a very secluded spot, as you well know. Let us take advantage of the night, when there are no people around, to transport the body in your boat and secretly bury it there. Neither man nor ghost will know." After a moment's thought, Zhou the Fourth replied, "There is much reason in what you say, but how do you intend to thank me for doing this?" Scholar Wang gave him the package of silver. However, Zhou the Fourth thought it too little, and said, "Is a man's life worth only this bit of silver? Since he happens to have died in my boat, it is Heaven's will that I should derive some profit from this affair. I will accept no less than one hundred taels of silver."

Eager to see the matter settled, Scholar Wang dared not dispute the boatman's demand. He nodded, and then went back in his chambers. In a while he came out again with some silver, clothing and jewelry and handed these to Zhou the Fourth, saying, "These things are worth about sixty taels of silver. I am not wealthy, and I hope you will bear with me." When Zhou the Fourth saw all the things Scholar Wang had brought, he relented and said grudgingly, "All right, all right. You are but a scholar and I shall not haggle with you. However, in the future be sure to keep my interests in mind!"

Scholar Wang, who had up to now been racked with anxiety, now felt somewhat relieved. He partook of some food and wine with the boatman; then he instructed two house servants to look for hoes and spades. One of these house servants was a man named Hu. Brutal and endowed with great strength, he bore the nickname "Hu the Tiger."

When everything was ready, all boarded the boat, which took them to the graveyard. A vacant plot was chosen, a hole was dug there and the corpse buried, after which all boarded the boat again. The expedition had taken the better part of the night, and dawn was breaking when they returned to Scholar Wang's house. Wang Jie treated the boatman to breakfast, and then bade him farewell. The servants were told to shut the front gate, and all retired to their respective quarters.

Scholar Wang went to the inner chambers and said to his wife, Mistress Liu, "I am from an old family and have always wished to do everything the right way. How was I to expect that such a disaster would be visited on me, and that I would be exposed to coercion by that knave?" He wept, and his tears fell like rain. Mistress Liu comforted him, saying, "My husband, it was fated that you should suffer such a fright and forfeit some property. But do not worry. With Heaven's blessings, all will be well, and we should consider ourselves lucky nothing worse has happened. You must be tired after your night's exertions and had better rest now." She brought him tea and refreshments, and after he had eaten they went to sleep.

After a few days had gone by and all appeared to be quiet, Scholar Wang purchased some sacrificial objects and offered these to the gods and his ancestors. Zhou the Fourth would come from time to time, ostensibly on friendly visits. And when he did so, Scholar Wang could only show him courtesy and dared not rebuff him. The boatman would also ask for small loans, which Scholar Wang gave him, albeit with reluctance. This went on until Zhou the Fourth's fortunes improved and he sold his boat to open up a shop, after which no more mention was made of the affair.

Let me say this to my listeners: Scholar Wang was, after all, a pedant and a bookworm and possessed little worldly wisdom. Since he had already bribed the boatman to transport the body to the graveyard that night, he should have gathered some firewood and burned the body. No trace would have remained of it, leaving things neat and tidy. He failed to think of this, however, and, as the saying goes: "Weeds that are not pulled up by the roots will surely sprout again in spring."

And indeed, about a year later, as it so often happens, "disasters assail him who is unprotected by Fortune." Scholar Wang's three-year-old daughter came down with a grave case of chickenpox. Her parents prayed to the gods, consulted fortune-tellers, and engaged medical practioners to provide treatment, all to no avail. Scholar Wang had only this one daughter, and both he and his wife doted on her. Greatly worried, they sat at her bedside day and night, weeping. Then one day a relative came with a box of delicacies for the sick girl. Scholar Wang entertained the visitor with tea and mentioned that his daughter was so severely ill that she might not survive. The relative said, "There is a children's physician by the name of Feng in this county whose skill is such that he can truly bring the dead back to life. He lives but thirty *li* from here, so why not invite him here for a consultation?" Scholar Wang replied, "I shall indeed do so!" He then invited the relative to stay for dinner before seeing him off.

Scholar Wang informed Mistress Liu of his decision and wrote out a letter of invitation. That very night, he called in Hu the Tiger and instructed him, "Leave at daybreak with this letter and deliver it to Physician Feng. Ask him to come at once to see a patient with chickenpox. I shall prepare lunch for him and shall wait for him, standing on my feet until he arrives." Hu the Tiger promised to do as he was instructed, and all retired for the night.

The next day, Scholar Wang had lunch prepared, but even after midday there was no sign of the physician. The day went by, and when Scholar Wang went to see his daughter it was obvious that her condition was growing worse. By the middle of the night she could only exhale and no longer inhale, and soon she departed from her parents for the domains of Yama, the King of the Dead. Scholar Wang and his wife wept till they nearly fainted, so great was their grief at losing this treasured child. Then they laid out the body in full funereal regalia and cremated it.

Hu the Tiger did not report back until around midday the day after. He declared, "Physician Feng is not at home. I waited for him another half day, which is why I have only returned today." Tears trickled from Scholar Wang's eyes, and he sighed, "That was clearly the fate of our daughter, so there is nothing more to say."

A few days later, however, others among the servants divulged the truth, which was that Hu the Tiger had become sodden drunk on the way to the physician, lost the letter, and therefore tarried until the day after, and then had concocted that big lie. Scholar Wang, still in deep sorrow over the death his daughter, flew into a towering rage when he learned the true facts. He at once summoned Hu the Tiger and brought out a bamboo lathe with which to punish the servant, whereupon Hu the Tiger remonstrated, "Why am I being treated in such fashion? I have not killed anyone!" But these words merely exacerbated Scholar Wang's wrath, and his spleen drove him once more to ill-considered violence. Ordering some other servants to hold Hu the Tiger down, he administered more than fifty strokes with the bamboo lathe before desisting and returning to his chambers.

Hu the Tiger, his skin and flesh torn by the beating, limped back to his quarters, fuming, "Why should I be made the object of his ire? His daughter's illness was incurable, and she did not die because I failed to bring the physician. I did not deserve such a vicious beating. I detest him! I detest him!" After some reflection, he said to himself, "Not to worry! I have the upper hand. Wait until the injuries I have suffered from your blows are healed, and you shall know of what I am capable. Then we shall see who comes out on top! However, I must keep my counsel for the time being, so that he will not be prepared."

Let us, for the moment, leave Hu the Tiger to brood on his cruel revenge and return to Scholar Wang.

A month went by after the death of his daughter, and as friends and relatives frequently treated him to good wine and food to comfort him, he gradually laid his grief to rest. One day as he was strolling in his courtyard, a band of bailiffs, bearing ropes and chains, swarmed in and, ignoring Scholar Wang's protests, threw the shackles around his neck and shoulders. Greatly alarmed, Scholar Wang asked, "Why are you humiliating me in this way? I am a scholar! Why are you doing this?" One of the bailiffs spat on the ground and retorted, "A scholar indeed! One who kills people and takes other's lives! In any case, if a mistake has been made, it was made by the yamen officials and not by us. Go plead your case before the county magistrate!" Mistress Liu and the house servants heard and saw what was happening, but knew not the cause. They could only stand numbly, and none dared to step forward.

No longer master of his own actions, Wang Jie was pushed and pulled by the band of ferocious bailiffs all the way to the yamen of Yongjia County. In the righthand corner of the hall knelt a plaintiff, and when Scholar Wang raised his head to look at the man, he recognized Hu the Tiger. He knew now that it was his servant who, out of spite and a desire for revenge, had denounced him.

The county magistrate addressed Wang Jie, saying, "Hu the Tiger has accused you of beating to death a merchant from Huzhou. What have you to say to this?" Wang replied, "Most fair and impartial judge, do not listen to his lies. How could I, Wang Jie, a weak and timid pedant, beat someone to death? Hu the Tiger is my manservant and he was severely punished according to family rules not long ago for committing a wrong, for which reason he now harbors hatred against me and has brought me to such a sorry pass! I hope that My Lord will clarify the circumstances."

Hu the Tiger then kowtowed and declared, "Most fair and impartial judge, do not listen to his one-sided testimony. Masters frequently beat their servants, so why would I hate him for that? As for the body of the dead man, it now rests in a hole on the lefthand side of a graveyard. I beg My Lord to send someone to dig there. Should they find a body, then what I am saying is true. If they do not, then what I say is untrue, and I will gladly plead guilty to the crime of lodging false accusations."

The county magistrate acted accordingly. He dispatched men who took Hu the Tiger with them to dig for the body, and with Hu the Tiger providing directions, they soon found the corpse and brought it back to the county yamen. The country magistrate rose to his feet and examined it, then said to Scholar Wang, "This is indeed a corpse. Now what else have you to say?"

The county magistrate was just about to order that torture be applied, when Scholar Wang cried, "My Lord, allow me to defend myself! The body is decomposed and was manifestly not done to death just recently. If the man were killed a long time ago, why did Hu the Tiger not file his complaint then but wait until now? It is clear that he has found this body merely to falsely incriminate me." To which the magistrate replied, "There is reason in what you say."

Hu the Tiger responded, "This corpse is indeed of a man killed a year ago. However, I did not bring forth accusations then on account of the sentiments between my master and myself. Besides, a servant is already deemed to be in the wrong if he accuses his master, and for that reason I have kept silent about the matter. But lately I have found that my master has not changed his violent ways, and I am afraid I might be implicated if anything else should happen. Hence, I am now bringing up a charge about that old affair. If My Lord does not believe what I have said, you need only to summon the neighbors and ask them whether someone was beaten to death on a certain day of a certain moon. It will then be seen whether or not I speak the truth."

The county magistrate again did as Hu the Tiger suggested, and before long, all of Scholar Wang's neighbors arrived. The county magistrate questioned them one by one, and they all said, "On a certain day of a certain moon last year, a merchant who sold ginger roots was beaten unconscious by Scholar Wang. He was brought back to his senses for a while, but we do not know how he fared afterward."

As neighbor after neighbor accused him, Scholar Wang's face turned pale, and he carped and caviled and denied all that they said. The magistrate stopped him, saying, "The facts are clear and the accusation is just. What else have you to say for yourself? This fellow will not confess unless he is beaten!" He thereupon snatched up a mandate slip, tossed it before Scholar Wang and roared, "Beat him!"

With fierce shouts, yamen beadles seized Wang Jie, threw him to the ground, and gave him twenty blows with their staves. That puny scholar had never suffered such harsh treatment and, unable to bear the pain, admitted to doing all of which he was accused. The magistrate had his verbal confessions placed on record; he then declared: "There is no question that the man was killed by him. However, no one has come forward yet from the man's family, so I cannot yet pass sentence. The defendant will first be placed in detention, pending such time as someone comes to identify the body, after which I shall sentence him." He had Wang Jie cast in prison and ordered that the body be taken out and buried, though it was not to be cremated before further examination and verification. All the neighbors were allowed to go home, and the magistrate returned to his chambers.

Hu the Tiger was highly pleased, as he had obtained his revenge. However, he did not dare go back to the Wang's house and face the mistress, so he gathered up his possessions and moved elsewhere.

The other servants of the Wang family, who had waited outside the yamen for news, were so shocked to learn that their master had been thrown in prison that their very ears turned pale. They hurried back to the house to inform Mistress Liu, and when she heard the evil tidings it was as though her spirit flew out of her body. She gave a loud cry and fell down in a faint. Her maidservants, seized with panic, anxiously called out to her, and after a while Mistress Liu regained consciousness. She cried out, "Oh, my Master!" and sobbed several hours without cease. Then she assembled some pieces of silver, attired herself in somber garments, and asked a maidservant to accompany her. A manservant took them to the gates of the Yongjia county prison.

Once there, Mistress Liu met her husband, and the two wept aloud. Scholar Wang said tearfully, "It is that knave, Hu the Tiger, who has caused me such suffering!" Mistress Liu ground her teeth in anger and fiercely cursed Hu. Then she took out the silver she had brought and handed it to her husband with the words, "Give this to the warden and guards so that they may accord you better treatment and not make you suffer too much." Scholar Wang accepted the money and, as it was getting dark, Mistress Liu took her leave. She went home, sobbing all the way, and after a haphazard evening meal went unhappily to bed. She thought to herself, "Just last night I shared this bed with my husband. How were we to know that disaster would befall us and we would be forced apart!" She wept miserably before falling asleep.

Scholar Wang was not whipped or beaten in prison because of the silver he passed out to the warden and the guards, but with only the companionship of unkempt and unwashed prisoners he felt deeply depressed. Besides, he had not been sentenced yet and knew not whether he was fated to live or die. And although well-wishers brought him some food and clothing, it was unavoidable that he should suffer somewhat from hunger and cold, and he became increasingly hollow-eyed and thin. Mistress Liu brought some more silver and paid it to officials high and low in an attempt to have her husband set free on bail, but she was told, "The prisoner cannot be released as this case concerns a human life." And so, Scholar Wang had, perforce, to wait patiently in prison.

Time flew by, and as the sun and moon shuttled across the Heavens, the ailing Scholar Wang had spent a full six moons in prison. Exhaustion and anxiety conspired to render him gravely ill, and all the physicians and medications Mistress Liu sent to him appeared to be of little avail. It seemed he would soon die.

One day, when a manservant brought him a morning meal, he instructed the man, "Go back and tell the Mistress that I am grievously ill and that death is not far off. Tell her to come quickly to visit me, as I shall soon depart forever." The manservant did as he was told, and the news struck fear in Mistress Liu's heart. Afraid that she might be too late, she hired a sedan chair and rushed off to the county yamen. She asked to be set down a short distance from the prison gate, and then walked over to see Scholar Wang. Needless to say, tears welled from their eyes when they met. Scholar Wang said, "It is because your stupid dolt of a husband unintentionally killed a man that I now rot in chains and that you, my virtuous wife, have suffered such humiliations. My ailments are becoming steadily worse, but now that I have seen you once more, I am ready to die. However, I cannot forgive that knave, Hu the Tiger, and will never have mercy on him, not even in the nether regions!"

Mistress Liu replied, "My husband, do not utter such ill-omened words. You should take heart and look to your health. After all, the man's death was an accident, and no one from his family has put in an appearance yet. And even if I have to sell all our land and property, I shall try to get you out of prison so that we may be together again. As for that knave, Hu the Tiger—the laws of Heaven will not countenance him and there shall be a day of requital. Do not worry yourself about that!"

Scholar Wang sighed, and said, "My good wife. That you put so much heart into restoring my freedom to me gives my ailing body some relief. But I fear I am too weak and may not last too much longer." Mistress Liu comforted him as best she could, then tearfully took leave of him and went home.

Later that morning, as she sat in her room pondering what to do, and as some menservants were playing dominoes in the courtyard, a middle-age man with a brace of boxes slung at both ends of a tote pole walked through the gate. Setting down his load, he inquired of the menservants, "Is the master at home?" The menservants stared at him, and then yelled "A ghost! A ghost!" and scattered in all directions.

Can you guess who it was? It was Merchant Lu, the seller of ginger roots from Huzhou who had come a year earlier! He now seized one of the menservants by the arm and asked, "Why do you call me a ghost? I have simply come to pay my respects to your master!"

Mistress Liu, who had heard the commotion, came out of the house to see what was going on, and Merchant Lu stepped forward to greet her, saying, "Madam, please listen to me. I am the ginger root merchant, Lu, from Huzhou. Some time ago, your husband treated me to wine and food and presented me with a bolt of white silk, for all of which I was most grateful. After we parted, I returned to Huzhou, then conducted some business in other places for a year and a half. I happened to be passing through your prefecture today, so I purchased some local specialties and came here to pay a call on your husband. I fail to understand why your honorable servants called me a ghost!"

A young servant who was standing nearby cried, "Mistress, do not listen to him! He must have learned that you intend to set the master free, so he has appeared today in human form to claim the master's life!"

Mistress Liu brusquely ordered the servant to stand back, then said to the visitor reproachfully, "So it seems that you are not a ghost after all. But do you know how much suffering you have brought to my husband?" Thunderstruck, Merchant Lu inquired, "Where is your husband? And how have I made him suffer?"

Mistress Liu recounted in detail everything that had transpired—how Zhou the Fourth had moored his boat at the pier before their house and displayed the silk and the basket as evidence the merchant's demise, how her husband had bribed the boatman to bury the corpse, how Hu the Tiger had denounced her husband, and how her husband had confessed under torture.

The merchant struck his breast with his fists and cried, "Alas! Alas, that there should be such injustice in this world! I did indeed board the ferry after I left your house last year. The boatman espied the bolt of white silk and asked me how it had come into my possession, and in my improvidence, I recounted to him how your husband pummeled me so badly I nearly died and how he subsequently treated me to dinner and gave me the silk to make amends. The boatman insisted on purchasing the silk and, as he offered me a fair price, I sold it to him then and there. He also asked me for the basket, so I surrendered it to him as payment for using his boat. How was I to know that he desired these two things for such an evil purpose?! But it is my fault that I have not returned to Wenzhou for so long, and by that omission caused your husband to suffer so!"

Mollified, Mistress Liu said, "Had you not come today, even I would not know that my husband was unjustly accused of your death. So the boatman tricked you into giving him the silk and the basket! But where did he obtain the corpse?"

Merchant Lu thought for a moment, and then exclaimed, "Yes, that is it! As I rode in his boat and told him what had happened, I noticed a dead body floating by the bank of the river. I observed, too, that the boatman was staring at it, but I did not suspect that he had any purpose in mind. It must have been then that he conceived his nefarious scheme. Oh! The hateful scoundrel! But we have no time to lose! Please put away the gifts I have brought and come with me to the Yongjia County yamen to right this injustice and have your husband released from prison. That is the matter of first importance!"

Mistress Liu took this advice, accepted the gifts, and had a meal prepared for the visitor. She then composed a plea to be submitted to the magistrate. Being the daughter of a scholar, she was adept with brush and ink and thus had no need to engage the services of a scrivener. This done, she hired a sedan chair and, together with Merchant Lu and a household servant, set out for the Yongjia County yamen.

Soon after they arrived, the county magistrate appeared in court for his afternoon session. Mistress Liu and Merchant Lu both called out loudly for justice, and then submitted the plea. Having carefully read it from beginning to end, the magistrate first called up Mistress Liu for questioning. Mistress Liu related in full and meticulous detail how her husband had inadvertently pummeled a merchant senseless during an argument over prices, how the boatman had been richly remunerated for transporting and burying the body, and how a servant had denounced her husband out of rancor and a desire for revenge. She also said, "It was not until this very morning, when the ginger root merchant returned, that I knew my husband had been wrongfully accused."

The magistrate then called Merchant Lu up for questioning; he too recounted how he had been beaten and how he sold the silk. The magistrate asked him, "Have you been paid to say this by Mistress Liu?"

Merchant Lu kowtowed and replied, "My Lord, although I am from Huzhou, I have done business in these parts for many years and have many acquaintances here. There is no way I could deceive My Lord. If I were on the verge of dying last year, why would I not ask the boatman to find some acquaintance of mine whom I could entrust with seeking redress for me, instead of charging a mere boatman with this matter? One might claim that I was so near death at the time that I had no opportunity to do so. But why is it that if I had left for so long and not returned not a single blood kin of mine has come from Huzhou to seek news about me? Had any of them heard that I had been beaten to death, they would surely have come to this yamen to file suit. And why is it that an accusation was brought forward only a year later, and by a servant of the Wang family at that? I arrived here just today and have only now been apprised of this injustice. Although I was not the one to falsely accuse Scholar Wang Jie, his misfortunes began with me, and I cannot bear to see him accused of a crime he did not commit, which is why I am here before My Lord with this plea. I beg My Lord to spare Wang Jie's life when writing out your sentence."

The magistrate commanded, "Since you claim to have acquaintances here, name some names!" Merchant Lu, counting them off on his fingers, produced ten names. The magistrate jotted these down with his brush, then summoned two bailiffs and, pointing to the last four names, instructed them, "Go quickly, and bring me these four, together with those neighbors who previously bore witness." With these orders, the bailiffs left the yamen.

Some time later, both groups of people arrived, and when the four acquaintances whom Merchant Lu had named caught sight of him, they cried out as one man, "Why, is this not Elder Brother Lu from Huzhou? How is it that you are here? So you have not died!" The country magistrate instructed the neighbors to step closer and identify Merchant Lu, and all exclaimed in astonishment, "Are our eyes deceiving us? This is without question the ginger root merchant Scholar Wang beat to death. Was he brought back to life, or is this his double?" One among them remarked, "No two persons can resemble one another so closely. Once I set eyes on a face I never forget it. This is, without doubt, Merchant Lu."

By now, the magistrate had by and large deduced where the problem lay. He accepted Mistress Liu's plea and instructed all those present, "After you leave this room, you must not reveal what you have seen and heard here. Anyone who disobeys this order will be severely punished." All promised to do as they were told and left the yamen. The magistrate then called in a number of bailiffs and ordered: "Mount a secret search for the boatman, Zhou the Fourth, and when you find him, coax him with honeyed words to come here. But do not say why I seek him. The plaintiff, Hu the Tiger, is out on bail. See to it that both are here for the hearing tomorrow afternoon." With these orders, the bailiffs went out, each in a different direction.

The magistrate also told Mistress Liu and Merchant Lu to return the next day for the afternoon hearing. Both kowtowed and departed. Mistress Liu led Merchant Lu to the prison gate where they saw Scholar Wang and told him everything that had transpired. The elated Scholar Wang felt as though his head were bathed in balm and his heart sprinkled with sweet dew, washing away most of his woes. He said, "I blamed only Hu the Tiger for this and never suspect the boatman of being so evil. Had you not come, sir, even I would not know that I was falsely accused."

Mistress Liu then took leave of her husband, walked out of the county yamen, and took a small sedan chair. Merchant Lu and the servant followed on foot all the way to her house. Mistress Liu retired to her rooms and instructed her manservants to sup with her visitor, who later lay down to sleep in the front hall.

When they returned to the county yamen in the afternoon of the next day, the county magistrate had already taken his seat in the hall. A short time later, two bailiffs brought in Zhou the Fourth. With the silver he had obtained from Scholar Wang, he had opened a draper's shop in the county, and the bailiffs, true to their instructions, had told him, "The county magistrate wishes to purchase some fabrics." He had thus been deluded into coming to the county yamen. Yet it was also in accordance with Heaven's will that his iniquities should be exposed. The sight of Merchant Lu in the yamen took him completely by surprise, and his ears flamed a bright red. Merchant Lu addressed him, saying, "Boatmaster, we have not seen one another since the time you purchased my white silk and my basket. Are your affairs going well?" Zhou the Fourth could find nothing to say, and his countenance became as haggard as withered wood.

A short time later, Hu the Tiger was also led in. He had moved elsewhere but had recently come back to the county to visit relatives. The bailiff who had happened upon him by chance had tricked him into coming to the yamen by saying, "A member from the victim's family has now come forward in your master's murder case, and sentence will be passed as soon as you, as the original plaintiff, appear in court." Hu the Tiger, believing these words, blithely followed the bailiff into the hall and knelt down before the magistrate.

The county magistrate pointed at Merchant Lu, asking, "Do you recognize this person?" Hu the Tiger took a close look and recoiled in shock. He hesitated, undecided as to what to say. The country magistrate had carefully observed the reactions of both Hu the Tiger and Zhou the Fourth. He now berated Hu the Tiger, saying, "You knave with the heart of a wolf and the ways of a cur! What ill did your master do to you that you should scheme with the boatman to find a corpse and bring false charges against your master?" Hu the Tiger protested, "The man was truly beaten to death by my master. I am not telling a lie." Angered, the magistrate shouted, "So your mouth still refuses to yield! If Merchant Lu is dead, who then is the person kneeling over there?" He then ordered the his attendants to apply vises to Hu the Tiger and roared, "Confess, and be quick about it!"

As the vises were tightened, Hu the Tiger cried loudly, "My Lord, I would willingly admit guilt were it said that I should not have accused my master out of a wish for revenge. But I would die rather than confess that I conspired against him! After Merchant Lu was knocked down by my master, he was revived with hot soup, given food and wine, and presented with a bolt of white silk, after which he walked by himself to the ferry crossing. At about the time of the second watch that night, Zhou the Fourth brought a body to the gate and produced the white silk and a bamboo basket as evidence, and everyone took him at his word when he announced that the body was that of Merchant Lu. My master then bribed the boatman with money and valuables to transport myself and others to the family cemetery to bury the body. I, in all honesty, was unaware of the truth about that body. Nor did I know even later, after the master sorely beat me and I, seeking revenge, came before My Lord with my accusation. And if Merchant Lu had not come here today, I would still be ignorant of the circumstance that my master has been wrongly accused of beating him to death. Only the boatman knows from where he obtained that body."

The magistrate had Hu the Tiger's confessions recorded, then ordered him to stand down and called Zhou the Fourth to come forward.

At the outset, the boatman attempted to deny everything. He was, however, confronted with Merchant Lu and, when the magistrate had torture applied, he could do little else but admit to all his machinations. He said, "On a certain day of a certain month last year, Merchant Lu boarded my boat, bearing a bolt of white silk. I happened to ask him about it, and that was how I learned of the beating he had received. Then, when I saw a corpse floating by the riverbank at the ferry landing, I conceived the notion of extorting some money from Scholar Wang. So I purchased the silk from Merchant Lu, prevailed on him to give me his basket, and fished the corpse out of the water and placed it in my boat. That done, I proceeded to the residence of Scholar Wang. He not only believed what I said to him and gave me some silver, but also had the corpse buried in his cemetery. That is the truth, and nothing but the truth."

The county magistrate said, "That may be so, but there is one thing that still remains unclear to me. How is it that there happened to be a body in the water, and that the body happened to resemble Merchant Lu? You must have murdered the man in some other place, and then used the body to further your scheme of blackmailing Scholar Wang."

Zhou the Fourth at once cried in a loud voice, "I am innocent of that, My Lord! Had this small person intended to murder someone, why would I not have simply killed Merchant Lu? The scheme occurred to me when I saw the floating corpse, after which I obtained the silk and the basket. But I did indeed think at the time that 'the deception may not succeed, since the faces do not look alike.' Yet again, it might succeed, because, first, Scholar Wang had a guilty conscience to start with. Second, because he had had but one previous encounter with Merchant Lu, and the night was dark, and in general it is difficult to clearly identify a body in dim light. And third, because there was no question that the silk and basket had belonged to Merchant Lu and no reason for Scholar Wang to suspect otherwise. Hence, I was emboldened to attempt the deception and he was, indeed, taken in. Nor did any of his servants see anything wrong with the corpse. As for the body itself, it may have been that of someone who fell into the river by accident, but I have no way of knowing."

At this juncture, Merchant Lu approached the magistrate on his knees and stated, "I did indeed notice a body floating in the river during the time I was on Zhou the Fourth's boat. He is speaking the truth." The magistrate also had these words recorded.

Zhou the Fourth appealed to the magistrate, saying, "This small person merely wished to extort some money and valuables from Scholar Wang and had no intention of harming him otherwise. I beg My Lord to deal with me leniently." However, the magistrate loudly rebuked him with the words, "You are but a villainous thief who violates the laws of Heaven! Your greed for another man's silver well nigh caused him to lose his home and his life. How many others have you ensnared with your wicked schemes? Today, I shall rid Yongjia County of an evil. As for Hu the Tiger, a house slave, he has taken advantage of a matter of grave consequence to betray his master and has turned his back on his master's benevolence, both of which circumstances are most despicable!"

He forthwith ordered that both be thrown to the ground, that Hu the Tiger be administered forty heavy strokes with a stave, and that Zhou the Fourth be given as many strokes as would be needed to end his life. Tiger Hu, who had not yet recovered from a recent bout of febrile fever occasioned by a chill, was unable to endure such punishment. Besides, the laws of Heaven would not countenance a servant's betrayal of his master, and he expired in the yamen hall before his forty strokes were done. Zhou the Fourth lost consciousness and breathed his last only after more than seventy strokes were dealt. And in this manner both these evil wretches died pitiably under the stave.

The magistrate then ordered that the families of the deceased come and recover the bodies. He also ordered that Scholar Wang be brought from prison and then and there set him free. The lengths of fabric confiscated from Zhou the Fourth's shop were valued at one hundred taels of silver, and being the proceeds of coercion, would as a rule have entered the county's coffers. However, the magistrate pitied Wang Jie—a scholar wronged for so long—for the gratuitous sufferings he had undergone, and bent the rules to give the confiscated goods to him instead. This was, indeed, a mark of consideration on the magistrate's part.

As for the body unearthed in the cemetery, it was once more disinterred, and grains of sand were found under its fingernails, proving that it was indeed that of a person who had drowned. However, since no one came forward to claim the corpse, the coroner was instructed to lay it to rest in a public burial ground.

Scholar Wang, Mistress Liu, and Merchant Lu thanked the magistrate and returned to Wang Jie's house. The scholar and his wife fell into each other's arms and wept out their pain. Then Scholar Wang went to the main room with Merchant Lu to go through the process of making formal acquaintance with one another. Merchant Lu recognized that he was in part to blame for the injustice Scholar Wang had suffered, and Scholar Wang, in turn, recognized that it was the merchant who had stood forward to clear his name. The two expressed, one to the other, their apologies, and their gratitude. As the saying goes, "friendships often grow out of a fight," and in later days there were constant comings and goings between the two.

From then on, Scholar Wang reined in his temper and was most friendly and amiable to all persons he encountered, even beggars and mendicants. In view of his previous experiences, and in the desire to gain honor and clear his reputation, he devoted himself to his studies and refrained from intercourse with casual acquaintances. And in ten years he passed the highest imperial examinations to become a *jinshi*.

We would like to say, in closing, that officials and officeholders in the government should on no account deal with human lives irresponsibly and as worth no more than weeds. In the legal case of Scholar Wang, only the boatman was aware of the whole truth. Had the merchant of ginger roots not returned to Wenzhou, no one would have known that Scholar Wang had been falsely accused. Not his servants, not his wife, not even Wang Jie himself. And it is not true that the sunshine of justice reaches into all tribunals. Men of honor and good will should keep this in mind!

The General's Daughter
Who Disguised Herself as a Man

同窗友認假作真
女秀才移花接木

In the days of the Song dynasty there lived in Mianzhu County near Chengdu in Sichuan a military officer by the name of Wen Que. Successor to a family of hereditary army commanders, he had twice passed government examinations on military skills and won promotions until he was now a general and commander of the local army garrison.

General Wen, as he was popularly known, possessed considerable wealth and was known for his magnanimity and generosity. As his wife had passed away, he kept a harem of concubines, many of whom were adept in the arts of music and dance. He had but one son, born of one of his concubines and not yet three years old at the time of this story.

General Wen also had a daughter, Fei'e. Seventeen years of age and exceedingly comely, she had since childhood learned to ride and to shoot with bow and arrow, and could pierce the leaf of a poplar tree at a hundred paces.

From an early age, however, Fei'e became conscious of the fact that her father's military provenance earned his household scant regard from other local dignitaries, who were wont to call them "that soldier's family." And she understood that her family would never be accepted in genteel society or escape disparagement unless it succeeded in producing a scholar. Unwilling to wait for her younger brother to fulfill that role, she began to dress like a boy and attended school as such, appearing in public as a young student and only reverting to female garb when she was at home.

Over the the years, she acquired much knowledge of literature and the classics as well as a masculine-sounding style name—Shengjie, the connotation of which is "man of surpassing talent." In fact, by going about so long as a man, she came to be regarded as the "young master" of the Wen household.

When her scholastic excellence gained her the title of *xiucai*, people mistook her for the general's son and many came to offer their congratulations. At the end of the school term, the county government even had her escorted home as a budding local celebrity, and the general, making no effort to correct this misconception, gave a banquet in her honor.

Thereafter her father took her with him to all official functions for the assistance she could give him as well as for the honor reflected on his name. Indeed, everyone in the family seemed to close their eyes to the fact that Shengjie was really a "she," and even helped to maintain the pretense that this "she" was a "he."

Shengjie's best friends at school were Wei Zhuanzhi and Du Yi. Both were young men of exceptional talent, shared the same likes and dislikes as Shengjie, and stood academically on an even footing with her. They were also of about the same age. Zhuanzhi was nineteen, or two years Shengjie's senior, while Du Yi had been born in the same year as Shengjie, although a few months later. Like brothers, the three studied together in the same classroom and got along famously.

Although the other two regarded their relationship as one among good friends, Shengjie was secretly desirous of choosing between the two for a husband. Comparing them, she somewhat favored Du Yi since she felt she they had more in common and he was the more handsome. Du Yi, on his part, was greatly attracted to Shengjie for both her wit and her carriage, and he would say, "What a pity both of us are male. Were I a girl, I would give you my hand, and were you a girl I would certainly take you as my bride."

One day Zhuanzhi overheard these words and jested, "Carnality between men is quite common today, and *yin* and *yang* have long been reversed. So why should two males not marry?" Shengjie, however, replied unsmilingly, "As disciples of the teachings of Confucius, would it not be better for us to commune through literature and the arts and with mutual respect? Where would our honor be were we to indulge in lewd thoughts? Respectable men do not use their bodies like impudent boys. I propose that as punishment you take us out to dinner." Whereupon Zhuanzhi parried: "I ventured this jest only because I heard Du Yi's words. And I put forward my suggestion—of which Shengjie obviously disapproves—merely because it is clearly too late now for Du Yi to change into a woman." Du Yi protested: "My remarks were meant to apply to both of us, and I only uttered the first half. Now it seems I am the butt of the joke." Zhuanzhi shot back, "And since you are the youngest, you should resign yourself to coming out third best." All three laughed, and the incident was forgotten.

But when Shengjie went home and had changed into women's attire, she thought to herself, "I have consorted with males too long and it is now becoming inconvenient. If matters go on in this way, I may have to leave my schoolmates altogether and seek a husband elsewhere. Yet I feel my choice must be made between those two. Du Yi attracts me more, but Zhuanzhi is quite outstanding in his own way. I wonder which of them will turn out the better, and with whom my future marriage lies?" She was beset with indecision.

Now, there was in the Wen residence a small tower that overlooked the surrounding area. On a sudden whim, Shengjie climbed to the top of this tower. A crow happened to fly by and light on a tall tree a hundred or more paces away. It then proceeded to caw loudly and incessantly. Shengjie, seeing that the tree stood within the courtyard of her school, thought, "How insufferably that crow caws. I shall put an end to it."

She hastened to her room, took her bow and arrows, and returned to the tower. The crow was still cawing as before. "Let that creature decide my fortune," she said and, as she fitted an arrow to the bowstring, whispered, "Do not deceive me!" The arrow whistled on its way, and the crow fell to the ground. Confident that she had not missed her mark, Shengjie hurried to her chambers, changed into men's clothing and went to the school to retrieve her arrow.

It so happened that Du Yi had been taking a stroll near the school and heard the crow cawing. When it suddenly tumbled from the tree, he went to look and observed that an arrow had transfixed it through both eyes. He drew the arrow forth, asking himself, "Who has such skill as to pierce a bird right through the head?" Examining the arrow, he found two lines of small characters engraved on the shaft. He read: "My arrow will not miss; it hits its mark." "What arrogance!" thought Du Yi.

At this juncture, Zhuanzhi came by and asked to see the arrow. Du Yi gave it to him. As they inspected it together, however, a servant approached and informed Du Yi that he was wanted at home, so he left the arrow with Zhuanzhi and departed. Zhuanzhi then saw beneath the two lines of characters several smaller ones, which read: "Signed by Fei'e." "But that is a woman's name!" he reflected. "Are there truly such excellent marksmen among women? This is most amazing. Had Du Yi seen these characters, his surprise would have been even greater!"

As Zhuangzhi was thus marveling, Shengjie arrived and, observing the arrow in Zhuanzhi's hands, quickly asked, "Did you find this arrow?" Zhuanzhi countered, "Why do you ask? Do you know where it comes from?" Shengjie then inquired, "Do you see any writing on it?" Zhuanzhi replied, "There is a name, Fei'e, which is a cause for wonderment, since it belongs to a woman. Am I to believe that a woman can be such a skilled marksman?" Evasively, Shengjie answered, "She is my elder sister." Wei pursued, "Then she is most talented. Is she spoken for?" And when Shengjie replied in the negative, Zhuanzhi continued, "Does she resemble you?" "Very much so, indeed," said Shengjie.

"Then she must be exceedingly beautiful," averred Zhuanzhi. "People say, 'If you have never seen your bride-to-be, look at your prospective brother-in-law.' As you are aware, I am not yet engaged, so do you think you could arrange a match between her and myself?" Shengjie replied, "I believe I could easily persuade my father of the felicity of such a match, since I have much say in my family. I cannot, of course, say how my sister will respond." Zhuanzhi pleaded, "I can only hope you will intercede with her on my behalf. She cannot refuse, I am certain, once she learns how close you and I are." To which Shengjie replied, "I shall keep the matter in mind."

Zhuanzhi was overjoyed. "With your intervention, there should be eight or nine chances of success out of ten. To think that my marriage might depend on an arrow! I shall always treasure it!" So saying, he placed it in his personal casket, from which he then extracted a jade amulet, declaring, "I present this to your sister in exchange for the arrow. Let it serve as a token of troth." Shengjie accepted the amulet and secured it to her sash before taking her leave.

Thereafter, Zhuanzhi became obsessed with thoughts about Shengjie's beautiful and talented sister, whom he hoped to marry. But he kept these thoughts as well as the arrow well concealed from Du Yi, especially since his fellow-student had found the arrow first and might well demand that it be returned to him should he learn what it betokened.

The fact is that from the day Shengjie had begun to learn archery, she had been of a mind to use this arrow to determine her future husband. That, indeed, was the riddle behind the allusion to striking the "mark" she had engraved on it. She had loosed the arrow at the crow, knowing full well that it would be discovered by either Zhuanzhi or Du Yi, who were the sole occupants of the school, and had thus entrusted her matrimonial future to the outcome. She was, of course, unaware of what had transpired while she hastened to the school. Thus, when she came upon Zhuanzhi with the arrow in his hands, she assumed that Fate had thereby ordained the latter to be her mate. She was somewhat loath to forgo Du Yi, however, for she felt much affection for him. But, she murmured with a sigh, "One horse cannot wear two saddles, and I must bow to the will of Heaven. I shall attempt to requite Du Yi's love by other means."

The next day, she told Zhuanzhi, "I have done my utmost to persuade my father and sister, who now seem inclined to agree, and have left the amulet with my sister. My father, however, feels that any further consideration of the matter should wait until the autumn examinations, after you have obtained an advancement." Zhuanzhi replied, "That's just as well. I only hope this is in the nature of a promise and that they will not change their minds." Shengjie assured him, "With me here, that will not happen." Zhuanzhi was greatly pleased.

The time for the autumn examinations came, and since Shengjie, Zhuanzhi and Du Yi had done well in their studies, all three were chosen to take the county examinations. Shengjie, however, consulted her father on the matter. "I am after all a girl, and can maintain my disguise only as long as I remain a low-ranking scholar. If indeed I qualify for the higher title of *juren* and should the truth about me be exposed, an inquiry will certainly be undertaken. An incident of such proportions would not be lightly dismissed and should be avoided at all costs."

Thus when Shengjie's schoolmates tried to persuade her to go with them, she pleaded ill health and the two left without her. Both successfully passed the examinations. Shengjie was happy for their sake, and resolved to inform her father about Zhuanzhi's request for her hand as soon as her schoolmates returned to their native township.

It so happened, however, that the military commissioner of Anmian had a falling out with General Wen. Taking advantage of a government investigation of military and administrative affairs, the commissioner submitted a report to the procuratorate in which he accused the general of abusing his position to misappropriate vast quantities of military supplies and of falsely reporting achievements. The procuratorate sent up the report and subsequently received an imperial edict instructing it to examine the case.

No sooner did the matter become known than the Wen household was plunged into confusion. Worse still, even some of the general's colleagues and associates commenced to needle and harass them. Only the fact that Shengjie was a noted *xiucai* kept the gossipers from becoming excessively intemperate and unbridled.

Soon a summons arrived and the general was taken to prison to await trial. Shengjie submitted an appeal and applied to post bail for her father. The appeal was accepted, but bail was denied. Shengjie then asked her two former schoolmates, now newly elevated to the position of *juren*, to intercede with the authorities, but the reply they received was, "No favors may be granted, for the orders have come from above."

In the meantime, Zhuanzhi had realized that, owing to the disastrous turn of events for the Wen family, further discussion of the proposed marriage would be inopportune for the moment; better that he wait until after the national examinations. Both Zhuanzhi and Du Yi came to bid farewell to Shengjie before setting out for the capital. Zhuanzhi said, "We are three bosom friends, yet owing to ill-health you were unable to become a *juren* like the two of us, and now troubles have overtaken your family. Our hearts bleed for you as we depart for the capital, but we have no other choice. Please tell your father to attend the hearings with his mind at peace. No sooner shall we have gained even the least official advancement than we shall do our utmost to clear up the false accusations."

Then Du Yi spoke, saying, "The local officials have connived to set a trap for your father. There is little you can do here to help him. Should the two of us gain promotions at the examinations, you would do well to come to us at the capital to seek to exonerate your father. It is easier in the capital to have cases reviewed, and we would be there to assist you. Mark my words!"

Zhuanzhi then took Shengjie aside and entreated her, "By all means keep the matter of your sister in mind. I wish to carry through with it when I return, whether or not I succeed in the examinations." Shengjie replied, "With the amulet as testimony, I see no reason that you should be disappointed." The three then parted tearfully.

After her two schoolmates were gone, Shengjie was left with no one to consult about rescuing her father. Fortunately, "officials hasten no more than three days, but tarry at least seven." The authorities took their time dealing with the case and left it unresolved for the time being. Meanwhile, some silver, judiciously dispensed in high and low places, ensured that the prisoner would suffer no hardships.

One day, the general confided a plan to his daughter: "Since there is no sign of my case being taken to court yet, we are left with some time in which to maneuver. I intend to write an appeal with the full details of my case and have it sent to the capital. Yet I have hesitated to do so because I know of no person capable of executing such a mission."

Shengjie replied, "This matter requires that I go in person. Before my friends Zhuanzhi and Du Yi left, they counseled me to go to the capital to seek opportunities. And should even but one of them succeed in the examinations, he could be of much help." The general agreed, saying, "You are a man among women, and it is indeed best that you go. But the journey is long and there would be many inconveniences."

Shengjie replied, "There is the tale of Tisuo, who became legendary for saving her father. She too, was a woman. Besides, I have long dressed like a man and have gained a reputation as being one, so I see no reason I should not go. The journey is indeed long, but I am able defend myself with my skill with the bow, and my knowledge of worldly matters is such that I would have no difficulty parrying importunate questions. However, I would require a man to accompany me, and that would indeed pose an inconvenience. Yet I have a solution. Among our servants is a couple who are both of the Miao people and therefore skilled at riding and using the bow and arrow. The wife could be garbed as a man. Then there would be three of us. With the woman to attend to my needs and the man to serve as a male escort, I would have little to fear."

The general then spoke, saying, "Since you have anticipated all contingencies, I propose that you set out at the earliest possible moment. The matter brooks no delay."

As Shengjie passed through the streets on her way home, she heard a public reading of the names of successful candidates at the national examinations. Zhuanzhi and Du Yi had both attained the rank of *jinshi*, the highest for scholars in the imperial civil service. She was delighted. As she later told her father, "Their presence and assistance in the capital will greatly facilitate my task."

Having selected a date for her departure, Shengjie applied for and obtained a safe-conduct pass which testified to her status as a journeying scholar. She stopped briefly in the regional capital to glean what news she could in official quarters, then continued on her way.

How was the young lady garbed? Her long hair was covered with a flowing silk headdress, high boots encased her slim legs, and the short jacket of her riding habit was gathered at the waist with a wide silken sash knotted to one side. A bow slung across her back needed but a nimble twist of her shoulders to rest in her hands, where a goose-feathered arrow could be swiftly notched on the bowstring and sent unerringly to its mark. She looked every inch a young gentleman trained in both the literary and martial arts, and none would have suspected her of being a woman disguised as a man.

The travelers soon approached the city of Chengdu, and Wen Long, the manservant, rode ahead to seek out a quiet hostel. When Shengjie arrived and the baggage was unloaded, she instructed Wen Long's wife to take out some home-prepared viands they had brought along and to set them out in dishes. Then, having obtained a pot of wine from the hostel, she sat down to a leisurely meal.

Few are the stories that are not woven around coincidences. The table at which Shengjie was seated faced a neighbor's window, with only a narrow courtyard intervening. As Shengjie drank and dined, a young woman appeared at the half-open window and gazed fixedly at her. Only when Shengjie looked up did the woman hastily withdraw. This occurred several times until, by chance, the two looked each other full in the face. The young woman was of such extraordinary beauty that Shengjie thought to herself, "To think that such perfection exists in the world!"

Had Shengjie been a man, she would certainly have become aroused and, with looks and gestures, forthwith embarked on a flirtation. But being a woman, she remained unmoved. Ordering some cooked rice from the hostel, she finished her meal and departed for the yamen to attend to more serious affairs.

When, however, Shengjie returned to the hostel that evening and seated herself at the same table, the neighbor, hearing movement, reappeared at the window. Shengjie smiled to herself, "Would you look at me thus if you knew that you and I are the same?" As she was thinking these thoughts, an elderly maidservant appeared at the door, bearing a box in her hands. She placed the box before Shengjie and greeted her, saying, "Miss Jing, who lives next door, saw you drinking alone, and sends you some fruit to supplement your repast."

Opening the box, Shengjie saw a dozen each of the most luscious tangerines and pears.

Shengjie remarked, "This humble scholar is only passing by and is neither family nor kin to the young lady. I could hardly accept this favor." The elderly maidservant replied, "My young mistress says she has observed thousands of passers-by, but never one as striking as you. Surmising you to be from an illustrious family, she has made inquiries and was told you are the young master of General Wen's household. She said this lowly hostel has nothing worthy to offer you, so she asked me to bring you this fruit to quench your thirst."

Intrigued, Shengjie asked, "Who is this young lady, and why does she live next to the hostel?" The elderly woman replied, "My young mistress is the daughter of the vice-prefect of Jingyan. Since both her parents have passed away, she now lives with her maternal grandparents. Her family possesses tens of thousands of taels of silver, though she has not married for lack of a suitable match. Her grandfather is a wealthy man who owns a dozen of the best hostels in this city and earns much profit from them. He and his family reside next to this hostel because of its quiet and secluded location. He dares not decide on a husband for his granddaughter for fear that she will never forgive him should he make a poor choice. Hence he has told her to inform him when she has found the man of her heart, and he will then oversee the nuptials. But our young lady is most discriminating and has never expressed her approval of any suitor. She was, however, full of praise for you the instant she laid eyes on you. Perhaps she is of a mind to marry you." At loss for a reply, Shengjie merely smiled and said, "Such good fortune would hardly come my way." She then asked the elderly maidservant to convey her thanks to the young lady for her generosity.

When the maidservant had left, Shengjie could not help laughing. "The young lady is merely wasting her sentiments if she has designs on me," she reflected wryly, then composed a poem which set forth her own feelings on the matter:

> *Believing him a man of pride,*
> *She plies him with the choicest fruit.*
> *But he, alas, seeks not a bride;*
> *The lonely lute must still be mute.*

The old woman reappeared the next morning, this time with a bowl containing four hard-boiled eggs with their shells removed and a pot of fine tea. "For your breakfast," she explained. But when Shengjie thanked her she said, "It is the young lady who told me last night to bring these. I am but obeying her behests." Whereupon Shengjie protested, "How can I continue to accept such graciousness from the young lady? I have composed a poem of thanks, which I pray you to convey to her." Shengjie wrote the poem on a sheet of paper. This she sealed and entrusted to the old maidservant.

The poem was clearly meant as a rejection of the young lady's advances, but Miss Jing, in her infatuation for Shengjie, took it as a sign of acquiescence and assumed the last two lines of the poem to be merely expressions of modesty and self-effacement. She thereupon composed a poem in reply, wrote it on a sheet of silk paper, and asked the maidservant to take it to Shengjie. The poem read:

> *Her heart has flown beyond this wall,*
> *She yearns for wings to share his nest.*
> *His songs suffice to soothe her soul,*
> *So let the lute remain at rest.*

Shengjie smiled as she read the poem and thought, "Rare indeed is the young lady's talent!" But she was beginning to feel hard-pressed by the young lady's advances, so she devised a subterfuge.

To the maidservant, she said, "I thank the young lady for her praiseworthy sentiments. I am not unaffected by them, but I must confess that I am already engaged and dare not abuse her hopes. Please tell her we can only look forward to a union in our next life." The old maidservant replied, "That being the case, I will inform the young mistress so that she will not entertain false expectations and be sorely disappointed."

The maidservant left, whereupon Shengjie went again to the yamen to seek an extension of the proceedings against her father. It was fairly late when she returned to the hostel.

The next morning, the old maidservant appeared again. With a smile she said, "How is it that a person as young as you is so adept at deception? And why do you forswear a wife who tumbles into your arms? Having heard your reply yesterday evening, the young lady made inquiries from your two servants. Both said you are not engaged. The young lady was overjoyed and informed the old master, who is coming to see you very soon to arrange the match."

Shengjie was flabbergasted. "What a fine kettle of fish!" she reflected. "The only way out is to pack up and leave!" She instructed her manservant, Wen Long, to settle accounts with the hostel and prepare to depart. Hardly had she done this, however, than the hosteler came to announce, "The old master, owner of this establishment, is here to call on you."

A moment later, an elderly man, apparently in his seventies, entered the front hall. His face was wreathed in smiles, and he was obviously pleased when he saw Shengjie. "You must be Young Master Wen?" he inquired. The old woman, who had not yet left the hostel, approached and confirmed this with the words, "This is indeed he."

After exchanging obeisances with the old master, Shengjie invited the latter to be seated. The old master then stated, "I would not have taken the liberty of disturbing you had I not occasion to do so. I have a granddaughter whose father, my late son-in-law, was vice-prefect of Jingyan. She is as yet unspoken for as she is determined not to give her hand lightly to a man of commonplace qualities. Hence, I have not presumed to decide a match for her, but have left the matter to her own choice. She told me yesterday that a certain young master Wen had taken up lodgings in this hostel, that he was of uncommon talent and good looks, and that she wished to become his wife. That is the reason for my presence here. And I now see that you are indeed extraordinarily handsome and cultured. Since she, too, is not ill-favored and knows something about the art of letters, I see no reason for letting such a felicitous match slip."

Shengjie replied, "To be honest with you, I cannot honorably refuse such an offer of love from your granddaughter. However, it would hardly be an equal match, since she springs from such a distinguished family while mine is merely a military one. Moreover, my father is in grievous trouble and I am on my way to the capital to appeal his case. This match should first be communicated to my father, yet I cannot tarry here for this purpose. Hence, I am unable to pledge my troth."

"But your family is well-established and you yourself are a scholar who will some day become a man of importance," argued the old master. "So the distinction between a civil and a military background has no relevance. But since you must hasten to the capital for your father's sake, I propose that we confirm the engagement and that you inform your father about the wedding on your return. My granddaughter would thus be at peace and your affairs would not be delayed."

Shengjie could find no other excuses. She thought to herself, "They would not insist if they knew my predicament. On the other hand, I risk exposing my deception by refusing too strenuously. Were I not pledged to Wei Zhuanzhi by the arrow, I could recommend him as a suitor. Yet there is Du Yi, to whom I am still closer but have had to relinquish. I have long entertained the thought of compensating him by finding him a good match among my female friends. And, matters being as they are, would it not be an excellent idea to accept the engagement and then substitute Du Yi for myself? Then these people will perhaps not be overly censorious when they discover I have been less than truthful. Even if Du Yi will not do, I shall better be able to extricate myself from this sorry mess."

Having decided on this course of action, Shengjie said to the old master: "The noble sentiments displayed by you and your granddaughter leave me no choice but to accede. I leave this amulet as a pledge, and shall come to ask for her hand as soon as I return from the capital." So saying, Shengjie untied the jade amulet from her sash and proffered it with both hands to the old master. The latter accepted it with elation, then sent the old woman back to the granddaughter with the message: "It has been agreed."

The old master then instructed the hosteler to bring food and drink to send Shengjie on her way. Unable to decline, Shengjie partook of a hearty meal, and then bid her farewells.

The trio resumed their travels, seeking lodgings at night and setting out again at dawn, and not infrequently sleeping and eating under open skies, unprotected from the elements.

When they finally arrived in the capital, Shengjie dispatched Wen Long to discover the whereabouts of Wei and Du, the two new officials. The servant found Du Yi's residence, but learned that Wei Zhuanzhi had taken a leave of absence to visit his family. Du, in the meantime, was overjoyed by the news of Shengjie's arrival and forthwith ordered his housekeeper to bring her to his residence.

Following a brief exchange of small talk, Shengjie said, "I have come on behalf of my father. I remember that you told me, when we took leave of each other, to come to you if ever I came to the capital. I hear that both you and Zhuanzhi have succeeded in the exams, so I have come all this way to seek your assistance. Zhuanzhi, I'm told, has gone home. Fortunately you are still here, so I shall not be disappointed."

Du Yi suggested, "You would do well to compose a handbill with the details of how your father was falsely accused, then have it printed and distributed to all who pass by the gates of the imperial palace. When the public is apprised of the facts, I shall ask a co-examiner who is now in the Ministry of Military Affairs to include this case when others are examined. Then it will be possible to secure a reprieve at the local court." Shengjie asked, "Will it serve any good purpose to submit my father's original appeal?" To which Du replied, "Nowadays the literati are in greater favor than the military. Your father's case was brought up by the provincial procuratorate, and they would hardly accept an appeal submitted by a military official on his own behalf. Indeed, they might become incensed, which would jeopardize any chance of success. Mine is the best course of action, so you had best refrain from any ill-considered moves."

Shengjie said, "I am grateful for your advice. I see things from a pedant's point of view, and it behooves me to listen to you." Whereupon Du protested, "We are brothers albeit with different surnames. It goes without saying that I have a duty toward you."

Shengjie then asked why Zhuanzhi had gone home. Du Yi replied, "He and I have lived in the same house for a long time, and he kept telling me there was something he must discuss with you, though he would not tell me what it is. I told him you would most likely visit the capital when you learned of our success at the examinations. But he said there was no predicting when you would come and, moreover, the matter had to be addressed at home, and as soon as possible, so he asked for leave. Little did he know that you were on the way here and that he would miss you. May I ask you what this is all about?" Shengjie knew full well that it was about their marriage, but she feigned ignorance. "I do not know. It must be some family matter." Du Yi remarked, "That is my guess as well, but why was he in such haste?"

Du Yi then gave orders that dinner be prepared to welcome his friend and instructed Shengjie's servants to bring the luggage into the house, saying it was not necessary for them to seek lodgings elsewhere as he could put them up at his residence. The house was shared by Du Yi and Zhuanzhi, and since Zhuanzhi was absent there was ample room for Shengjie and her servants. Du Yi also instructed his servants to prepare a chamber for Shengjie and to place his own bed across from Shengjie's in the same chamber so that they could converse at night.

Consternated, Shengjie thought, "When he and I were schoolmates we met only in the daytime to talk about books and share a pot of wine. He did not see through my disguise since he never saw me in bed. But now that we will be sharing a room, concealment may become impossible and I could very well betray myself!" But she found no excuse to sleep in separate chambers, and could do little else but resolve to exercise greater caution.

Despite the best of resolutions, however, deceptions are, as a rule, hard to maintain. Constant association made it harder to dissemble various details of behavior as well as the extreme inconvenience thus created for Shengjie. She could engage convincingly in masculine pursuits in daytime as she distributed handbills in the streets of the capital, but when she repaired to her bed at night there were many telltale signs that Du Yi could not fail to notice. Du Yi was an intelligent and knowledgeable person in whom the inexplicable only served to whet greater curiosity. The more he watched, the stronger his suspicions became.

One day, Shengjie neglected to lock her personal casket when she went out. Du Yi stole a look at its contents and found a collection of writing effects, among which was this draft: "I, Wen of Mianzhu, a woman who believes in the True God Guan Gong, burn incense before his image in supplication for the exoneration of my father Wen Que and for my safe return. May the commitment of the arrow and the engagement of the jade amulet both be duly resolved."

Du Yi clapped his hands in glee. "The evidence is right before my eyes!" he exclaimed. "How can I, a man, have been deceived by her for so many years?! She can fly to high heavens now, for all the good it will do her. But what does the second sentence signify? Can it be that she is engaged to another?" The very thought set his heart aflutter.

Just then Shengjie returned. Du Yi preceded her into their chamber, and then sat there grinning at her. Mystified, Shengjie looked herself up and down and front and back, then inquired, "What have I done wrong, that you smile at me so?" To which Du Yi replied, "I am smiling at the manner in which you kept me in the dark."

Shengjie protested, "I have not kept you in the dark about anything I am doing here." But Du Yi retorted, "Yes, you have, and very much so! Think about it." Shengjie insisted, "No. Truly I have not." Whereupon Du Yi said, "Do you remember that conversation we had at school? I said at the time that were I a girl I would give you my hand, and were you a girl I would certainly take you as my bride. I said it was a pity you were not a girl. However, it seems you are a girl after all, and had you not kept me in the dark about that, I would have married you long ago."

Shengjie blushed hotly and asked, "Who told you about me?" Du Yi extracted from his sleeve the slip of paper he had found in the casket, saying, "You wrote this, I assume." Wen bowed her head and fell silent. Laughing, Du Yi moved across to sit beside her. "I once said I regretted that two men could not marry. But now it seems my wish is about to be fulfilled."

Shengjie rose to her feet, saying, "I can no longer deny the truth of what you have discovered. You have always been fond of me, and I must admit that I admire you. But since fate has ordained it that I should belong to Zhuanzhi, I may not give myself to you. I hope you can forgive me." Stunned, Du Yi protested, "Zhuanzhi and I were both schoolmates of yours, but by all indications I was a cut above him in your affections. For what reason have you favored him over me? Besides which, Zhuanzhi is away, so why should you smelt bronze when a ready-made bell is here for you to ring?"

Shengjie said, "There is something of which you are not aware. Have you remarked that I wrote about a certain commitment?" Du Yi replied, "Yes, and I was perplexed by that statement." Shengjie continued, "Since I knew you both well and could not decide to whom I should belong, I decided to leave that decision to Fate. I vowed to Heaven that I would marry the first man to pick up the arrow. It was in Zhuanzhi's hands. But I lied to him and said the arrow belonged to my sister. Zhuanzhi at once became enamored of her and offered a jade amulet as a token of betrothal. Although I did not tell him the truth, it is I who am committed. It is the will of Heaven, not a matter of whom I favor or do not favor."

Du Yi burst out laughing. "If that is the case, then you incontestably belong to me." Mystified, Shengjie inquired, "Why is that so?" To which Du Yi replied, "It was I who retrieved the arrow. Surprised to see two lines of writing on it, I was reading them aloud when Zhuanzhi heard me. He came and took the arrow out of my hands to examine the inscription. Just then a servant arrived with a message for me to go home, so I left the arrow with Zhuanzhi. Since then I have never asked him to return it. No, he did not pick it up. And if the will of Heaven is to be invoked, then I should be the beneficiary. You may ask Zhuanzhi about this matter. I trust he will not try to deny the truth."

Shengjie again asked, "Since you have seen the inscription, do you remember it?" Du Yi replied, "Although I had but a hasty and cursory glance, I recall the words as 'My arrow will not miss; it hits its mark.' Surely I could not have made that up, could I?"

Convinced, now, that Du Yi was speaking the truth, Shengjie relented. "If such is the case, then it was meant by Heaven that we should be betrothed. My only regret is that Zhuanzhi's long-cherished expectations will be disappointed, even as he hurries home to fulfill them. I wonder what he will think when he learns of this?" To which Du Yi replied, "That is beside the point. As the saying goes: First come, first served. Besides, you were mine in the first place!"

So saying, Du Yi put his arms around Shengjie and entreated her to make love with him, saying, "Even as brothers we loved each other. I can think of no greater joy in heaven and on earth than sharing a coverlet and pillow with you." Shengjie could not refuse. Shyly, she walked with him over to the canopied bed and let him have his way.

A folk ditty describes the events that ensued:

> *The handsome young student was somewhat peculiar,*
> *And only in bed did he show his true face.*

This scholarly writer of erudite trivia
In truth was a maiden of ravishing grace!

The innocent friendship of intimate brothers,
Gave way to the passion of fleshly desire.
While once they communed over volumes and papers,
The brush they had used was replaced by a spear.

She furrowed her brow but suffered in silence,
For driving the spear was her favorite mate.
He fondled her breast and her sweet inflorescence,
Enjoying the rapture of joining their fate.

Her whispers and love cries, so seemingly distant,
Disclosed but the depths of her ardent consent.
So swift was his thrusting, so stormy and urgent,
He well-nigh confounded the vale and the vent!

When they were done, Shengjie rose and straightened her attire, sighing, "Now my life belongs to you and I am content. But Zhuanzhi will be sorely deceived. What shall I say to him?" Then, after a moment's reflection, she struck the bed with her palm and exclaimed, "I know what to do!" Doubtfully, Du Yi inquired, "And what, pray, can be done about this matter?"

Shengjie proceeded to explain, "There is something you should know. As I was staying at a hostel in Chengdu, the owner's granddaughter spied on me, then prevailed upon her grandfather to press me into an engagement with her. I resorted to a subterfuge and left a token, promising to return later to culminate the marriage. I was mindful that you would feel slighted by my pledge to Zhuanzhi. And since the girl has both talent and beauty and would have made a good match for you, I resolved to keep this betrothal in reserve. But now that I am yours, would it not be opportune to pass on this match to Zhuanzhi when he returns and asks me about my pledge to him? In any case I would not be playing him false, for I had told him it was my sister he would marry; he had no inkling that it would be me."

Du Yi agreed, "This is the best solution. It attests to your concern for your friends, and should your idea be feasible I would feel less contrite before Zhuanzhi when I marry you. What a stroke of fortune you had such an encounter on your journey! But I have one question: Granted that you were able to hide your womanly nature by dressing up as a man, traveling with two manservants surely presented many inconveniences!" Shengjie smiled, saying, "Who told you they were both men? They are husband and wife, a man and a woman, both clothed like men so as to serve me without arousing suspicion." Du Yi laughed and exclaimed, "Like master, like servant. Ingenious persons are wont to do bizarre things!"

Shengjie then brought out the verses written by Miss Jing and showed them to Du Yi, who remarked, "I had not imagined there were women such as she. Zhuanzhi should be well content to have her."

Shengjie then took up the matter of her father. Du Yi said, "Since he will now be my father-in-law, it will be all the easier for me to solicit support. I have an acquaintance at the Ministry of Official Personnel Affairs whom I will entreat to have the hostile official transferred. Then the rest will be easy." To which Shengjie agreed, saying, "That would seem to be the best solution. Please do it."

Du Yi proceeded accordingly, and in a few days the hostile official was named in the Notice of Promotions for transferal to a higher posting in Guangxi. Du Yi informed Shengjie of this circumstance, saying, "The hostile official is gone. I will now request to be sent on a mission, and then return with you to secure the general's release. The case is settled and the procuratorate will deal with it leniently. All is in order." Shengjie's gratitude to Du Yi translated itself into greater love for him.

Du Yi was duly dispatched to escort an army paymaster to Shandong, after which he could go home. Attired as a man, Shengjie rode beside the official sedan chair with her two servants and was once again addressed as the Young Master.

A few days later, as the company was passing through an uninhabited region near Mozhou, an arrow whistled by the sedan chair. Realizing that they were being attacked, Shengjie instructed the bearers not to stop. She said, "I shall deal with the matter." With complete composure she unslung her bow and fitted an arrow to the string. A horseman was galloping swiftly toward her at a hundred paces' distance. Uttering a warlike cry, Shengjie drew her bow and loosed the arrow. It flew straight at the unsuspecting horseman, who fell, writhing, to the ground. Shengjie whipped her mount forward to take a look at the man. Then she called back, "The bandit will cause us no more trouble. Continue to advance." Her companions were full of praise for her marksmanship, and all regarded her with awe. Du Yi, it goes without saying, was highly pleased.

Their mission completed, Du Yi and Shengjie arrived home without further incident. General Wen had been freed on bail, now that the hostile official was gone. After Shengjie recounted Du Yi's efforts to secure his release and the official's transfer, the general was exceedingly grateful and asked, "How can I recompense him for such a great service?"

Shengjie then told him how she had been discovered by Du Yi, how she had surrendered herself to him, and for what purpose they had come back together. Elated, the general exclaimed, "This is a most felicitous match of talent and grace! Make haste to change your garb, and I shall take advantage of this auspicious day of Du Yi's triumphant return to deliver you to him as his bride!"

But Shengjie demurred, saying, "I would prefer not to change my attire yet, as I wish to have Zhuanzhi see me thus." Whereupon the general said, "I was about to speak to you about Zhuanzhi. Ever since he returned from the capital, he has been sending emissaries here to inquire about a daughter of mine and to declare his intention of marrying her. I thought he had probably heard some rumors and must have been seeking you. But after I had asked a few more questions, it appears that a certain young master of this house had pledged him a sister in marriage, but that Zhuanzhi was completely unaware of your circumstances. Not knowing how to respond, I procrastinated, suggesting that he await your return. Why do you wish to meet him?" Shengjie replied, "There are many ramifications to this matter which I cannot explain now, Father. You will understand in good time."

As they were speaking, Wei Zhuanzhi arrived to pay his respects. In truth, Zhuanzhi had returned to Mianzhu because he was anxious about his proposed marriage. But when he inquired after Young Master Wen, he was told that the latter had gone to the capital, and his questions about Young Master Wen's sister only elicited conflicting and puzzling replies. Some pointed out, "The general has two sons, one older and one younger, but no daughters." Others insisted, "The general has a daughter, who is in fact the young master." The effect was to fill Zhuanzhi's mind with suspicions and wild conjectures. Having learned just now about Shengjie's return, he hasten to pay his respects and to clarify matters.

Shengjie received him in her customary fashion and, once the amenities were done with, Zhuanzhi asked with great urgency, "Brother, how goes it with your elder sister? I came back expressly for that matter." Shengjie answered, "Rest assured that you will have a good wife." But Zhuanzhi pressed on, "I had some inquiries made and obtained nothing but conflicting reports. Why is that?" To which Shengjie replied, "Set your doubts at rest. The jade amulet is in good hands, and once I have made some arrangements you may make ready to meet your bride."

But Zhuanzhi continued, "Your manner of speaking would seem to indicate that the bride is not your sister." Shengjie said, "Du Yi is fully apprised of the matter. Ask him, and you will understand." Zhuanzhi protested, "Why not tell me now, instead having me ask him?" Shengjie said, "There are many intricacies which I cannot talk about and only Du Yi can explain." Her words only served to deepen Zhuanzhi's suspicions.

Since Zhuanzhi had intended to visit Du Yi anyway, he took his leave and went directly to the latter's house. Dispensing with preliminaries, he came straight to the point, whereupon Du Yi gave him a full account of how he and Shengjie had shared the same room, how he had discovered her true gender, and how they had consummated their relationship as man and woman.

Zhuanzhi was thunderstruck. "I was told some time ago that Shengjie was a woman, but would not believe it. But now it seems she really is one! Though this marriage has slipped by me, by rights it should have been mine." Whereupon Du Yi inquired, "And why should it have been yours?"

Zhuanzhi proceeded to recount how he had retrieved the arrow and presented Shengjie with the jade amulet as a pledge. Du Yi demurred, saying, "But it was I who first retrieved the arrow. I was unaware at the time that Shengjie had staked her destiny on that arrow, so I neglected to ask you for it later. Thus it is Heaven's will that Shengjie should belong to me. Furthermore, you were intent on having Shengjie's elder sister, and not Shengjie herself. But have no regrets, your amulet has not been pledged in vain."

Puzzled, Zhuanzhi inquired, "The affair is terminated now, so why do you say the amulet has not been pledged in vain? Does Shengjie indeed have an elder sister?" Du Yi then related Shengjie's encounter with the Jing family during her journey to the capital. "The girl is extraordinarily talented and beautiful, and since Shengjie was unable to extricate herself she left your amulet with the girl. Looking back today, this occurrence would seem to be foreordained; the match should be yours, should it not?" Zhuanzhi exclaimed, "Little wonder Shengjie was unwilling to tell me about these things! But I foresee one difficulty. The Jing family was unaware of what was transpiring when Shengjie agreed to the match, and I can hardly present myself as my own go-between. How should I proceed?"

Du Yi replied, "Although Shengjie and I are already betrothed, I have yet to meet my father-in-law. We intend to wed today and shall of course need a go-between. We would be much obliged if you would assume that role, and after we are married I shall reciprocate the favor and serve you as your go-between." Zhuanzhi laughed, saying, "Done! It's a deal! Only, I find it most amusing that I spent my time dreaming while you made off with the prize! However, all is well since you are not leaving me high and dry. That being the case, I shall go now to the Wen residence, and you may come somewhat later." Zhuanzhi borrowed a suit of formal clothing, changed into it, and then set forth in a sedan chair. Shengjie, having already donned women's attire, did not come out to meet him. Instead, it was the general himself who performed the honors. When Zhuanzhi had stated Du Yi's intentions, the general said, "My daughter has always been enamored of book-learning and scholars. Thus it is most fitting and proper that your friend should choose her as his helpmate. I am greatly pleased to accept his proposal."

Having been forewarned by Shengjie, the general had had time to make all his preparations. So when the gateman announced Du Yi's arrival, there was a lively chorus of drums and cymbals to meet the bridegroom as he was carried in on a sedan chair, clad in a bright red robe. All present admired the noble bearing of the young scholar. The procession entered the main hall where Du Yi took his place and made his obeisance to the general. Shengjie was invited out of her rooms and the young couple together performed the requisite kowtows, thanked Zhuanzhi, then departed in the sedan chair. When they came to Du Yi's residence, they kowtowed again to Heaven and Earth and visited the family's ancestral shrine. Thus this pair of old friends, now a newly wed couple, happily fulfilled their wedding rites.

Zhuanzhi, however, felt somewhat envious. He brooded, thinking to himself, "Whereas all three of us were once boon companions, now the two of them have become a pair. Du Yi loved her so much he even wished one of them could change gender so that they could become husband and wife. By some strange twist of fate his wish has come true. But what about their promises to me?"

He broached the subject to Du Yi when he went the next day to offer his congratulations. Du Yi said, "My wife and I made plans last night to go to Chengdu today expressly to resolve this matter. My wife has sworn to fulfill her promise to you and not to return until she can bring you good news." Zhuanzhi replied, "I am most grateful. We were all three of us boon companions, so you must appreciate how lonely I feel now. But I am curious to know what this girl is like."

Repairing to his bedchamber, Du Yi soon returned with the verses written by Miss Jing and handed them to Zhuanzhi. Having read them, Zhuanzhi exclaimed, "I would no longer be envious of you if I could have her!" Du Yi smiled, "If Shengjie's descriptions are to be believed, you will certainly not be disappointed." Zhuanzhi replied, "And if this matter comes to fruition, it would be a marvelous thing. I am on tenterhooks." Both laughed, and then took leave of each other. Du Yi related this conversation to Shengjie, who observed, "It is not surprising. He has waited for a long time. Let us go in haste to Chengdu and settle this matter."

Shengjie set out with Du Yi for Chengdu, taking along the servant couple who had accompanied her earlier. They took up lodgings at the same hostel as before and Du Yi had the manservant deliver a message to the old master. Surprised that a newly appointed *jinshi* should be calling on him, the old master hurried out to meet the visitors. When all were seated, he inquired, "To what do I owe your eminent presence in my humble establishment?" Du Yi replied, "I was passing by and learned that you have a granddaughter of great beauty and talent. The reason for my visit is that I have a friend, also a newly appointed *jinshi*, who desires her hand in marriage."

The Old Master said, "It is true I have a granddaughter, but she wishes to choose her own husband. Not long ago she settled on a certain Young Master Wen, who was journeying to the capital and accepted a jade amulet from him as a pledge. So Your Excellency has come too late." To which Du Yi replied, "Young Master Wen happens to be a friend of mine, and I am aware that he is otherwise committed, for which reason I have the temerity to make this proposal." The old master exclaimed indignantly, "But Young Master Wen is a man of learning, how could he ill-use my granddaughter like this? It goes without saying that she will expect an explanation from him!"

Du Yi produced the verses written by Miss Jing, saying, "Be so kind as to examine this. I believe it was written by Miss Jing to Young Master Wen. Being unable to marry your granddaughter, he gave this to me to present as a testimonial when asking for the hand of your granddaughter for my friend. In other words, this is Young Master Wen's reply."

The old master recognized his granddaughter's writing on the paper. He mused, "Young Master Wen did indeed say he was already engaged, but we did not believe him and left him with no choice but to commit himself. So he was telling the truth after all. Allow me to confer with my granddaughter. I shall return at once and tell Your Excellency what she thinks." Whereupon the Old Master took his leave.

He returned after a while to say, "My granddaughter was greatly distressed by what I told her. She insists that, even if Young Master Wen has had a change of heart, he should come in person to retrieve the jade amulet and terminate the matter before there can be any further talk of a marriage." Du Yi replied, "If the truth be told, the amulet was a pledge of betrothal from my friend Wei Zhuanzhi, and not from Young Master Wen. Since Young Master Wen had already been pledged, yet could not decline your proposal, he accepted it on behalf of my friend Zhuanzhi. That was the hidden intention, so I have not come here today without good cause."

But the old master said, "I am certain my granddaughter will not be content in spite of Your Excellency's protestations. The matter can only be laid to rest by the young master offering a personal explanation." To which Du Yi replied, "Young Master Wen is no longer able to come. However, my wife here could go in to see your granddaughter. Once my wife has told her all the ins and outs of the matter, she will surely understand." The old master agreed, saying, "It would indeed be best that your wife speak face to face with my granddaughter. That would save the trouble of passing messages back and forth."

The elderly maidservant was summoned to take Lady Du into the house. When she laid eyes on Shengjie, she felt there was something familiar about the younger woman's demeanor and appearance, but could not be certain on account of Shengjie's change of attire. She puzzled about this as she led Shengjie into the inner chambers.

Miss Jing came out to receive her visitor, and the two exchanged formal greetings. Shengjie then asked Miss Jing, "Do you know Young Master Wen?" Miss Jing had observed a resemblance, but assumed that the young woman was Young Master Wen's sister, so she merely asked, "Are you related to Young Master Wen?" Shengjie replied, "For all the discernment you possess, can your eyesight be really so dim? I am the young master who passed through here and with whom you fell in love!"

Astounded, Miss Jing took a closer look and saw that this was indeed the case. The old maidservant, who was standing to one side, clapped her hands together and exclaimed, "Yes, Yes! I thought you looked familiar, but who would have suspected you were the young master?!"

Miss Jing said, "Madam, may I ask why you were attired in such a manner?" Shengjie replied, "I was traveling to the capital to submit an appeal in behalf of my father, who had been wrongfully accused, and I dressed as a man for convenience on the road. That is the reason I repeatedly rejected your expressions of love. But when I could find no more excuses, yet dared not tell the truth, I decided to make the pledge on behalf of my friend and explain at a later date. This friend has become a *jinshi* and is of a suitable age, so my husband and I have come to ask for you for your hand, to make good a promise I have made, and to repay you for your sincere sentiments."

Miss Jing remained silent. After a while, the old maidservant spoke up, "We are thankful to you for your good intentions, but could you tell us the name of the gentleman and why you call him a friend?" Shengjie replied, "He and I were schoolmates since childhood, and together we passed the examinations to qualify as *xiucai*. Being of similar ages and dispositions, he, my husband and I were like brothers with different surnames. And since he is as yet unbetrothed, I resolved to seek a match for him. His name is Wei, he is a most personable man, and he became a *jinshi* at the same time as my husband. I believe he is worthy of you. Moreover, by marrying him you would become a lady of rank."

Miss Jing was extremely gratified by this account, and especially by the news that her proposed betrothed held such an eminent position. Leaving the old maidservant to entertain Shengjie, she slipped away to inform her grandfather of the details of the conversation described above. The old master, too, was all in favor of the match when he learned that his prospective grandson-in-law happened to be a *jinshi*. Who would not?

And so, with one giving permission and the other willing, Shengjie and, through her, Du Yi were informed that the matter had been decided. The old master gave a banquet to thank the matchmakers—he entertaining Du Yi in the outer hall and Miss Jing playing host to Lady Du in an inner chamber. The two women found they had much in common and parted company on the best of terms.

When the couple returned to Mianzhu, the first thing they did was to instruct Wei Zhuanzhi to deliver the bride money and select an auspicious date to bring his betrothed back home. And when Zhuanzhi saw her on his wedding night, one might have surmised from his behavior that he had obtained a goddess from Heaven!

When the jade amulet was mentioned, Zhuanzhi remarked, "That, in truth, is mine." His wife asked, "Then how did it land in Shengjie's hands?" Zhuanzhi thereupon recounted how Du Yi had retrieved the arrow with the inscription and then passed it on to him, how Shengjie had made up a story about an elder sister, and how he had given her the jade amulet as a pledge of betrothal. When Zhuanzhi had done telling this story, he and his new bride laughed happily and said, "Matches are made in Heaven, so all these twists and turns were meant to be."

Thereafter the two families consorted with each other as brothers and sisters. The two new officials together contrived to clear General Wen of the false charges brought against him, after which the general retired. Du Yi and Zhuanzhi both became high-ranking officials, their wives gave birth to sons and daughters who married among one another, and the friendship between the households spanned several generations.

What Happened after Academician Quan Found Half of a Vanity Case

權學士權認遠鄉姑
白孺人白嫁親生女

The story was first told in Jin times, one thousand years ago, about a certain Grand Minister Zhang Hua who was highly learned in astrology and who had a discerning eye for objects of great antiquity.

One night, as he was looking at the heavens, he saw a wondrous refulgence lighting up the sky between the Big Dipper and Altair constellations, which indicated to him that some great treasure lay in Fengcheng County in Henan.

Grand Minister Zhang Hua had a friend named Lei Huan who also had a wide knowledge about treasures, so Grand Minister Zhang appointed him to the position of Magistrate of Fengcheng and gave him a special assignment, which was to seek the treasure that had lighted up the heavens. He said to Lei Huan, "There was a cold and ominous aura to the refulgence, so I am convinced that the treasure is a sword."

With this assignment, Lei Huan went to Fengcheng County and observed that the refulgence emanated from the county prison. He took a number of retainers to the prison and proceeded to the end of a passageway, and there they dug up a pair of swords. The name inscribed on the masculine sword was "Chun Gou," and that on the feminine sword was "Zhan Lu." Lei Huan took one of the swords for himself and gave the other to Minister Zhang Hua. Needless to say, both the swords were greatly treasured by their owners.

Some time later, Zhang Hua, wearing his sword, was at the Yanping ferry crossing when the sword suddenly sprang out of its scabbard and fell into the river. As it did so, it turned into a dragon. Then another dragon shot out of the water, and the pair rose, dancing and whirling, into the sky. Zhang Hua was astounded, though he was fully aware that precious swords had supernatural qualities. He asked himself, "What was that thing that conjugated with my sword and emerged from the water?" He sent a messenger to ask Lei Huan, "Where is the other sword that you found?" And the messenger brought back the reply: "In a moment of carelessness I dropped it in the river at the Yanping ferry crossing." It was then that Zhang Hua realized the two swords had come together again after being separated.

Today, people still allude to the story called "The Swords That Reunited at Yanping" to describe predestined relationships made whole by a chance event. And the tale I tell today, although far removed in time and distance from that story, is also about such a predestined relationship.

*   *   *

In the time of our current Ming dynasty, there lived an official whose family name was Quan, whose personal name was Ciqing, and who went by the style name of Wenchang. A native of Ningguo Prefecture in the south part of Zhili, he had passed the imperial examinations at a fairly young age and been appointed Junior Compiler at the Hanlin Academy. This Junior Compiler, or "Hanlin" as he was addressed on account of his association with that prestigious academy, was a man of handsome and elegant appearance, of talented and romantic personality, and of multifarious skills and interests, and in these respects he could well rival the immortals in Heaven or the fairest men in the world of the living. At the time this story commences, more than a year had passed since he had passed the examinations and obtained his post in the national capital.

Now, it was the custom in the capital to hold temple fairs on the first, fifteenth, and twenty-fifth day of each moon. All manner of merchandise would be laid out for sale, both in front of the Temple of the City God and all the way to Xingbu Street, and the fairgrounds were thronged with people who came to do business. Even officials—those who had the time and inclination to do so—would don casual caps and clothing and, accompanied by one or two servants or retainers, stroll here and look around and occasionally purchase a few good objects or some old bric-a-brac. It so happened that the Hanlin Academy was the least busy department at the imperial court. Its members had little else to do but read books, play chess, drink wine, and pay calls on acquaintances. But Hanlin Quan was young and restless, so he would come on days when the fair was bustling with business in order to walk about the grounds.

One day, he noticed an elderly man sitting behind a table laden with many odds and ends, for the most part household articles such as lamp stands, copper ladles, teapots, vases, dishes and bowls, none of which would catch the fancy of a scholar. By chance, however, Hanlin Quan's eyes lit upon an object of unique color and appearance. He picked it up and saw that it was the lid of a gold-inlaid vanity case. He recognized it as an antique, though he thought it a pity that the case was incomplete. He said to the elderly man, "There should be a lower part to this object. Where is it?" The elderly man replied, "There is no lower part, only a lid." Hanlin Quan countered, "I see no reason why there should be no lower part. Tell me, where did this lid come from? We might then be able to find the other part."

The elderly man answered, "This old person has an unoccupied house near East Straight Gate which I let out to renters. Some time ago, one of the renters, a family of four or five, was struck down by a contagious disease. When the children began to die, the family panicked and moved away, ill as they were, leaving the objects you see here as payment for their rent. I put the objects away but am now selling them to eke out a living. This lid, which belonged to that family, was preserved in a paper box and had been wrapped in several layers of old paper with writing on them. I have no idea what purpose the other half of the case served, but I have placed the lid on this table in the hope that someone might wish to purchase it."

Hanlin Quan declared, "I am willing to purchase it, even though it is not a complete case. Show me the paper box you just mentioned!" The elderly man groped under the table and brought out a battered box, the pieces of which were pasted together with strips of paper. The Hanlin remarked, "None of these articles are of any use. But I shall take them if you'll let them go for a small price." The elderly man agreed, saying, "For these insignificant articles, My Lord can give me whatever he sees fit." The Hanlin instructed his retainer Quan Zhong to give the elderly man a hundred copper coins, and thus the deal was done. The elderly man took some old paper out of the box and wrapped up the lid of the vanity case, which he then laid in the box and respectfully handed to the Hanlin with both hands. The Hanlin told Quan Zhong to carry the box and then walked around some more and purchased a number of antique writing utensils.

When he returned to his quarters, Hanlin Quan laid all his purchases on a table of natural waterstone, scrutinized the articles one by one, and was content with them. The last he inspected were the contents of the paper box. Opening the box, he extracted the paper parcel and unwrapped it, proceeding then to examine the lid of the vanity case. As he turned it about in his hands, he could see from its brilliant gold luster that it indeed was of superior quality. Yet it was, after all, no more than a lid. He thought to himself, "Where could the other half have gone? I shall put this away for safekeeping since I might just come across the other half some day. Who knows?"

As he was about to wrap the lid up in its original layers of paper, he observed something red protruding from a tear in the wrappings. Removing the outer layers, he found a sheet of red paper with writing on it. This he took out and read, and then exclaimed, "So that's what it is!" The writing on it said:

> *Mistress Bai of the Xu household, a resident of Dashi Yongfang, has a daughter named Osmanthus who is just two years old. Also born in the same year was Liuge, the son of Bai the Elder, Mistress Bai's older brother. Mistress Bai's husband is a native of Suzhou, and in the case that the families become separated and no other evidence remains, each family shall have half of this gold-inlaid vanity case whereby to seek one another out and thus serve as proof.*

The year and the month were duly noted after the text, and below these a mark in lieu of a signature had been affixed.

Having read all this, the Hanlin said to himself, "So the lid is proof of a betrothal! But how is it that such an important thing was lost and then sold by someone else? The person or persons in this matter must be quite scatterbrained!" Then again, he reflected, "The writer of this slip of paper is a married woman. Since she had a husband, why was this not written in his name?" He counted off the years on his fingers and then smiled, thinking, "It is eighteen years since this agreement was written down, so the girl must be a nineteen-year-old maiden now. I wonder whether she is married." Then he laughed at himself and said, "Not that there could be anything in this for me! Nonetheless, I shall keep these objects." And he put the lid and message away with his other purchases.

When the next temple fair day came around, he took a walk through the fairgrounds and again saw the elderly man selling things there. He addressed the man, saying, "You said the vanity case you sold me a few days ago was left behind by some family. Do you know where this family moved?" The elderly man replied, "Who knows where they went? When the members of that family began to die, starting with the children, they were overcome with fear and fled in the middle of the night. It is my guess that all of them are deceased, but no one knows for certain." The Hanlin then asked, "Did any of their relatives visit them at the time they were your tenants?" The elderly man thought for a moment, then said, "The husband had a younger sister who was married to a man from some province along the lower reaches of the Yangzi River. They used to live near Qianmen Gate, but I do not know where they have gone now, and I have not seen them for many years."

The Hanlin thought to himself, "If I could find out where they live, I could return the articles to them and, in so doing, perform a good deed. However, I can only let the matter rest since there is no clue to their whereabouts."

When Hanlin Quan returned to his quarters, he found a letter from home informing him that his wife had passed away. The Hanlin wept bitterly for several days. Then, feeling deeply dispirited, he decided to go home. He wrote out an application for a leave of absence owing to poor health, and soon received an imperial edict that proclaimed: "Hanlin Quan is permitted to return to his place of origin to recuperate. He shall return to the capital after he recovers from his illness. Wherefore this Imperial Edict." Thereupon Hanlin Quan left the capital city and returned to his home county.

Now to the other side of this story and the origins of the vanity case.

There was, in Suzhou, a man from an old family of scholars whose surname was Xu. His given name was Fang, and he went by the style name Xiquan. A student at the Imperial University, he spent many years in the capital in order to fulfill his career ambitions. And as he felt lonely in his quarters, he sought a matchmaker and, through her, took as his concubine a girl from of a local family surnamed Bai. A daughter was born to them in the eighth moon. She was named Osmanthus, as that is the flower of the eighth moon. At about the same time a son was born to Mistress Bai's brother, Bai the Elder, and was given the pet name Liuge.

Mistress Bai, as is in the nature of women, inordinately favored members of her own family. Besides, residents of the capital know little about the ways of people in other parts if the country and do not wish to have outsiders as relatives. So her heart was set on marrying Osmanthus to her own nephew. To Scholar Xu, however, the capital city was merely a temporary place of abode. He intended to return to his native place sooner or later, and wished to save his daughter for establishing kinships over there. Thus he was very much opposed to his concubine's plans for the girl.

Then one day, Scholar Xu was chosen to serve as vice-governor of the central region of Fujian. He informed Mistress Bai that they would be leaving the capital and then packed his belongings to go home before setting out to assume his post. Seeing that her plans had gone awry, and loath to part with her own family, Mistress Bai secretly and without Vice-governor Xu's knowledge wrote out the aforesaid testimonial. She dared not openly mention marriage, but she separated the lid of a gold-inlaid vanity case from its lower section and left it with her nephew. This would, in the future, serve as an earnest if ever the Xu family returned to the capital or the two families met in some distant place.

Mistress Bai traveled with Scholar Xu to his home county, Wumen. As this newly appointed vice-governor did not have a legal wife, she was elevated to fill this vacancy and conferred with the honorific title "Dame," after which the two went to his posting. There they had a second child—a son, whom they named Gao-er. Scholar Xu returned to Wumen after serving for two terms as vice-governor, and then promised his daughter in marriage to a family surnamed Chen in the same county.

Constrained by distance and perverse timing, Dame Bai could do little else but push her plans to the back of her mind for the time being. Nevertheless she continued to harbor regrets and frequently offered silent prayers to Buddha that she might return to her birthplace and discover what had happened to the other half of the vanity case. Her thoughts of going back to the capital faded only a few years later when her husband, the vice-governor, passed away and Dame Bai was left a widow with two children. By then fifteen or sixteen years had elapsed since she had left the capital, and Osmanthus had turned into a young woman of exceptional beauty.

The Chen family's son, too, had grown up. However, just as the young man was about to present gifts and set a date for the nuptials, he suddenly came down with consumption owing to overindulgence, and died. This left Osmanthus in a precarious position. She had become a widow before even setting foot in the bridegroom's door, and it would be difficult to marry her off to someone else. She had no choice but to remain with her mother and brother, wear garments of subdued colors, and lead a dismal existence.

Let us, for the moment, leave Osmanthus to her bleak prospects and see how Hanlin Quan was faring.

More than a year had passed since his wife had died and he went home on sick leave, but he had not yet remarried. Filled with ennui, he decided to go to Wumen where he thought he might distract himself and, perhaps, find himself an attractive concubine. However, he feared that the county officials might learn of his visit and consequently welcome him and send him off with horses and carriages and ply him with banquets and gifts, which would insufferably hinder his movements. Hence, counting on his own youth and tender appearance and slender build, which might spare him from being recognized as a person of authority, he told people that he was a roving scholar and rented a quiet room next to Moonwave Temple just outside the city.

Moonwave Temple was a nunnery, and in it was an elderly nun known to all as The Reverend Miaotong. Sixty or more years of age, she was well-versed in the social graces, possessed much worldly wisdom, and consorted with all the better-known local families. Miaotong was struck by Hanlin Quan's noble appearance, and although she could not tell that he was an official traveling incognito but saw him merely as a youthful scholar, she felt he was destined for an illustrious future and thus treated him with respect. She often had tea sent to the Hanlin by the nunnery's old tender of incense burners, or invited him over to the nunnery for conversations. During one such visit, Hanlin Quan mentioned his desire to acquire a concubine and sought Miaotong's advice. However, she replied that "those who have taken their vows do not intervene in other people's worldly affairs." Hanlin Quan fell silent and no longer pursued the subject.

Soon it was the seventh day of the seventh moon, the day when, in the legend, the unfortunate lovers—the Cowherd and the Weaving Maid—meet once every year across the Milky Way. Hanlin Quan, alone in a strange place and with only his own shadow to keep him company, mused over the ancient legend and was assailed with feelings of loneliness.

He walked out of his silent room and was wandering about, reciting poetry to himself, when, by the light of the crescent moon, he noticed a young woman in somber clothing entering the temple courtyard. Hanlin Quan followed her and, concealing himself in the shadows, gazed at her. He saw the elderly nun Miaotong come out to greet the girl, who, before exchanging any amenities, lighted sticks of incense and placed these before a statue of Buddha. He could see that the young woman was exquisitely beautiful, with silky black hair and a jade-like complexion.

Holding a stick of incense between her fingers, she knelt before the statue of Buddha and mumbled a great many words, all in tones so low that Hanlin Quan could not discern what she said.

After a while the elderly nun stepped forward to end the moment of prayer, saying, "My dear young lady, with all those words you have not fully expressed what is in your heart. Let me put it more simply." The young woman asked, "More simply? How so?" So Miaotong said, " 'May Buddha in Heaven bless me with a good husband.' Is that not what you wish to say?" The young woman protested, "Do not make fun of me! I come to pray to Buddha in Heaven for protection and good fortune because my fate is so bitter: My father has died and my mother is old, and I have no one to support me." Miaotong laughed and replied, "That is not too different from what I just said." Whereupon the young woman also laughed.

Miaotong then laid out tea and confections. The young woman drank two cups of tea and then stood up to take her leave. As the Hanlin observed all of this from his place of concealment, flames almost flared from his eyes and he yearned to step forward and enfold the young woman in his arms. His heart ached unbearably when she departed.

As the Hanlin struggled to master his emotions, Miaotong, now coming back from seeing the young woman off, caught sight of him and asked, "Sir, have you not retired yet? How long have you been here?" The Hanlin replied, "I saw a white-robed goddess and came here to gaze reverently upon her." Miaotong smiled and said, "She is the daughter of a neighbor, the Xu family, and her name is Osmanthus. Her beauty is indeed of the sort that brings down city walls. A rare pleasure to the eyes!"

Hanlin Quan asked, "Is she married?" To which Miaotong replied, "How should I put it? When her father was alive, she was betrothed to Young Master Chen of this city. But by the time they were supposed to be married, that young man unfortunately died, which has placed her in the unenviable position of becoming a widow even before her wedding. She has had no suitors since." The Hanlin remarked, "No wonder she is clad in such somber clothing. But why did she come here so late in the evening?" Miaotong explained, "This being the seventh day of the seventh moon, and shorn as she is of a mate, she was overcome with a sense of frustration. So she told her mother she would come here to say nocturnal prayers."

"What kind of person is her mother?" asked the Hanlin. Miaotong replied, "Her mother is of the Bai family in the capital, and was married to old Master Xu while he was there waiting to be assigned an official position. Dame Bai is a straightforward and quite congenial person. She tells me she has an older brother in the capital and that when she left that city her brother had a two-year-old son, born in the same year as her daughter. There has been no news about them from the capital since they parted, and she does not know whether they are alive or dead. She often asks me to pray that Buddha might bless her kinsfolk."

The Hanlin listened, dumbstruck, and marveled, "The paper wrapped around the lid of that vanity case I purchased explicitly mentioned a Mistress Bai, married to Xu, their daughter Osmanthus, the older brother Bai the Elder, and his son Bai Liuge. Now it seems this girl's name is Osmanthus, and her mother is of the Bai family. These are obviously the same people. The elderly man who sold me the lid said the parents fled in the middle of the night and left that earnest after two children in the family had died. Needless to say, one of those children was quite probably Mistress Bai's nephew, Liuge. Who would have imagined that the girl had become such a ravishing beauty and that her betrothal to another man would come to an abrupt end! And what a coincidence it is that the earnest should fall into my hands and that we should meet in this place! It could just be that this is the way I am destined to find my spouse!" Having reflected a moment longer, he stamped his foot and told himself, "As the events took place almost twenty years ago and several thousand *li* from here, no one will be able to check back on them. I have only to . . ."

Having decided on his plan, Hanlin Quan asked Miaotong, "That Dame Bai you mentioned earlier, how old is she?" Miaotong replied, "She is in her forties." The Hanlin continued, "Is her brother named Bai the Elder? And is her nephew called Liuge?" Astonished, Miaotong exclaimed, "Yes, yes! But how do you know these things?" The Hanlin replied, "Dame Bai is my aunt, and I am her nephew, Bai Liuge." Whereupon Miaotong declared, "You must be jesting! Your surname is Quan. Why is it Bai now?" The Hanlin said, "I left the capital when I was still young to pursue learning in all corners of the country. And I changed my name and made my way to this place because I was enchanted by the scenery in the south, and also for convenience in seeking my relatives. By chance you have told me about them today, and I believe our meeting is Heaven's will. Besides, how would I know the names of persons in that family if I were not their kinsman?" Miaotong conceded, "This is indeed a rare coincidence! I shall congratulate both of you after you have your reunion with your aunt tomorrow."

The Hanlin then took leave of the nun and went to his room, where he spent the night giving free rein to his fantasies.

Rising at dawn the next morning, Hanlin Quan roused his retainer Quan Zhong and gave him careful instructions as to what he should say. Then, having attired himself neatly, he set out with his retainer for the Xu family's residence, asking for directions along the way.

As they approached the house, they saw an old man sitting idly by the gate. On the Hanlin's instructions, Quan Zhong went up to the man and said, "Kindly go in and announce Master Bai from the capital." The old man replied, "Our old master has passed away, and the young master is but a child. Whom do you wish to see?" The Hanlin asked, "Is the old mistress from the Bai family in the capital?" The old man replied, "She is of the Bai family." Quan Zhong declared, "Master Bai, whom I serve, is Dame Bai's nephew." Whereupon the old man said to Quan Zhong, "In that case, come in with me to do the announcing."

The old man led Quan Zhong straight to Dame Bai, and the retainer, who was a man of much experience, kowtowed to her and stated, "Master Bai, whom I serve, has come from the capital and stands at your gate." Dame Bai inquired, "Is he Liuge?" Quan Zhong replied, "That is my master's childhood name." Dame Bai's face lit up with delight, and she exclaimed, "What a happy event!" Hastily calling in her son, she said, "Gao-er, your elder brother has come. Go and welcome him!" Hopping and skipping, the child went out and led Hanlin Quan into the house.

The Hanlin walked meekly and hesitantly into the main room. When he saw Dame Bai rising from her chair, he cried "Auntie!" and was about to kowtow, but she restrained him and said, "You must be exhausted after the long journey. There is no need for the full ritual." Dame Bai looked at the Hanlin with tears in her eyes, and was greatly pleased to see his uncommonly handsome countenance. She said, "When this old person left the capital, you were only two years old. What a fine man you have turned out to be! Is your father still in sound health?" Feigning tears, the Hanlin replied, "He passed away a long time ago! I came here both to seek learning and to search for you, because I have no more near kin in the capital and because my father said before he died that an aunt of mine was married to someone in the south. However, only when I mentioned this to Reverend Miaotong of Moonwave Temple yesterday did I learn that you were here, which is why I have come to pay my respects to you."

Dame Bai asked curiously, "Why is your accent not like that of someone from the north?" The Hanlin hastened to explain, "I have wandered around these parts for a long time and have tried hard to learn the southern manner of speech. That is why I have lost my native accent."

He then told Quan Zhong to present some gifts he had brought along. Dame Bai happily accepted them, insisting all the while, however: "We are the closest of kin, and it is enough that we should meet again. There is no need for gifts!" To which the Hanlin said, "Do not stand on ceremony. I have little to offer my Aunt, since I am constantly moving from place to place. But I am gratified to know that you are in good health. Miaotong informed me yesterday that Uncle has passed away. I have just met my young cousin. I believe I also have a female cousin who was born in the same year as I was. Is she still with you?" Dame Bai replied, "When your uncle was alive he betrothed her to another family, but the match was not meant to be, and the man died before the wedding took place. She is still unmarried." The Hanlin said, "I would be pleased to meet her." But Dame Bai declined, saying, "She went out yesterday to burn incense and caught a cold, so she has not risen from her bed or washed and combed herself yet. However, you will presumably stay here for some time, so the two of you will have many opportunities to see one another. Now, before we do anything else, let us have your luggage taken to the West Hall."

Dame Bai gave orders that food be prepared and then took the Hanlin by the hand and led him to the West Hall. As they passed by a small courtyard, Dame Bai pointed to it and said, "Your sister's bedchamber is in here." Hanlin Quan felt a thrill of excitement as a whiff of magnolia and musk titillated his nostrils. Dame Bai shared a meal with him, then saw to it that his luggage was installed in the study at the West Hall and that all else was in order before going back to her own chambers.

Alone now in the study, the Hanlin thought to himself, "I have not yet had a chance to meet the young woman, though it is for that purpose that I passed myself off as Dame Bai's nephew. Fortunately the mother already believes I am indeed her nephew and is permitting me to stay here. I should not be too impatient, for opportunities will present themselves. We shall see what happens when I meet the girl tomorrow."

And now to Osmanthus.

Downhearted because the best years of her life were going to waste, and thrown into a bad mood by contemplations about the Cowherd and the Weaving Maid as well as by the chill she had caught when burning incense the night before, Osmanthus stayed in bed the next morning. She was told that a cousin had come from the capital, and she remembered her mother saying that there had been thoughts of making a pair of them when both of them were quite young. Then she heard that this cousin was quite handsome, and this stirred in her a desire to meet him. And so, overcoming feelings of lassitude, she forced herself to rise and perform her toilette. As she did so, she examined her reflection in the mirror and sighed, "Such a comely countenance, but who is there to enjoy it?"

Having completed her toilette, she was just about to go forth and pay her respects to her cousin, when Gao-er, her brother, rushed in, saying, "Mother has had a sudden pain in her chest and fainted. I must go out to get some medicine. Sister, go quickly to mother and see what you can do for her!" Osmanthus hurried out of her chambers, neglecting even to close her toilet case or lock the door, and went straight to Dame Bai.

Hanlin Quan, too, had completed his ablutions and was preparing himself to meet his cousin when he overheard someone saying, "Dame Bai has suffered a sudden chest pain and has fainted." Hearing these words, he thought, "The only medicine that has an instant effect on this illness is the Spirit Stabilizing Elixir of Qipan Street by Qianmen Gate. It so happens that I have some among my personal effects. I shall go as her nephew to inquire after her health and present her with one of the pills. If it does her any good, I shall quite naturally be in her good graces." He took a pill and thrust it in one of his sleeves and then set forth to see Dame Bai.

As he walked past the small courtyard on the eastern side, the one that Dame Bai had told him contained Osmanthus' bedchamber, he observed that the door was open and thought to himself, "Osmanthus must surely be in there. I can feign ignorance and simply enter, then offer some excuse when I see her." He summoned up his courage and went in.

What met his eyes was an array of perfumes, powders, ointments, rouges and eyebrow darkeners scattered about the dressing table, enticing and intoxicating. Like a drunken man, Hanlin Quan picked up some of the articles and put them to his nose, reveling in their scents. He then became aware of a heady, musk-like fragrance and, looking around, saw an embroidered canopy over an ivory bedstead with satin coverlets and cushions, all most neat and tidy. He thought to himself, "Let me lie on her bed and breathe in that fragrance. It will seem like being next to her bare flesh."

He lay down on the bed with his head on a pillow and fantasized for a few minutes, waiting for something to happen. But as nothing happened, he soon lost interest, rose from the bed and reluctantly left the room.

As he walked toward Dame Bai's chambers, he reached into his sleeve and realized that the medicine was no longer there. Where had he lost it? Having no recollection, he could only retrace his steps all the way back to the study.

Osmanthus remained with her mother until the pains in her chest had receded somewhat. Then, remembering that she had failed to lock her door or put away her toileteries, she hurried back to her chambers. When she had finished putting things in order, she felt tired and drew aside the canopy over her bed to lie down and rest. As she did so, she noticed a paper packet lying among the bedclothes. She picked up the packet and opened it, and found that it contained a pill. There were words written on the paper, which said, "Spirit Stabilizing Elixir. Special Remedy for Chest Pains. Miraculously Effective." Osmanthus thought to herself, "Where did this come from? If my brother brought this back, why did he leave it on my bed instead of taking it to our mother? Yet who else but my brother would come to this room? And this is a special medication for chest pains! This is indeed strange! I shall show the pill to my mother and ask her if she knows anything about it."

Taking the packet, she locked her door and went to Dame Bai's chambers. "Mother," she asked, "has my brother come back with your medicine?" Dame Bai replied, "I have been waiting expectantly all this while. That boy must have gone to play somewhere and forgotten to return." Osmanthus then said, "I come to tell Mother that when I went back to my chambers just now, I found a medicinal pill on my bed. It was wrapped in a piece of paper on which is written, 'Spirit Stabilizing Elixir. Special Remedy for Chest Pains. Miraculously Effective.' I presume it was bought by my brother, but why would he not bring it to you and instead leave it in my room? Since he has not returned, I am at loss to explain where this pill came from."

Dame Bai replied, "My child, this Spirit Stabilizing Elixir can only be purchased on a street near Qianmen Gate in the capital. It is not to be found here. Clearly, this pill was given us by the gods who have been touched by your filial piety. Let me take it without delay!" Osmanthus brought a cup of hot water, and Dame Bai used it to wash the pill down. Before long, her chest pains ceased, to the great delight of both mother and daughter. Although Dame Bai now no longer felt any pain, she was exhausted and soon dozed off. Not daring to leave her alone, Osmanthus kept vigil at her bedside.

In the meantime, Hanlin Quan, unable to find the pill, returned empty-handed to pay his respects. He came upon Osthmanthus before she had time to avoid this stranger. Osmanthus quickly realized, however, that this was her cousin from the Bai family and did not attempt to evade him, since they would in any case meet one another sooner or later. Hanlin Quan approached her, his face wreathed in an ingratiating smile, and with a deep bow he announced, "My obeisances to you, Younger Sister." Osmanthus returned the greeting, saying, "May all happiness be yours, Elder Brother!"

The Hanlin inquired, "How is my aunt's health?" Osmanthus replied, "She is feeling better, and has just fallen asleep." The Hanlin continued, "I had hoped to see my younger sister's beauteous countenance when I came to this house yesterday, but I was told that you were indisposed, so I dared not disturb you." Osmanthus assured him, "I too desired greatly to make acquaintance with my elder brother yesterday, but I did not have time to do my toilette and was in no state to meet you. Today, I was just going to see you when my mother suddenly fell ill, and I have not been able to get away. Now that you have come to inquire about my mother, however, it gives me pleasure to behold your felicitous presence." The Hanlin declared, "I have come from afar, but the sight of your jade countenance has truly made all my wanderings worthwhile." Osmanthus responded, "You and my mother are aunt and nephew, and it is, of course, you and she who share the closest relationship. A luckless girl like your younger sister is beneath your notice." The Hanlin replied, "Why do you say that? You are in the best and most beautiful time of your life; good fortune lies before you and your luck will soon change."

The two thus traded comments and compliments. Osmanthus was, at her age, no stranger to certain stirrings, and she had already been much taken by the Hanlin's handsome and elegant bearing. Besides, they were close cousins—or so she believed—and she did not feel embarrassed by his soft and sweet blandishments. She told the Hanlin, "You are new to our home, so let me know if there is anything less than satisfactory with your accommodations, and I shall try to remedy the matter."

Hanlin Quan asked, "What do you mean by less than satisfactory?" Osmanthus replied, "I mean, is there anything wanting." The Hanlin stated, "There is something wanting, but I cannot tell you what it is." Osmanthus asked, "Why can you not tell me?" The Hanlin said, "What is wanting, you cannot remedy. Yet no one but you can remedy what is wanting." Curious, Osmanthus inquired, "And what might that be?" The Hanlin smiled and said, "Someone to keep me company at night!"

Osmanthus did not speak. Blushing hotly, she turned and walked away. Hanlin Quan caught up with her and seized her by the arm, pleading, "Could you not take me to your chambers and let me pay my respects to you there?" Now that the Hanlin had begun to take physical liberties with her, Osmanthus was at loss as to what to do. At this juncture, Dame Bai's voice was heard calling from within the canopy, "Who is talking there?"

The Hanlin loosened his grip and turned back to say, "It is your nephew. I have come to inquire about your health." Osmanthus, availing herself of the opportunity to free her arm, ran out of the room.

Dame Bai drew aside the curtains of the canopy, and seeing the Hanlin, she said, "So it is my nephew. Your little brother went out and has not yet returned. But why has your sister not come to show you around? And with whom were you speaking just now?" With a guilty conscience, the Hanlin lied, "I am alone here. There is no one else." Dame Bai said, "If that is so, then my old ears were deceiving me." She wished to converse further, but the Hanlin was preoccupied and left after uttering a few desultory remarks.

Dame Bai had observed the academician's flustered and disconcerted manner, and suspicions rose in her mind. She thought, "That Spirit Stabilizing Elixir I took comes from the capital, so it was surely brought here by my nephew. Yet how did it get into my daughter's bedchamber? And I clearly heard him speaking to her, but he insisted there was no one else. It may be that, having learned what transpired in the past, they are in secret communication, or have even had an assignation. They are, of course, both of age now, and I have always wished to make a couple of them. But my nephew has just arrived and I know nothing about him. I do not even know if he is married. In any case, it is too early to broach the matter. Better to wait a while, as there might still be an opportunity to bring this matter to fulfillment."

As Dame Bai was pondering this, Gao-er came in with a package of medicines and grumbled, "That accursed physician! He went out, and I had to wait until now for him to draw this medicine." Annoyed with Gao-er for returning so late, Dame Bai snapped, "If I had had to wait for your medicine, I would be dead by now! Fortunately the pain is gone and I don't need it any longer. Go keep your elder brother company!"

Gao-er remarked, "That elder brother of mine is behaving rather suspiciously. I bumped into him as I came in the house. He was loitering in front of my sister's chambers, and withdrew only after he saw me." Dame Bai reproved him, saying, "Enough of that idle chatter!" But Gao-er would not be hushed and he persisted, "I think this older brother of mine is a handsome fellow. Since my sister has lost her husband, why not marry her off to him and be done with it? Then he will cease to roam around with that restless and hungry look." Dame Bai shouted peremptorily, "What does a child like you know about such things! I have my own plans!" Although she had silenced her son, Dame Bai knew that there was reason to what he had said, and she turned the matter about in her mind. However, it was too early to say anything yet.

After the first time Hanlin Quan and Osmanthus talked to one another, they had frequent encounters, and on each occasion the amorous glances they exchanged bespoke their sentiments. The Hanlin was like a man possessed, all day scribbling who-knows-what with his brush and showing no interest in either tea or food. Osmanthus, on her part, was moody and listless, kept dozing off, and left needle and thread untouched. None of this passed unnoticed by Dame

Bai. Both, however, kept their desires to themselves and made no overt advances to one another as there were too many eyes and ears around them.

One day, as the Hanlin was on his way to see Dame Bai, Osmanthus happened to come out of her chambers after completing her toilette. The Hanlin stopped and stood before the door, preventing Osmanthus from coming out. After greeting her, he said, "I have long heard that your chambers are well appointed though I have not had the occasion to visit them. Now that I have the luck to meet you here, I insist on seeing them." Without so much as a by-your-leave, he slipped through the door and into the room, and Osmanthus could only follow him in. Having ascertained that no one else was around, the Hanlin threw his arms around Osmanthus and pleaded, "Have pity on me, your elder brother and guest, and save me from death!"

Osmanthus dared not cry out, so she said in a low voice, "Show me some respect, elder brother! If you do not reject me, why do you not have someone go to my mother and ask for my hand in marriage? She would surely give her consent, and there would be no need for such frivolous behavior." But the Hanlin would not be put off. He said, "I thank you for your advice, which only shows the depth of your sentiments. However, distant water cannot quench an immediate fire, and I cannot wait so long for that to happen." Osmanthus sternly rebuked him: "If what you seek is an illicit affair, I flatly refuse! For when and if we become a couple, you will surely despise me for it!"

Osmanthus freed herself from his embrace and walked out of the door, the bun of hair atop her head askew and her earlocks in disarray. She hurried, almost running, to Dame Bai's chambers and was still panting when she entered. Dame Bai noticed that she was not her usual self and asked, "Why are you like this?" Osmanthus replied, "I saw my cousin coming up behind me as I stepped out of my door, and I walked quite rapidly to stay ahead of him." Dame Bai remarked, "We are all of the same family, so why do you try to avoid him?"

Dame Bai fully expected her nephew to follow in Osmanthus' wake but he failed to appear. The truth is, he was smarting from Osmanthus' rebuff and had returned to his study. However, Dame Bai's suspicions only grew stronger, and she thought it best to have them marry as soon as possible. What was lacking was an intermediary. All at once, Dame Bai thought of someone. She recalled, "The day my nephew came here, he stated he had found our family because The Reverend Miaotong told him about us. Would it not be a good idea to ask Miaotong to come and discuss this matter with her?" She forthwith instructed Gao-er to go to the nunnery and bring Miaotong back with him. Gao-er did so accordingly.

And now, back to Hanlin Quan.

Having returned to the study, he felt most melancholy as he recalled what had happened. He mused, "Osmanthus is attracted to me even though she would not let me have my way. And what she said was right, although she does not know I am an imposter. But whom can I ask to speak for me?" Then again, he thought, "Her mother and she both believe me to be Bai the Elder's son, for which I must of course thank the vanity case. If only I produce the evidence of that vanity case, there is no danger that my design will not succeed." But another thought occurred to him, and he told himself, "Not so! Not so! If, by some chance, the names happen to be the same but the vanity case does not belong to their family, all my pretences will come to naught. I should not do anything to jeopardize what I have already achieved. What I must do is continue to enhance feelings of cordiality and warmth between us, and she will be mine."

As he thought all these thoughts, he stepped out of his room and strolled around in front of the main hall to clear the turmoil from his mind. Suddenly, he saw The Reverend Miaotong coming through the front gate. At the sight of Hanlin Quan, the elderly nun made a gesture of greetings and said reprovingly, "Sir, now that you have found your kinsfolk and a pleasurable place to stay, you no longer visit our humble little nunnery."

With a laugh the Hanlin returned her greetings and said, "If the truth be told, my aunt wishes me to be at her side. And second, as a lonely man who has had only my shadow to keep me company, I crave the companionship of my own flesh and blood and have little desire to go out now." Miaotong declared, "Since you are unhappy about being alone, let this older person be your matchmaker!" Surprised, the Hanlin said, "I have long wanted to purchase a concubine, but you told me the other day that you do not intervene in other people's worldly affairs, so I have not dared to importune you again. But I would be most pleased if you were to arrange a match for me."

Miaotong conceded, "I do, in fact, have a match in mind. But it so happens that Dame Bai has asked me to come to her about some matter. Let me first see her, after which I will talk with you in greater detail." Hanlin Quan said, "I, too, have someone in mind, for whom I shall be needing a go-between. So your presence is most opportune. Be sure to come to the study after you have met my aunt. I have something to ask of you." Miaotong replied, "I shall do so."

With that, Miaotong proceeded to the inner chambers and saw Dame Bai, who greeted her with the words, "It is a long time since you have last visited us." Miaotong explained, "I had heard that you were indisposed and was just about to come and see you when your young master came to get me. So here I am." Dame Bai said, "My nephew arrived a few days ago, and the joy and sorrow I felt on seeing him, added to some overexertion on my part, made me unwell. But that has passed and you need not be concerned. There is, however, something I wish to discuss with you." Miaotong asked, "And what might that be?"

Dame Bai said, "I worry day and night because my daughter is still not spoken for." Miaotong parried, "It is no easy matter to find someone suitable." Dame Bai assured her, "I do have someone, and that is why I need to confer with you." Miaotong smiled and asked, "And who might it be, that you would wish to discuss him with a nun?"

Dame Bai hastened to say, "I shall not say who he is! I only wish to ask you one thing. My nephew from the capital tells me that he was first acquainted with you. Do you know anything about that?" Miaotong replied, "Of course I do. He resided next to the nunnery for quite some time, and he came to you only after I mentioned your name. I might say, too, that I find him a most handsome and refined person."

Dame Bai continued, "This nephew was born in the same year as my daughter, as I once told you. Before we left the capital, I had intended to betroth my daughter to him, but my late husband disapproved. And so when we left the capital I secretly separated a vanity case into two parts and had his family and my family each keep one part, to be used in the future as an earnest. I also wrote out a testimonial on a sheet of paper. My nephew was very young at the time, and I know not whether the vanity case or the sheet of paper are still in existence, yet I do know that he is the right person. My daughter has no marriage agreement now with any family, and that may just be Heaven's will. I very much desire to fulfill that former pledge, but it is difficult for me to bring up the subject with him. Besides, I do not even know whether he has taken a wife in the capital. So could you do me the favor of going to the West Hall and asking him about this? If he is not married, I would like to see this matter happily resolved. What do you say?"

Miaotong replied, "I can do that, and I am confident the matter will be resolved in short order. But let me take along your half of the vanity case. I can use it to bring up a matter or two." Dame Bai said, "You are quite right." She went to her bedchamber and brought back the bottom half of a vanity case, which she handed to Miaotong.

Miaotong put the object in one of her sleeves and walked over to the study in the West Hall. The Hanlin met her with the words, "Have you seen my aunt?" Miaotong replied, "Yes, I have." The Hanlin inquired, "What did you talk about?" Miaotong said, "Nothing in particular. We have not seen one another for some time."

The Hanlin then asked, "Did you see my younger sister, too?" Miaotong replied, "I did not, but I shall visit her in her chambers in a little while." Hanlin

Quan remarked, "She has such well-appointed rooms. It is a pity she is there by herself." Miaotong assured him, "A man will soon be found for her."

Changing the subject, the Hanlin asked, "You said earlier that you had a match in mind for me, and that you wished to confer with me. From which family is she?" Miaotong replied, "Her family is one of my alms-giving patrons. This young lady is of the most attractive appearance, and she will make a good match for you. However, you wish to take a concubine, which must mean you already have a wife. This family will not consent to her becoming a concubine."

The Hanlin explained, "I had a wife once, but she died more than a year ago. I said I wished to have a concubine because I did not think I would be able soon to find a good wife of appropriate social status. However, if she comes from a family that meets my approval, I shall of course take her as my wife." Miaotong asked, "As far as physical appearances go, what kind of girl would meet your approval?" Hanlin Quan pointed toward the small courtyard and said, "To be frank with you, it would be best if she looks like that cousin of mine." Miaotong smiled and said, "I should say they are quite similar in appearance."

The Hanlin then asked, "How much betrothal money are they seeking?" Miaotong took the vanity case from her sleeve and said, "None at all, but they have asked that a puzzle be solved. They have half of a gold case, and will give the girl in marriage if it is matched with the other half."

The Hanlin took the object in his hands and at once recognized it as the bottom half of the vanity case. He was overjoyed, yet pointedly inquired, "There must be some reason why they are seeking the other half of this case. Do you know what that reason is?" Miaotong replied, "This family once lived in the capital. The mother had a nephew to whom it was agreed that the girl should be married, and each family retained one half of the case as an earnest. So the person who has the other half of this case is the one destined to marry the girl."

The Hanlin declared, "As far as vanity cases go, I do have the lid of one such case. I wonder if it would be a match." He quickly took the lid out of his box of valuables and placed it together with the lower part. The two were a perfect match. Miaotong exclaimed, "So these make up one single case! It is fortunate that you have kept it!"

The Hanlin then demanded, "Tell me now, to which family does the lower half belong?" Miaotong looked at him quizzically before replying, "To whom else would it belong? You pretend not to know and think you can fool me. Are you still trying to say you are unaware that it belongs to your cousin Osmanthus' family?" The Hanlin said defensively, "I feigned ignorance, though only in jest, because you did not ask me outright and kept part of the truth from me. However, I would like to know why my aunt had you address me in such a roundabout fashion, considering that she had already promised me Osmanthus' hand in marriage while we were still infants." Miaotong explained, "Your aunt said that too many years have gone by since that time, that she did not know whether you had already married someone else, and that it would be embarrassing for her to ask you. That is why she charged me with finding out. Anyhow, since your wife has died and you have not remarried, and since the two parts of the vanity case match one another, I shall go back and report these things to Dame Bai, and all that remains is for you two to become husband and wife."

The Hanlin hastened to say, "I am most grateful to you for your kind offices on our behalf. But when can the wedding take place? Even one day earlier would do me pleasure!" Miaotong replied with a smile, "What a impatient groom you make! Now, tomorrow is the Mid-autumn Festival, and I shall see if I can persuade Dame Bai to bring this matter to fruition. I see no reason to wait any longer." Whereupon the Hanlin thanked her effusively.

Miaotong then secreted the two parts of the vanity case in her sleeves and happily returned to Dame Bai to report what she had learned. Dame Bai was overjoyed. Flesh and blood were now reunited, she stated, and old connections made whole, and all she desired now was to hold the nuptials the next day and drink at the wedding banquet. Among all the ten thousand thoughts that filled her mind at this time, however, there was not a glimmer of suspicion that the groom might not be her nephew.

All night long, the ecstatic Hanlin did not sleep a wink. Rising at the crack of dawn, he instructed his man Quan Zhong to find a pawnshop and rent a scholar's cap and gown in readiness for the forthcoming formal wedding vows. Dame Bai, too, was up and about very early to make arrangements for the banquet and to urge her daughter to hurry through her toilette. For the guests would be arriving soon and the bride and groom were to bow and kowtow to them. The Hanlin, now clad in ordinary scholar's clothing, tried to conceal his amusement over his attire, which was far below that of his real station. Even Quan Zhong smiled. However, onlookers attributed the Hanlin's merriment merely to joy over this auspicious event. How were they to know the truth?

Then the wedding candles were lit, and in a dream-like ambience of silvery candles, bright red lanterns and fragrant incense, the handsome groom and beautiful bride were joined under the full moon, in an elegant hall filled with cheerful well-wishers.

Having drunk toasts to the guests, the newlyweds were escorted to the wedding chamber. This happened to be Osmanthus' bedchamber in the Eastern Courtyard, and was precisely the room that Hanlin Quan had slipped into earlier and lain on the bed, and later barged into to seek some stolen favors. Now that he could sleep in it all night long, his delight can well be imagined. In truth, the Hanlin felt for all the world as though he was being transported to the Isle of Penglai, the fabled abode of the immortals!

Husband and wife entered the embroidered canopy, and within its silken curtains the man satisfied his passions and the woman her craving for love and, needless to say, both were amply fulfilled.

When they had done making clouds and rain, the Hanlin gently caressed Osmanthus and said, "The thousand-*li* bond between you and me has now been marvelously fulfilled. Our fortune is such that it will last three incarnations." Osmanthus responded, "It is not surprising that we should marry, since you and I were betrothed when we were both young. What gives me the greatest joy is that after so many years and across such distances were have finally been reunited. It would seem that Heaven's will is on our side. There is, however, one question in my mind. You are not from these parts but have married into my family. I do not know where your footsteps will take us. I do not even know who you are and what you do. Are you a scholar? A merchant? As people say, 'marry a chicken and follow the chicken; marry a dog and follow the dog.' I shall remain with you whatever your lot in life. But we should discuss arrangements for the future. More is needed than the moment's pleasure and love."

The Hanlin reassured her, saying, "You need not worry. My only fear has been that you would not marry me. But now that you have done so, I promise you many good things." Osmanthus inquired, "What sort of good things? I hardly expect to become the wife of an official with a five-flower mandate!" The Hanlin laughed and declared, "Had you asked for anything else, you might have caused me some embarrassment. But if the mandate of a five-flower official is what you desire, I can find one for you in my effects." Osmanthus chided him, asking, "Do you not blush when you say such things?" She did not take his words in earnest as she assumed he was merely boasting. The Hanlin, however, smiled enigmatically and offered no clarification. He continued with his tender and caring attentions, and the two passed the night as blissfully as fish in water.

When they had risen the next morning and completed their ablutions, they donned formal dress and went to greet Dame Bai and to thank Miaotong for acting as matchmaker. Just as they were performing the rituals, a clamor of gongs and what sounded like a dozen men shouting shattered the silence in front of the hall, so alarming the boy Gao-er that he scampered away into hiding. The Hanlin strode out of the hall and asked, "Who is creating such a row?"

He had hardly spoken these words when an old household steward named Quan Xiao came forward with a number of special emissaries from the capital.

Seeing the Hanlin, the emissaries fell to their knees and kowtowed, and Quan Xiao announced, "These are emissaries from the capital who have come to proclaim Your Excellency's promotion. They could not find you, and only when they met Quan Zhong in the street did they learn that you had taken up residence here. But why are you dressed in this manner? Please change at once into more appropriate attire!"

The Hanlin hurriedly waved his hands to prevent the emissaries from revealing his true identity, but none would listen. One and all shouted without cease "My Lord Quan!" Then they produced a proclamation to the effect that the Hanlin had been raised to the position of Academician, and vociferously demanded to be rewarded for bringing the good tidings. The Hanlin sternly requested that they refrain from using his family name, Quan, but the emissaries were not to be deterred, and instead pasted a congratulatory red-colored poster high up in the hall. It was inscribed with the words:

Urgent proclamation: Lord Quan of this residence has been officially promoted and is now Academician of the Hanlin Academy

By this time the retainer Quan Zhong had brought out the Hanlin's official cap and gown, and he said to the Hanlin, now an Academician, "I presume the truth can no longer be hidden, so you might as well put these on." With a smile, the Academician divested himself of his scholar's cap and gown and donned his official garb. Then, having requested that a table with incense be laid out, he thanked the Emperor for his indulgence. That done, he instructed the special emissaries to wait outside the gate for their reward.

He then went back into the house and asked once more to kowtow to his mother-in-law. Dame Bai, however, had been taken completely by surprise. The news had come out of nowhere, like a clap of thunder in a clear sky, and she was all aflutter and didn't know what to do. And when she saw the Academician going down on his knees, she cried, "You will be the death of me! I had no idea your name was Quan and that you were such a important official at the imperial court! How could my eyes have failed to discern such an illustrious person? I beg you not to be too harsh with me and to forgive me for having been so discourteous!" The Academician said soothingly, "There is no need to say such things. We are all one family now."

Somewhat reassured, Dame Bai continued, "May I be so bold as to ask my worthy son-in-law a question? Since your name is not Bai, why did you feign to be my nephew and honor my poor abode with your presence? There must be a reason." The Academician explained, "As I was residing at the nunnery and taking a stroll by moonlight one evening, I happened to see your beautiful daughter and was filled with admiration. From The Reverend Miaotong I learned her name, place of residence, and sundry details about her family and then came to you under false pretenses and claimed to be your kinsman. To my surprise, you did not suspect anything and readily accepted me. That was truly the greatest fortune of three incarnations."

Miaotong confirmed his account, saying, "When the academician first came to the nunnery, he told me his name was Quan. Later, as we conversed about your family, he corrected himself and said his name was Bai. I, too, asked him about that, and he explained he had changed his name for convenience in seeking his relatives. How was I to know he was beguiling me? In fact, he made dunces of all of us. A capital joke indeed!"

Dame Bai then stated, "There is another question I wish to ask my son-in-law. Where does the lid of the vanity case come from? Are you perchance in league with the gods?" The Academician laughed and declared, "This nephew may be an imposter, but the lid is real. Whatever has happened, however, it is indeed Heaven that intervened in this matter, not the will of man." Dame Bai and Miaotong looked at him uncomprehendingly, and Dame Bai said, "Kindly explain!"

The Academician told her, "It was by sheer chance that your humble son-in-law purchased the lid of that vanity case at a temple fair in the capital. Among it wrappings was the testimonial you had written for your nephew, Liuge, and it bore the name of your daughter. It is this testimonial, which is now in my possession, that gave me the audacity to falsely present myself as your nephew. I beg your forgiveness for having committed such deceit and fraud."

Dame Bai replied, "There is no need to say such things now. But why would my nephew's family sell the lid of the vanity case? Who was the person who sold it to you? You must surely know something about that." The academician said, "The lid was sold to me by an elderly man who told me he was once your brother's landlord. He said that your brother's entire family had come down with a plague, that the young ones had died, leaving only the parents, who hastily fled the city, and that he was selling the things they had left behind."

Dame Bai sighed, saying, "So my elder brother and nephew have in all probability passed away. How true is the saying that 'the objects remain after the owners are gone'!" And she broke into tears. Miaotong hastened to console her, saying, "Dame Bai, this marriage was decided by Heaven, and it matters little whether he is or not your nephew, or whether his name is Quan or Bai. What does matter is that you now have a Hanlin Academician as your son-in-law, which, I would think, brings no disgrace upon your daughter." Dame Bai concurred, saying, "What you say is true." And all those present were happy for Dame Bai.

Osmanthus, who was at her mother's side, heard everything that had been said. Although she did not say anything, she knew now that her husband had promised in good faith that she would become the wife of an official with a five-flower mandate and that he had not been exaggerating. She also knew that their marriage, for which she had to thank the vanity case, was indeed a stroke of good fortune. It is needless, here, to describe her contentment.

Academician Quan, on his part, adored his beautiful wife and knew full well that their marriage, occasioned as it had been by the vanity case, was nothing short of a miracle. Consequently he and Osmanthus loved one another dearly.

Before long, Academician Quan presented handsome gifts to The Reverend Miaotong and departed for his new position in the capital together with his wife, mother-in-law, and brother-in-law. Osmanthus was in due course conferred the honorific title Lady of Befitting Gentility, and she and her husband both lived to a ripe old age.

The Thief Who Was Both a Prankster and a Gentleman

神偷寄興一支梅
俠盜慣性三昧戲

There was in the city of Lin'an, during the Song dynasty some four hundred years before our present Ming dynasty, a thief of surpassing skill who was known simply as "I Was Here." No one knew either his name or his surname. When he robbed a house, he left no clues to himself other than the three words " I Was Here" written in large characters on a wall, and only when the residents of the house saw these words the next day and checked their possessions did they know that their belongings had been stolen. So masterfully did he practice his calling that, had he not announced his presence, neither gods nor demons would have known he had been there!

The residents of Lin'an were so vexed by his depredations that they submitted innumerable complaints. The prefectural magistrate charged his minions with the task of instituting a rigorous search and arresting, within a set time limit, the thief called "I Was Here." But no one knew his identity or so much as his real name, and without these, what thief would admit to his misdeeds even if he were caught?

However, fearing the sanctions they might suffer when the time limit expired, the minions and the yamen bailiffs under them put all their heart into locating the culprit. Yamen bailiffs have, after all, their ways of sniffing the winds, and a thief, no matter how astute, cannot escape their attention forever and is sooner or later bound to arouse suspicion. And so it was that in the course of their investigations, the yamen bailiffs somehow apprehended the thief and brought him to the Lin'an yamen.

When the prefectural magistrate had ascended to his bench, a minion declared, "We have seized the real 'I Was Here,' and though we do not know his real name, he is undoubtedly the man who has written those three words." The magistrate inquired, "How can you be so certain?" Whereupon the minion replied, "We have been most assiduous in our investigations, and there can be no mistake."

But the man protested, "This insignificant person is an honest subject and by no means the thief 'I Was Here.' Your minions have arrested me and are passing me off as the culprit because they fear being punished for their failure to catch the real villain."

The minions hastened to deny this accusation, saying, "That is what all thieves say. Do not listen to him." The magistrate still had his doubts, but his minions pleaded, "We have spent a great deal of time and effort on finding him. Should he succeed with his artful words in talking himself out of custody, we will never be able to catch him again!"

The magistrate was not fully convinced by his minions' arguments and was inclined to let the man go. But he also feared that the man might indeed be the thief and that it would be impossible to find him again were he released. Besides, he, as magistrate, would have no excuse for admonishing his minions if he himself set the man free. So the magistrate temporized and ordered that the man be kept in detention.

Once the man arrived in jail, he lost no time ingratiating himself with the jail guard. He said, "The custom in prisons is to pay a gratuity to the guards, but the bailiffs have taken everything I had on my person. However, I do have some silver cached under a broken brick next to the pedestal in the temple of the patriot Yue Fei, and I would be pleased to present that to you, my elder brother, as a mark of my regard for you. You may retrieve the silver when you go to the temple to burn incense." The guard was skeptical. Nevertheless he went to see if what the man said was true, and he found a parcel which contained some twenty taels of silver. Highly pleased, the guard thereafter took good care of the man, and the two gradually became close friends.

Some time later, the man said to the guard, "For the great kindness and good treatment you, my brother, have accorded me, I have nothing with which to repay you. However, I have concealed another parcel with sundry articles under the pier of such-and-such a bridge. You may take these articles as a token of my respect for you." The guard, however, replied doubtfully, "There is much traffic as well as many eyes at the place you have just mentioned, and I do not know how I could collect the parcel unnoticed." Whereupon the man said, "Take a basketful of clothes and wash them in the river under the bridge. Once you have found the parcel, place it in the basket and cover it with the clothes. That way you can bring back the parcel unobserved." The guard did as the man suggested and, unnoticed by any passers-by, retrieved the parcel. Upon examining it, he found that the articles it contained were worth more than a hundred taels of silver. The guard was exceedingly grateful, and he now felt as much affection for the man as he would for his own flesh and blood.

That evening, the guard bought wine and treated the man to a good meal. After they had been drinking for a while, the man said, "I wish to go home tonight to attend to some matter and shall be back before dawn. Will you indulge me just this once?" Taken by surprise, the guard did not reply. He thought to himself, "Having accepted so many things from him, I cannot very well deny him this request. But what will happen should he not return?"

Observing his irresolution, the man continued, "You need not have any doubts, my brother. I was seized by the bailiffs and have now been confined here under the presumption that I am the person called 'I Was Here.' However, with neither evidence nor even a name to go by, what charges can be brought against me? I have no desire to become a fugitive, as I will surely argue successfully for my release. So please put your mind at ease. I require only the four hours between the third and fifth watches tonight, and shall be back without fail."

The guard found the man's reasoning to be sound. He also reflected, "As this man has not been charged with any crime, it would be of no great consequence even if he did abscond. He has, moreover, given me much money, and if worse comes to worst I can use some of that money to have the matter glossed over. In any case, it is not certain that he will fail to return." So the guard granted the man's request. The latter, however, did not leave through the prison gate but instead sprang onto the eaves of the jailhouse and soundlessly vanished across the roof tiles.

Just before daybreak, as the guard was still sleeping off his hangover from the previous night's drinking, the man jumped down from the roof and shook his shoulder, saying, "I am back." The guard awoke with a start and, seeing who it was, exclaimed, "You are indeed a trustworthy person!" To which the man replied, "How could I fail to come back and leave you to suffer the consequences? I am most grateful to you for allowing me to go out last night, and I have left some small tokens of my gratitude at your home. Go home without delay and put these articles safely away. This small person will be bidding you farewell soon, as I will be officially released from jail."

Not knowing what the man was talking about, the guard hurried home, where his wife said to him: "I have been waiting for you to come back. Something strange happened last night. Just before the last beating of the watch drum I heard some noise on the rafters of the house, after which a bundle suddenly fell from above. When I opened it, I discovered it was filled with objects made of gold and silver. Is it conceivable that these were given us by Heaven?"

The guard knew now what the man had meant, and he hastily motioned for his wife to hold her tongue. "Do not utter a word about this to anyone," he instructed her. "Store the objects in a safe place, and we shall make use of them at our leisure." He then quickly returned to the jailhouse and once more thanked the man profusely.

A short time later, when the magistrate ascended to his bench for the morning hearings, he received complaints about a spate of thefts. In fact, six or seven households were pleading for the arrest of a burglar who had robbed them of their belongings the night before and inscribed on their walls the legend "I Was Here."

The magistrate announced, "I had doubted all along whether the person currently being held in jail is truly the thief known as 'I Was Here.' But now there is proof that the thief is another man, and that the one in jail is suffering an injustice." He forthwith ordered the prison warden to release the detainee without delay, and then instructed the bailiffs to apprehend the real "I Was Here" within a fixed time limit, failing which they would be subject to sanctions. Never did it cross the magistrate's mind that he might be allowing the real culprit to go free. The only person who knew the truth of the matter was the jail guard, who now woke up to the fact that the man had made ingenious use of him. But having accepted munificent bribes, he, of course, could not breathe a word about what he knew.

Esteemed listeners, do you not think that this was a most clever burglar, and that his manifest talents could very well have been otherwise employed?

That, however, is past history.

*　　*　　*

I wish to tell you now about another most gifted thief who lived in Suzhou city during the Jiaqing reign [1522–1556] of our current Ming dynasty. He is known for his many exploits, and although a thief, he was not lacking in a certain gallantry combined with a good deal of roguishness, and the stories about him make amusing listening.

This man lived in Alley No. 1 in front of East Xuanmiao Temple in the Yazi area of Suzhou. No one knows his true name, but he called himself "Lazy Dragon" and was known to all by this nickname. It is said that his mother, a peasant woman, was out walking one day when it started to rain. She sought shelter in a dilapidated temple to wait out the rain, and when it did not stop she dozed off and dreamed that the god of that temple lay with her, and indeed she eventually became pregnant. Ten moons later she gave birth to Lazy Dragon.

Lazy Dragon was small in body but large in courage. He was known to be clever and witty as well as magnanimous. He not only excelled at the usual tricks of his trade but displayed some unique abilities and quirks. He had, since childhood, learned to walk swiftly on walls without removing his boots. He was able to speak the dialects of all the regions in our Empire. He could go without sleep for several nights running, but when he did sleep he would do so for many days on end, without taking tea or food. If he ate and drank without restraint, he could put away pitchers of wine and jars of rice and still complain he had not had his fill; yet at other times he fasted for days without feeling hunger. He lined his shoes with the ash of burnt straw so that he could walk without making a sound. When he grappled and fought with another man, his fists whirled like the wind. Lazy Dragon's abilities endeared him to many young ruffians. Indeed, he himself acquired the ways of a thief, but all his peers respected him for his prowess and admitted they were no match for him.

Lazy Dragon had neither a place to live nor any visible means of livelihood, and he simply made his home wherever he happened to be. No one knew where he could be found. In the daytime, he was sometimes seen walking in a marketplace or entering someone's home, yet what people actually discerned was more his shadow than his physical shape. At night, he would slip into some rich family's mansion to seek a place to sleep, be it under the rafters of the roof, or in the chambers of a newlywed couple, or behind a screen in a woman's boudoir, or in a pavilion with paintings, and there he would lie curled up like a hedgehog. Any place served him as a place to rest, and when he went away he might spirit away something or other if it suited him. It was because he slept so much, and because he was as elusive as the dragon is to ordinary mortals, that he gained the nickname "Lazy Dragon." Wherever he committed a theft, he would invariably leave his signature on a wall by drawing a sprig of plum blossoms, which he did with white chalk if the wall was black and with charcoal if the wall was white, and for this reason he was also known as "Plum Blossoms."

In the early years of the Jiaqing reign, heavy rains brought waters roaring down from the hills in the Dongting area. Some of the cliffs around Lake Tai crumbled and collapsed, revealing an ancient tomb that contained a vermilion-painted coffin. Also in the tomb were innumerable treasures, all of which, however, were soon stolen. Stories of this treasure reached the city, and one day when Lazy Dragon happened to be boating on the lake with some friends he stopped by the tomb. In it he saw the coffin which had been riven open and now lay overgrown with vines. A skeleton lay within the coffin, but the name on the broken and weathered tombstone was undecipherable. Lazy Dragon remarked, "This was undoubtedly the tomb of some ancient king or prince." He felt saddened and, after closing up the coffin, hired some locals to bury it and then poured a bowl of wine on the grave as an offering to the deceased.

When this was done and Lazy Dragon turned to leave, he stubbed his foot on an object in the grass. Leaning down, he saw that it was an ancient mirror. This he quickly hid in one of his socks when no one was looking. After returning to the city, he sought a secluded spot, scrubbed off the mud that covered the mirror and examined the object. The mirror was no larger than his palm. Its face shone bright and clear, and on its back and edges were relief depictions of various monsters and dragons and waves, all done in green and black and chased with cinnabar and silver. He gave the mirror a tap, and when it gave off a cold ringing tone he knew he had a real treasure.

Thereafter he kept the mirror on his person, since all things reflected in it at night stood out as clearly as if lit up by the light of day. Once he had acquired this mirror, Lazy Dragon was never without it for he had no more need of a torch or lantern, which was indeed a convenience. Places that others feared to go in the dark, he traversed unconcerned, as though in broad daylight, and he could steal things with much greater ease.

Despite Lazy Dragon's calling as a thief, there were a number of laudable things to be said about him. He never molested any women in the houses he entered; nor did he break into the houses of good and honest people or of the unfortunate, and he never went back on his word. Moreover, he gave generously to the poor and casually distributed things he stole among people who were in dire need. He delighted in taunting the avaricious wealthy and the unrighteous rich, taking every opportunity to play jokes on them and hold them up to ridicule. For these reasons, many people in the places he frequented looked up to and, indeed, worshiped him as a most benevolent and righteous man. Lazy Dragon, however, would laugh off such praise and declare, "I have neither parents nor a wife and children to support, so I might as well borrow some surplus wealth to assist the indigent. This is called 'making reasonable adjustments between the rich and the poor.' It is Heaven's way, and has nothing to do with either benevolence or righteousness on my part."

One day, Lazy Dragon learned that a big merchant had deposited a thousand taels of silver at the home of a prosperous maker of fabrics named Zhou Jia. Lazy Dragon resolved to take the silver, but having imbibed too much wine before he set forth, he entered another house by mistake. This was the house of a poor family, and as Lazy Dragon peered around the room, he saw no furniture of any value other than a sideboard. Since he was already in the room and could not leave just yet, he hid himself under the sideboard, and from there watched the husband and wife of this poor family sharing their evening meal. There was woefully little in their dishes. The husband's face was gloomy and overcast with anxiety as he told his wife, "The customer is pressing me for the debt I owe him and there is no way in which I can repay him. I would be better off dead." To which his wife replied, "How can you say such a thing? You would do better to sell me, so that you would have some money for your business." And after they had said this, their tears fell like rain.

At this moment, Lazy Dragon hopped out of his hiding place, causing the couple to shrink back in alarm. Lazy Dragon cried, "Do not be afraid. I am Lazy Dragon. I came to seek a rich merchant but have come to the wrong house. I overheard you speak of your sad plight, and shall present you with two hundred taels of silver to help you with your business. Pray do not think of doing anything untoward or abandon yourselves to despair."

The couple had often heard Lazy Dragon's name, and they now fell to their knees, exclaiming, "Oh, righteous person that you are! If you favor us with such benevolence, you will have given us a new lease on life!" Lazy Dragon then walked out of the door, and about two hours later a clinking sound was heard outside. The husband and wife went to look and, lo and behold, they found a cloth sack containing two hundred taels of silver, which was part of the booty Lazy Dragon had obtained that night from the merchant's home! The overjoyed couple subsequently wrote out a memorial tablet to Lazy Dragon and made offerings before it as long as they lived.

Then there is the story of a poor man who had been one of Lazy Dragon's childhood companions and had fallen on evil days. One day the man encountered Lazy Dragon on the street, but clad as he was in ragged clothing, he felt so ashamed that he covered his face with his fan and attempted to walk away. Lazy Dragon caught him by the sleeve and inquired, "Are you not Master So-and-So?" And the man replied in embarrassment, "Yes, to my great mortification!" Lazy Dragon said, "How have you landed in such poverty? Come with me to a rich man's house tomorrow and we shall get you something that you can use. You must, however, hold your tongue about this matter!" This person had heard about Lazy Dragon's skills and knew that the thief was a man of his word, so he sought him out the next evening.

Lazy Dragon took the man to the residence of a high official, a mansion with many pavilions and ponds. Having enjoined the man to wait outside, he climbed into a tree and from there leaped across the wall into the grounds of the residence. He was gone for a long time. His friend, meanwhile, squatted outside the wall and waited with bated breath for him to return. Once, when a pack of dogs ran up, barking frenziedly and gnashing their teeth, he circled about the wall to throw them off.

Then he heard the sound of splashing water within the wall, and soon afterward an object plunged out of the treetops like a diving cormorant. He took a closer look and saw that it was Lazy Dragon, soaked from head to toe and quite bedraggled. Lazy Dragon informed the man, "I well nigh lost my life for your sake. The gold and silver in that house are to be measured by the bushel, and I had already laid my hands on it when the loud barking of dogs outside woke up the people in the house and they began to give chase. I was obliged to abandon the gold and silver on the way out so that I could escape unencumbered. That is your bad luck." The man sighed sorrowfully and said, "You have usually but to stretch out your hand to take whatever you wish. That such a thing should have happened today shows how thin is my fortune!" Lazy Dragon consoled him, saying, "Do not be upset. We will succeed the next time!" The man departed, shaking his head disconsolately.

A month or so later, Lazy Dragon met the man in the street again, and the latter said to him dolefully, "I could no longer bear my poverty, so I went to see a soothsayer who told me that my fortunes are in the ascendancy and my wealth line is in motion. He said someone would soon bring me great riches, and I thought, who else can I look to other than Lazy Dragon?"

Lazy Dragon laughed and said, "I almost forgot! The other day I had already secured a box full of gold and silver, but I feared things might go amiss if I gave it to you then and there and the family discovered the loss and you failed to conceal the money properly. So I hid the box, for the time being, in one of the family's ponds and have waited to see what would transpire. Now a month has gone by with nothing happening, so I presume the family does not intend to mount a search and we may safely retrieve the box. Let us go again tonight."

The man waited until dusk, and then went to the residence together with Lazy Dragon. Once there, Lazy Dragon vanished among the trees and shrubbery as nimbly as a bird, and in a short time returned, bearing the box on his shoulder. Quickly finding a secluded spot, Lazy Dragon opened the box and looked inside it with his magic mirror. It was filled with gold and silver. Lazy Dragon did not take any of the money for himself; nor did he even count it. Instead, he gave the entire amount to his friend, saying, "This wealth should last you for the rest of your life. Use it wisely, and do not take me, Lazy Dragon, as an example, for I have frittered away half my life and failed even to set up a household of my own." The friend thanked Lazy Dragon for his advice, and after taking home the gold and silver, he invested it in a business and eventually became a rich man. Many were the times that Lazy Dragon performed deeds such as these.

One might ask, since Lazy Dragon was so clever and ingenious, did he always carry off his schemes so effortlessly and smoothly? Or were there times when he found himself in peril? This storyteller has learned that Lazy Dragon had his share of mishaps and misadventures, but that he was resourceful enough in times of emergency to extricate himself unscathed, as the following stories will show.

There was, in the same city, a family whose business was spinning and weaving fabrics and whose clients paid them silver in advance for the fabrics they made. The man and his wife kept the silver in a coffer which they placed on the far side of the bed they shared, and every night the two kept close watch over the silver.

Having learned of this circumstance, Lazy Dragon made up his mind to take the silver. One night, he crept into their room and, placing one foot on the edge of the bed, extended an arm over the bed to lift the coffer. The women awoke with a start and sensed that there was something on the edge of the bed, and when she reached out in the dark to touch the thing she felt a man's foot! Clutching it with both hands, she cried out to her husband, "Get up! Get up! I have caught the foot of a thief!"

Lazy Dragon at once seized the husband's foot and pinched it, whereupon the man cried out in pain, "Ouch! That is my foot! That is my foot!" Believing that she was indeed holding her husband's foot, the wife loosened her hold on it. Lazy Dragon then snatched up the coffer and in a trice was out of the room while the man and his wife were still arguing with one another.

The wife said accusingly, "That was clearly the foot of a thief, yet you made me let go of it!" To which the man replied, "That was no thief's foot! You pinched my foot so hard it still hurts!" The wife reasoned, "Your feet were on the inner side of the bed, but the foot I caught was on the outer side. Besides, I did not pinch the foot." Whereupon the man cried, "All right, then it was the thief who pinched my foot! You should not have released his foot!" And the wife cried back, "Your yelling so confused me that I let go of his foot, which is why he was able to get away! It seems we have been taken in by that wily thief, and I fear the worst."

They groped for the coffer that should have been on the inner side of the bed and found that it was indeed gone. For the rest of the night the two continued to reproach one another, each insisting the other was to blame.

And there was that occasion when Lazy Dragon entered a house and found a large clothespress wide open. He slipped into the clothespress to sequester some of the garments therein. Never did he expect that the owners of the house would shut the doors of the clothespress before they retired for the night, and that they would even affix a large padlock to the door, locking him inside! When Lazy Dragon had ascertained that he could not get out, he sat down to think, and soon came up with a stratagem.

He wrapped many of the garments and accessories in the press around his body and made up a big bundle with the remainder. Then, stationing himself and the bundle by the door of the clothespress, he proceeded to mimic the sounds of mice gnawing at fabrics. The master of the house heard these sounds and woke up his wife, saying, "How did you happen to shut a mouse in the clothespress? It will ruin our garments. Get up, open the press, and drive it out!"

The wife lit a lamp and opened the door of the press, whereupon the bundle tumbled out on the ground. Quick as a flash, Lazy Dragon curled himself up in a ball and rolled out after the bundle. As he did so he contrived to blow out the lamp held by the woman, so frightening her that she cried out. Fearing that other people would come in and make escape impossible, Lazy Dragon threw the bundle at the woman, knocking her to the ground, then ran out of the house. By this time, a few members of the household had rushed into the room and, in the dark, stumbled over the woman. Believing her to be the thief, they belabored her with their fists and feet. The woman shrieked, and others in the household, awakened by the shouting and yelling, came running with lanterns and torches. Only then was it discovered that members of the household were beating one another. Orders were shouted to stop fighting, but by then Lazy Dragon had long since disappeared.

On yet another occasion, Lazy Dragon entered a clothing shop and sought out its storehouse. His intention was to choose a few rich garments to take away, but it was too dark to determine which ones were of the best quality. Thus he produced his precious mirror and used it to examine the goods. It so happened, however, that a man living next door was repairing an upstairs window and observed a flash of light issuing from the storehouse. He felt that something was amiss, so he rapped loudly on his window and called toward the clothing store, "Neighbors, beware! There may be a thief in your store!" Roused from their slumbers, the clerks in the store cried, "Stop thief! Stop thief!"

Lazy Dragon heard the commotion and knew that he must find a place to hide. Looking around, he saw in the courtyard a large lidded jar used for storing fermented soybean paste. Hastily lifting the lid, he jumped into the jar and lowered the lid over his head. Moments later, the clerks arrived with lanterns and ransacked the premises. Finding nothing, however, they went to look behind the storehouse.

As he squatted in the jar, Lazy Dragon thought to himself, "This jar is the only place they have not examined. Once they fail to find anything in the back, they will surely return. I had best conceal myself in some spot they have already searched." It then occurred to him that his clothing was coated with brown beanpaste and he would be leaving smears of it wherever he went. So he removed all his clothes and, naked as the day he was born, clambered out of the jar. Then, intentionally leaving footprints of beanpaste, he trotted toward the gate and opened it. That done, he retraced his steps, entered the storehouse, and hid himself among the garments.

Before long, the clerks, having looked vainly in the rear of the premises, returned with their lanterns to the front courtyard. Opening the lid of the jar, they saw articles of clothing in it, and since no one recognized these, they knew the thief had left them there. Then they found the footprints leading to the now opened gate, and they concluded, "The thief was frightened when we came to look for him and hid in this jar. And when we searched the back courtyard, he took off his clothes and ran out of the gate. However, he has not gotten very far, and we may still be able to catch him." But the shop owner said, "We have chased him away, so leave it at that. Let us shut the gate and go back to bed." The clerks and members of the owner's family all assumed that the thief had decamped and, weary after their exertions, they lay down and fell sound asleep. No one suspected that the thief was still in their midst.

Meanwhile, Lazy Dragon, safely ensconced among stacks of silken and embroidered garments, wrapped the best of these tightly around his body, and over all of this donned an old black gown. Then he wrapped some small but valuable accessories in a quilt cover, tying these into a bundle. He was busy half the night, and when he was satisfied he leapt from the eaves of the storehouse into the street without the people in the house being any the wiser.

Dawn was breaking, and as Lazy Dragon hurried away from the shop he encountered three or four early risers. The sight of Lazy Dragon walking alone and bearing a large bundle aroused their suspicions, and they asked, "Who are you? Where do you come from? Explain yourself, or we shall not let you pass!" Lazy Dragon made no reply. Instead, he drew from behind his back a bundle bound in the shape of a large ball. This he cast on the ground and took to his heels. The passers-by gathered around to look at the bundle, and when they saw how tightly it was bound they presumed that it contained valuables and vied with one another to open it up. Layer by tight layer they unwrapped it, as though peeling a bamboo shoot. After they had removed more than a foot's thickness of wrappings and all that remained was a ball the size of a man's fist, they wondered, "What can be in there?" Their curiosity was so whetted that no one was willing to desist, and they tussled among themselves to undo the last knots. By this time, the wrappings of the bundle—for the most part torn garments and ragged clumps of wadding—lay scattered in heaps on the ground.

As they shouted and jostled one another, a group of men ran up to them, crying, "You stole those garments from our store! What are you doing? Dividing up the loot?" The newcomers, fiercely brandishing sticks and stones, would not listen to any explanations, and when no cries or pleas could stop them, the passers-by scattered and turned tail. The attackers only managed to detain an old man whose features they could not see in the dim light. They hustled him back to the store, pummeling him every step of the way. The old man kept crying out, "Do not hit me! Do not hit me! You have the wrong person!" But carried away by the fury of the moment, the group of men paid no attention to his entreaties. As the sky grew brighter, however, the shop owner took a closer look and found that the old man was one of his in-laws who lived in the countryside. The owner halted the beating at once, but by then the old man's head and countenance were puffed and swollen from the blows he had received. Apologizing profusely, the owner set out food and wine and sought the old man's forgiveness, pleading that this had happened only because his store had been robbed.

The old man then recounted what had happened. He said, "I was coming here with two or three of my fellow villagers. It was before daybreak, and we saw a person walking along with a big bag across his shoulders. We detained the man and were about to question him when he threw down a bundle before us. And while we all contended to see what was in it, he slipped away during the confusion. Who could have surmised that the bundle consisted of nothing else but layers of rags and old wadding! He fooled us, and instead of apprehending him, we received a drubbing from your men, who set upon us without inquiring into the hows and whys of the matter. My companions have fled, and there is no knowing how far that thief has gone by now!"

All those present were shocked and chastened by this account, and the incident became a source of much derision among the neighbors when they heard that people in this shop had thrashed one of the owner's in-laws instead of catching the thief!

The ball had been made by Lazy Dragon while he was hidden in the storehouse, to serve as a diversion in case he was followed when he departed from the store. This was but one of his many devices for extricating himself if he found himself in peril.

Lazy Dragon's reputation as a "wonder thief" spread far and wide—so much so that Commander Zhang of the local constabulary had his agents arrest him. Commander Zhang then proceeded to question Lazy Dragon, and asked, "Are you the leader of a band of thieves?" To which Lazy Dragon replied, "This small person has never been indicted by any tribunal for thievery; nor have I ever been accused of associating with thieves, burglars or robbers, so how could I be a leader of thieves? However, this small person does indeed possess a few petty skills with which I do no more than play an occasional prank upon my friends and relatives. My Lord, do not take exception to what I say, because you may find me useful some day, in which case I would be ready to go through fire and water for you."

The commander had already taken a liking to this person of small and nimble build and forthright disposition. Besides, he had no evidence or stolen goods with which to bring charges against Lazy Dragon. And now that Lazy Dragon had offered his services, it could very well be that some use could eventually be made of him. So the commander had no intention of making things difficult for Lazy Dragon.

As they were conversing, a man who lived near West Gate came to present the commander with a parrot with a red beak and green feathers. The commander had the parrot chained to a perch and hung under the rafters. Turning to Lazy Dragon, he said with a smile, "I hear you are extraordinarily proficient at the skills of burglars and thieves, and although you have professed to use such skills only for playing pranks, I am sure you must have pilfered many things from others. I am willing to forgive you your transgressions, but you must show me your skills. Should you succeed in taking this parrot tonight, and return it to me tomorrow, I shall wipe out all past accounts with you." Lazy Dragon replied, "That presents no difficulty. Allow me to go, and I shall return with the parrot tomorrow." He then kowtowed and took his leave.

The commander summoned two night watchmen and said to them, "Maintain close vigil over the parrot on that perch. Should anything go amiss, you shall be severely punished." The two stood guard under the rafters, not daring to move one step, and although their eyelids drooped heavily they tried to resist the urge to fall asleep. Now and then they dozed off, but woke up with a start at the slightest noise. It was a miserable night for them.

When the fifth watch drum sounded just before dawn, Lazy Dragon appeared on the roof of the commander's study. Removing some tiles and pushing aside a rafter, he lowered himself into the room. There he saw an aloe-colored cape hanging on a clothes rack and an official's headdress lying on the desk. There was also a small portable lantern bearing the words "Suzhou Constabulary." An idea occurred to Lazy Dragon. He donned the cape and headdress, then extracted a box with live cinders from his sleeve and, blowing on them, lit the lantern. That done, he stepped forth from the study, bearing the lantern and mimicking the gait and demeanor of Commander Zhang to such perfection that no one could have told the difference. Thus he approached the main hall, opened the door and, holding the lantern away from his face, walked over to the eaves of the room. By this time the moon was growing pale in a graying sky, and both the watchmen were sound asleep. Lazy Dragon nudged them with his foot, saying, "It will be light soon, so you no longer need to stand guard." As he spoke, he stretched out his hand and took the parrot's perch, then walked nonchalantly out of the door. To the weary watchmen, the permission to leave was like a reprieve from the Ninth Heaven. With no other thought in mind they hurried away.

Soon it was daylight, and Commander Zhang came out from his chambers, only to see that the parrot was no longer beneath the eaves and even the watchmen were gone. He hastily had the two guards summoned. When they arrived, still half in their dreams, the commander roared, "I ordered you to keep watch over the parrot. Now where is it? And why did you leave your posts?" A guard replied, "Your Lordship, you came yourself after the fifth watch, took the parrot, and told us to leave. Why do you now ask us for the parrot?" The commander cried, "Nonsense! When did I ever come out of my chambers? You were seeing things!" To which the guard protested, "Your Lordship, it was indeed you who came. Both of us were here. Our eyes would hardly deceive us both at the same time, would they?"

The commander knew now that he had been bested. He went to his study, and when he looked up and saw the hole among the rafters, he realized that that was where the thief had entered. As he was still musing over the matter, a guard reported, "Lazy Dragon is outside with the parrot."

The commander walked out with a smile and asked Lazy Dragon how he had made off with the parrot. Lazy Dragon recounted how he had disguised himself with the cape and headdress and taken away the bird. The commander was much amused, and from then on regarded Lazy Dragon with great favor. Thereafter, Lazy Dragon would occasionally do the commander some small services, and the commander, in turn, placed his trust in Lazy Dragon, so that the latter had little to fear from him. And thus did a constable take a thief under his wing, as has frequently been the practice with officers of the law everywhere under heaven.

Although Lazy Dragon was a thief, his adventures were more often than not in the nature of practical jokes. One day a gambler, who had had a streak of good fortune at a gaming house, was carrying home a thousand pieces of cash when he encountered Lazy Dragon on the road. Pointing to his money, the gambler said to Lazy Dragon in jest, "I shall place this cash under my pillow tonight, and if you succeed in taking it I shall treat you to wine and food tomorrow. If you do not succeed, you must treat me." Lazy Dragon laughed and replied, "So be it! So be it!"

Having returned to his home, the gambler said to his wife, "I have been lucky today and shall hide my winnings under my pillow." Much pleased, his wife killed a chicken and warmed a pot of wine, and the two shared these for supper. As they did not finish off the chicken, they placed the remainder in the kitchen larder before repairing to their bedchamber. There, the gambler told his wife about his wager with Lazy Dragon, and the two enjoined one another to remain on the lookout. Little did they know that Lazy Dragon was crouching under their window and listening to all they said.

Lazy Dragon knew that with both husband and wife on the alert taking the money would be no easy matter. He devised a plan on the spot. Entering the kitchen, he found a bone and crunched it between his teeth. The sound he made was like that of a cat eating chicken. The wife exclaimed in alarm, "More than half of that chicken is left, and I intended to make a meal of it for us tomorrow.

That wretched creature must not get away with it!" Hastily jumping out of bed, she went to look in the larder.

By this time, Lazy Dragon had gone out into the courtyard. Lifting a large stone, he dropped it in the well where it fell in the water with a loud splash. When the gambler heard this, he exclaimed in alarm, "Has she fallen into the well for the sake of a few pieces of chicken?" As he rushed out to seek his wife, Lazy Dragon slipped into the bedchamber, drew the money from under the pillow, and departed.

Husband and wife called out to one another in the dark and, having ascertained that both were safe and sound, returned hand in hand to the house. As they went back to bed, they saw that the pillow had been moved aside and that the coins were missing, whereupon they observed wryly, "He declared his intentions clearly and unmistakably, and neither of us was asleep. Yet he was able to bamboozle both of us. Truly, the joke is on us!"

The next day, Lazy Dragon brought back the money and asked to be treated. Laughing uproariously, the gambler thrust a few hundred cash in his sleeve and took Lazy Dragon to a tavern to treat him to wine and food. As they drank and dined, they recalled with much laughter and hand-clapping the details of the events of the previous night. The owner of the tavern became curious and came over to ask the reason for their merriment, and when they had told him, he said to Lazy Dragon, "Your fame has long since reached my ears, and it is indeed deserved." He pointed at the wine pot on the table and said, "If you can take that pot from me tonight, I shall treat you tomorrow to all the wine you can drink." Lazy Dragon laughed and declared, "I see no difficulty." The tavern owner then stipulated, "You must not damage any of my doors or windows. Other than that, you may employ any means you wish." Lazy Dragon replied, "It is agreed!" and thereupon took his leave.

That evening, the tavern owner latched the windows and doors and lit lamps in all corners of the room. Satisfied that Lazy Dragon could not enter unobserved, he said to himself, "I shall sit at the table with a lighted lamp and keep my eyes on that wine pot. Let us see what he can do!" The tavern keeper sat up most of the night and, as nothing happened, began to feel sleepy. His head started to nod, yet at first he managed to stay awake. After a while, however, he could no longer hold out and, stretching himself across the table, fell sound asleep. Soon he began to snore.

Lazy Dragon had been listening outside the door. He now stole onto the roof and pried up some tiles. Then he tied a pig's bladder to a long bamboo cane from which he had removed the partitions between each segment. This he lowered into the room and thrust into the pot. Like all the pots in wine taverns, this one had a wide belly and narrow mouth. Lazy Dragon took a deep breath and blew into the cane, causing the pig's bladder to swell until it filled the pot. He then plugged his end of the bamboo cane, lifted up the pot, and replaced the tiles he had removed, leaving everything as it had been. The tavern owner awoke with a start. The lamp on the table was still burning but the pot had vanished. Springing to his feet, he looked around and saw that the windows and door were still securely fastened. He never knew by what magical means the pot had been removed.

One other day, Lazy Dragon and two or three of his friends were standing before North Gate Restaurant, looking idly at the boats moored along the river below. In one of the boats, the young master of a wealthy family from Fujian had ordered his servants to air his garments and bedding on the prow of the boat, and all the onlookers clicked their tongues at the sight of the rich and colorful silks and brocades. One of the objects was a most unique quilt with a cover sewn of imported brocade. Incensed by such ostentation, Lazy Dragon's companions remarked, "Is there any way this can be taken from him? That would give us a good laugh!" Addressing Lazy Dragon, they said, "This is a good chance for you to show off your skills. What are you waiting for?" Lazy Dragon smiled and replied, "I shall take the quilt tonight, and all of us will come here tomorrow and return it. We will ask for a reward and then use the money to get drunk."

Having said this, Lazy Dragon went to a bathhouse, washed his body most thoroughly, and then returned to the place where the boat was moored. After taking stock of the situation, he waited until evening. By the time of the second watch the young master and his entourage were already besotted with drink. Spreading their bedding on the large common bunk in the boat's cabin, they blew out the lamp and lay down to sleep. In the darkness, Lazy Dragon slipped in among them and crept under a quilt shared by several sleepers, purposely jostling them and mumbling in Fujianese as though talking in his sleep. The other men, disturbed in their slumbers, complained and tossed about and pushed one another. Lazy Dragon took advantage of the confusion to snare the brocade quilt and roll it into a bundle. Then, feigning an urge to relieve himself, he opened the cabin door, walked out with the bundle, emptied his bladder, and jumped ashore without the men in the boat being aware of his coming or going.

The next morning, those on the boat found that the quilt was missing. A big uproar ensued. The young master was greatly put out by the loss and spoke with his companions. All wanted to report the matter to the authorities yet decided it was not worth the trouble, but they still sorely begrudged the loss of the quilt. So they announced a reward of a thousand cash to anyone who could furnish a clue to its whereabouts.

Lazy Dragon and his companions of the previous day then went aboard the boat and told the young master, "We have seen the quilt and know where it is. Give us the reward so we may buy some wine, and we guarantee that the quilt will be returned to you." The young master produced the one thousand cash and promised that they would have it once the quilt was returned. Whereupon Lazy Dragon said, "Have a retainer come with us to get the quilt."

The young master instructed a trusted retainer and several men to go with Lazy Dragon, and soon they arrived at a pawnshop where they saw a quilt. It was indeed the quilt they sought. The retainer said to the proprietor of the pawnshop, "This quilt comes from our boat. How did it get here?" The pawnshop proprietor replied, "A man brought it this morning to pawn it. Our suspicions were aroused when we saw that the brocade on the quilt is not of local manufacture, so we declined to give him any money. That man said, 'I see you do not trust me, so I shall bring some acquaintances of mine and I am certain we shall both get what money is owed us.' We said, 'So be it.' Then the man left, but has not come back. I had a feeling that the quilt was of questionable provenance, but since it belongs to your boat, take it back. When that person comes to retrieve it I shall have him apprehended and sent to you."

The retainer gave the pawnshop owner some money, then all returned to the boat and reported to the young master what the pawnshop owner had said. The young master declared, "We are visitors here, and since we have recovered the quilt I see no need to catch the thief or pursue the matter any further." He gave Lazy Dragon and his companions the promised one thousand cash, and they, after taking the money, went to a wine shop and spent it all. The man whom the pawnshop owner mentioned was, of course, someone Lazy Dragon had entrusted with depositing the brocade quilt so that he could claim the reward. These were not the only times Lazy Dragon played such practical jokes.

Although Lazy Dragon liked to make sport of people, he could also be quite mischievous, both in jest and in earnest, when he was displeased. Once, a band of petty thieves who were his drinking companions invited him for an outing at Tiger Hill. They sailed their boat across a lake between the hills and temporarily stopped at a wharf before a rice store, intending to purchase wine and kindling at a market behind the store. However, the clerks at the store deemed that the boat would be a hindrance to their business, so they harshly ordered it away and refused to let it be moored at the wharf. Lazy Dragon's companions entered into a heated altercation with the clerks, but Lazy Dragon cast a glance at his companions and said, "Since they do not allow us to stop here, let us go downstream and find a place to go ashore. There is no need to lose our tempers."

So they cast off and departed. The band of thieves were still greatly incensed, but Lazy Dragon said, "There is no need to argue with those scoundrels. I have a way to get even with them tonight." The thieves asked him what he intended to do, and he said, "Get a small boat for me tonight and place in it a jar of wine and a cup as well as a brazier with charcoal to warm the wine. On the return trip I shall enjoy myself by watching the moon until dawn, and by tomorrow morning you will know the answer. But do not tell anyone now what I have said."

That evening, the company had their banquet at Tiger Hill and then broke up. Lazy Dragon arranged to meet them again the next morning, keeping with himself only one of the thieves who was a convivial drinking companion and another who knew how to pole a boat. They boarded the small boat and set off on the return trip.

When they came to fork in the river next to the rice store, they found the store closed for the night. Floating on the water in front of the store were many pleasure boats from which came the sounds of music and singing. The people in the store, however, were fast asleep, and Lazy Dragon had his companions moor his boat alongside the store's plank wall. Earlier that day, Lazy Dragon had observed that a grain bin stood in the corner of the store, not far from the river and right next to the outer wall. Extracting a small knife from his sleeve, he dug at a knothole in one of the planks, and soon the knot fell out, leaving a sizeable hole in the plank. He then took from his waist a bamboo tube that had been cut at an angle at both ends. Sliding one end of the tube through the hole into the matting that formed the sides of the grain bin, he wiggled the other end around one or twice. With a swish, rice began to stream down the bamboo tube.

Lazy Dragon raised his wine cup to the moon and laughed and shouted drunkenly to cover up the sound of the grain pouring into the boat. Not a single person on the pleasure boats passing by noticed anything amiss. As for the men asleep in the rice store, not even in their dreams did they suspect that something was wrong.

After some time, the flow of rice dribbled to an end and Lazy Dragon assumed that the bin must be almost empty. His boat, too, was full, so he had his friends untether the boat. Taking their time, they poled it to a secluded spot where the other thieves joined them. Lazy Dragon recounted what he had done, and all the thieves laughed and rubbed their hands in glee. Lazy Dragon clasped his hands together and said to them, "Divide this rice among yourselves as repayment for the feast you gave me last night." He did not take any of it for himself.

As for the rice store, the clerks there found the bin empty when they opened it up much later. They never learned when or how the rice in it had disappeared.

Then there was the occasion when a number of Daoist priests from the White Clouds Hall of East Temple by the South Garden went on a tour of Tiger Hill and engaged a boat complete with wine and refreshments for that purpose. At that time, a new sort of headgear called the "hat of a hundred pillars" had become the fashion in Suzhou and was worn as an adornment by all local young fops. The Daoist priests too purchased such hats in private, so that they could pass themselves off as commoners when whey wished to go out and disport themselves.

Now, there was in Suzhou a certain Wang the Third, the third scion of Wang, the famous manufacturer of gauze. Wang the Third was normally on good terms with the Daoist priests and had always accompanied them on their outings and shared the costs. But the priests felt that he invariably sought petty advantages and created embarrassing scenes when he had too much to drink, so they decided to not to tell him about the current outing and to go on their own.

Wang the Third found out about their plans, however, and was greatly angered. He sought out Lazy Dragon and asked the latter if there were some way he could spoil the priests' fun. Lazy Dragon agreed to help and proceeded that night to the White Cloud Hall where he purloined all the bonnets usually worn by the priests. Wang the Third asked, "Why did you not take their new headwear instead of these everyday bonnets?" Whereupon Lazy Dragon replied, "If they lost their new hats they would simply refrain from going on their tour tomorrow, and that would be of little interest. Leave this matter to me and observe how I discomfit them tomorrow." He offered no further explanation, and Wang the Third could only wait to see what would happen.

The next day, the priests donned short garments like those worn by ordinary young men and went to their boat. Lazy Dragon, garbed in black, followed them on board and squatted down beside the rudder house. He did not excite anyone's suspicions, as the priests assumed he was one of the boat's crew while the boatmen thought he was a servant from the temple.

After the boat set sail, the priests removed their outer garments and hats and proceeded to drink and make merry. When no one was looking, Lazy Dragon rounded up the priests' new hats, placing in their stead the bonnets he had taken the day before. Then, as the boat approached Zhenzhuo Bridge and was preparing to dock, he hopped onto the bank. The priests now put on their clothing so as to go ashore and have a good time, but could not find their new hats. All they saw were their everyday bonnets neatly stacked in a pile. "This is really strange!" they cried. "Where did our hats go?" To which the crew replied, "Why ask us? It was you who put your things away. In any event, there should not be any problem, since not even a needle has ever been lost on our boats."

The priests conducted another futile search, and then said to the boat's crew, "You have a thin little man in black who just went ashore. Could you find him and ask whether he knows anything about our hats?" A crew member replied, "We do not have anyone like that on our boat. He came with you." The priests cried, "When did we ever bring servants with us? You must be in league with thieves who stole our new hats! Those hats cost several taels of silver apiece, and we shall not let you get away with them!"

So saying, they seized the boatmen and would not let go. The boatmen were not intimidated and argued loudly, and a large crowd of onlookers gathered to see what was happening.

A young man emerged from the crowd and jumped on the boat. "What is all this row about?" he asked. The priests and the boatmen both gave their accounts, and the priests, who knew the young man, assumed he would take their side. Little did they expect him to assume a severe expression and admonish them with the words, "You are all Daoist priests, and it is only natural that you should have worn bonnets when you came on this boat. And since all your bonnets are here, why would there be any hundred-pillar hats? You must be attempting to slander and defraud the boatmen."

Having heard that the passengers of the boat were Daoist priests, and that these had their regular headgear but insisted that the boatmen pay them for some hats, the onlookers started to mutter and shout. A number of busybodies and ruffians among them who had nothing better to do rolled up their sleeves and brandished their fists, yelling, "Those Daoist priests are blackguards! Let us beat them up and send them to the authorities!" But the man who had come on the boat waved his hands to stop them and cried, "Do not beat them! Do not beat them! Let them go!" Having said that, he quickly jumped ashore.

The Daoist priests, fearful that trouble would ensue, hurriedly ordered that the boat be sailed away. They departed with dampened spirits and much disappointment, because, for one, they had lost their new hats, and second, their disguise had been laid bare and they could not go up the hill to enjoy the wine and food they had prepared. As for that young man who jumped onto the boat—guess who he was! He was, of course, Wang the Third. Lazy Dragon had informed him once the Daoist priests' hats had been replaced so that he might unmask the priests during the dispute that was bound to follow and spoil their outing.

After the priests returned to Suzhou, they continued to importune the boatmen about their hats, so Wang the Third had a servant take the hats back to the priests with this message: "Be sure to notify me if you should wish to show off your hundred-pillar hats during some future excursion." The priests knew then that it was Wang the Third who had played this trick on them. They had also heard of Lazy Dragon and learned that Wang the Third was on good terms with him. So they surmised that it was Lazy Dragon who had engineered the entire affair.

At that time, there was in neighboring Wuxi a county magistrate who was more than usually venal and whose notoriety had spread far and wide. Someone once told Lazy Dragon, "There are piles of gold and treasure in the residence of Wuxi's county magistrate, and all are ill-gotten gains. Why not take some it from him? You would be doing a good thing by distributing it among the poor and the needy."

Thus informed, Lazy Dragon went to Wuxi and stole into the residence at night to see what was there. He saw trunks filled with silks and satins and shelves stacked with rare objects. Silver ingots lay unwrapped and lined up in rows. Pots brimmed over with gold and silver. Housemaids used ivory tusks to poke stoves and braziers, and the children drank soup out of rhinoceros horns. All these riches had been accumulated by the official for himself and his offspring by plundering the populace, yet he had the gall to demand that people address him as Father of the People!

As Lazy Dragon examined these treasures, he thought to himself, "All this wealth is guarded by gate after locked gate and many watchmen with bells and clappers, and I shall not be able to take very much." He saw a little coffer that was very heavy and surmised that it held gold and silver, so he took it with him. Then he thought, "This is the residence of an official, and I do not wish them to make wild guesses about who has taken this coffer and then wrongfully accuse innocent people." Picking up a brush, he painted a plum blossom on the wall next to the spot where the coffer had stood. Then he sprang onto the eaves of the building and departed from the rear of the residence.

Two or three days later, the magistrate took stock of his wealth and found that a small coffer used solely for storing gold was missing. It had contained around two hundred taels of gold, worth more than a thousand taels of silver. As the magistrate searched for the coffer, he was surprised to see a freshly painted sprig of plum blossoms on the wall next to the vacant spot. He said to himself, "The thief is evidently not an insider. But who could have entered my living quarters and painted this flower in such a leisurely manner? This is no ordinary thief, and he must be apprehended!"

He forthwith summoned a number of sharp-eyed, keen-witted constables to his residence to examine the scene of the crime. When the constables saw the painting, they exclaimed in consternation, "Your Excellency, we know about this thief, but it is not advisable to arrest him. He is a most ingenious thief from the city of Suzhou and is known as Lazy Dragon. Wherever he commits a theft, he always paints plum blossoms—his signature flower—on a wall. His skills are such that he leaves no a trace of how he enters or departs, and he has a large band of diehard followers because of his exceptional loyalty to his friends. It might be possible to apprehend him, but there would be serious consequences, more so than losing just a bit of gold and silver. So we would advise you to leave him alone, for he is not to be trifled with."

The magistrate flew into a rage and roared, "You knaves! Since you already know his name, why do you not seize him! You have always worked hand in glove with thieves and are using such excuses to protect this one. I should have all of you caned! Mark my words, I want you to arrest that thief, and if you do not bring him to me within ten days, I shall have your heads!" None of the constables dared to say another word.

The magistrate then instructed a secretary to write out a warrant for the arrest of the thief and dispatched two constables to carry it out. He also had requests for assistance addressed to neighboring counties. With no other choice but to obey, the constables set out for Suzhou.

Just as they were about to enter Suzhou, they saw Lazy Dragon standing by the city gate. One of the constables tapped him on the shoulder and said, "Old Dragon, you could have taken those things from our official and left it at that. Why did you have to flaunt your skills by painting that sprig of flowers? Now the two of us have been ordered to apprehend you and deliver you to the yamen. What else can we do?"

Lazy Dragon replied casually, "There is no need for you to worry. Let us talk about this matter in a tavern." He took the constables to a tavern and ordered wine; then he said, "I am discussing the matter with you because your official urgently wants me arrested, and I do not wish to put the two of you to any inconvenience. Just give me one day's grace. I shall send a message to your magistrate, and he will of his own accord withdraw the arrest warrant. What do you say?" The constables replied, "We have no objection to that, but you took too much from him. According to him, all of it is gold, and he will never forgive that. If we do not take you with us, we shall surely suffer for it."

Lazy Dragon remarked, "Even if you take me, the gold is already gone." The constables inquired, "Then where is it?" Lazy Dragon replied, "It has been divided up between the two of you." Frightened, the constables remonstrated,

"Stop joking! Such words would be no jesting matter if they reached the ears of the tribunal!" Lazy Dragon assured them, "I do not lie, and this is no joke. Go home, both of you, and see for yourselves." He leaned closer and whispered into their ears, "You will find the gold among the roof tiles at your homes."

Being well aware of Lazy Dragon's skills, the constables conferred between themselves and then decided that "if he says this before the tribunal and the loot is indeed at our homes, we cannot escape being incriminated!" So they said to Lazy Dragon, "We dare not ask you to go back with us. But tell us what we should do."

Lazy Dragon replied, "Go back to Wuxi, both of you, and I shall follow you in short order. I promise you your magistrate will not mention this matter any more and you will not be implicated." Having said this, he took from his sleeve a small packet of gold weighing about two taels and handed it to the constables with the words, "This is to pay for your traveling expenses."

It is said that money draws officials just as blood attracts flies, and indeed, the constables' eyes lit up at the sight of the glittering gold. All smiles, they accepted the gold although they were well aware that it might have come from their magistrate's stolen cache. And they no longer insisted that Lazy Dragon return with them. Thus they parted company.

Lazy Dragon left for Wuxi that very day and when night fell stole into the magistrate's residence. The magistrate had a wife and a concubine, and he happened to be sleeping in his wife's chambers that night. Thus the concubine was all by herself in her canopied bed. Lazy Dragon lifted the canopy, felt around with his hands and touched the bun of hair coiled like a reclining dragon atop the concubine's head. With a pair of scissors, he carefully clipped off the bun and then went in search of the casket that held the magistrate's official seal. When he had found the casket, he opened it, stuffed in the bun, and shut it again. Then he painted a sprig of plum blossoms on the wall. He touched nothing else and left as quietly as he had come.

The concubine woke up the next morning with her hair in complete disarray. Sensing that something was wrong, she felt her head and found that bun of hair was gone. Her shrieks aroused the entire household, and many people ran over to inquire what had taken place. The concubine wailed, "Someone has played this prank on me and cut off my hair!" The servants immediately reported the matter to the magistrate.

When the magistrate came in the room, he saw what looked like a beggar monk seated within the canopy and he wondered why this had happened. In his mind rose the image of his concubine's lovely long hair brushing the floor like a filmy cloud caressing the earth, and he was both chagrined and frightened by the sight she now presented. He thought, "I have yet to catch the thief who stole my gold, and now another scoundrel has entered my residence. However, these matters are less important than the safety of the county seal!"

The magistrate at once retrieved the casket that held the official seal. It seemed to be untouched, and the key was still in the lock. He opened the casket and saw with feelings of relief that the seal was still in its place. Then he noticed some hair in the box. Lifting the upper section of the casket, he found a bundle of hair in the lower section. After he had ascertained that nothing was missing, he looked up and noticed the painting on the wall. It was an exact replica of the one he had previously seen.

The magistrate was flabbergasted. "It is that thief again!" he reflected. "He knows I am on his heels and has played this trick to send me a message. If he can cut off someone's hair, he can just as well cut off a man's head. And by leaving the hair in the casket he is also saying that he can take the seal. What a formidable thief! Little wonder my constables advised me to leave him alone! I will be courting disaster if I do not stop pursuing him. The gold is a small matter, and I can easily make up the loss by bearing down on a few more wealthy households. I had best call off the search for that thief!" He at once wrote out a mandate slip recalling the two constables he had sent to Suzhou and canceling their mission.

As for the two constables, after they parted company with Lazy Dragon in Suzhou they both returned to Wuxi and, following Lazy Dragon's instructions, searched among the roof tiles at their homes. Both found packages of gold. The date inscribed on each package was the day on which the gold had been stolen, and they wondered when Lazy Dragon could have hidden the packages. The older constable chewed his own knuckles in apprehension as he thought, "It is fortunate that we did not insist on bringing in Lazy Dragon. Had we done so, and had he stated before the tribunal where he left the gold and the loot was found here, we could not clear ourselves even if we had a thousand mouths! But how are we to report back to the magistrate now?"

He called his junior colleague to his home, and the two were anxiously discussing what to say when a new order came from the magistrate. The two flew into a panic, as they believed the magistrate was demanding they meet the deadline, but the message merely instructed them to report in to have their mission canceled. They asked the messenger about the reason for this decision, and the latter recounted to them what had happened at the magistrate's residence the night before. He concluded, "The official is frightened out of his wits and dares not have the thief arrested." And thus the constables learned that Lazy

Dragon had been true to his word, that he had returned to Wuxi and once more demonstrated his amazing skills.

In the last year of the Jiaqing reign, there was a magistrate in Wujiang County whose greed and venality were rivaled only by his craftiness and cunning. One day, he had a trusted assistant go to Suzhou with gifts and invite Lazy Dragon to Wujiang County. Lazy Dragon accepted the invitation and, on meeting the magistrate, asked, "Why has Your Excellency summoned this small person? Can I be of any service to you?" The magistrate replied, "Having long heard of your fame, I have a highly confidential mission for you." Lazy Dragon demurred, saying, "This small person is but a footloose rascal. Since, however, Your Excellency deigns to notice me, what can I do for you? I would go through water and fire without hesitation."

The magistrate excused his staff and said to Lazy Dragon in private, "The regional inspector is now in this county and is picking fault with me. I want you to go to the yamen of the Investigation Bureau and steal his official seal. In that way he can no longer hold his position and I shall be able to avenge myself. When you will have accomplished this mission, I shall recompense you with one hundred taels of gold."

Lazy Dragon promised, "I shall get the seal without fail." He was gone for half the night, and when he returned he took the seal of the Inspection Bureau from his sleeve and proffered it to the magistrate with both hands.

Immensely pleased, the magistrate declared to Lazy Dragon, "Truly, you have magical hands. Even the most famous thieves in history are not your equal!" He produced one hundred taels of gold and gave them to Lazy Dragon, then instructed him to leave as soon as possible and not to tarry in the county.

Lazy Dragon said, "I thank Your Excellency for this munificent reward. But may I ask, what do you intend to do with that seal?" The magistrate replied, "Since it is in my possession now, he will not be able to get in my way." Lazy Dragon went on, "This small person is grateful to Your Excellency for holding me in such high esteem, so I would like to offer Your Excellency some sincere advice." Intrigued, the magistrate asked, "And what is that?"

Lazy Dragon continued, "I hid among the rafters of the Investigation Bureau's yamen for half the night and was able to spy on the regional inspector as he wrote instructions on reports by candlelight. His brush flew like the wind, and his dispositions were quite to the point. I believe him to be an unusually astute and keen-witted man who is not easily beguiled. Your Excellency had best return the seal to him and say it was recovered by your night watchmen from a thief who managed to escape. Even if the regional inspector would have his suspicions, he would be both thankful and fearful and would therefore make no trouble for you."

With a snort the magistrate said, "Return it to him so that he can go on doing as he pleases? Preposterous! You had better be on your way and leave me to my own devices!" Lazy Dragon said nothing more and quickly departed.

The next day, the regional inspector wished to use the seal and brought out the box that contained it. When he opened the box, however, he found it to be empty. He had his personal staff look in every conceivable place for the seal, and when this was not to be found the regional inspector thought to himself, "There is only one explanation for this. The magistrate of this county knows that I dislike him. I am in his territory and he surely has many spies. He must have had one of them steal the seal from me. I shall have to devise some way of dealing with him." He ordered his staff to keep quiet about the loss of the seal, then closed and sealed the box as usual.

That day, he did not go to his office, announcing that he was ill, and had an assistant temporarily take charge of all incoming documents. The same thing happened over the next few days, to the secret delight of the magistrate who knew what lay at the bottom of this "illness." As required by courtesy, however, the magistrate went to pay his respects and inquire about the regional inspector's health.

When informed of the magistrate's arrival, the regional inspector had his visitor brought in by a side door directly to his bedside. He then proceeded to chat vivaciously on subjects ranging from folk customs to local habits and from financial matters to political affairs, doing so with a great show of sincerity and interest. Cup after cup of tea was served as they spoke. This had the magistrate feeling uneasy, for he could not fathom the reason for such a cordial reception.

As they were conversing a fire suddenly broke out in the kitchen. Cooks, servants and staff members ran in one after the other, crying, "The fire is coming this way! Leave at once, My Lord!" The regional inspector, apparently quite shaken, quickly rose from his bed, took the sealed box that had held the official seal and thrust it into the hands of magistrate with the words, "My dear magistrate, please take this seal to the county treasury for safekeeping, and summon help at once to put out the fire!"

The magistrate could not very well refuse to accept the locked box during such an emergency, so he took it and left the residence. By now the local firemen had arrived and they soon extinguished the fire, which only burned down two rooms in the kitchen area and left the official residence unscathed. Orders were then given to shut the gates of the Inspection Bureau.

All this had, of course, taken place on instructions issued by the regional inspector after he discovered the theft of the seal.

The magistrate now found himself in a dilemma. He reflected, "The regional inspector has given me an empty box, and if I return the box to him as it is and he opens it in my presence, I shall have no way of accounting for the absence of the seal." He pondered the matter, but since he could find no other solution he moistened and lifted the seal on the box, unlocked it, put in the official seal, then sealed and locked the box again.

When the regional inspector held court the next day, the magistrate went to return the box. The regional inspector asked the magistrate to stay until he had opened the box and verified the presence of the seal. He then used the seal to stamp a large number of official documents that had not been issued during the past few days.

The regional inspector announced his departure from Wujiang County and set out the very same day, not, however, before informing the provincial governor's executive censor about all that had happened. The two together wrote out a report on the magistrate's many unlawful deeds, as a result of which the magistrate was relieved of his duties. On the day that the magistrate left his office, he said to his associates, "Lazy Dragon is a man of insight. Had I hearkened to his words, I would not have come to such an ignominious end."

As Lazy Dragon's fame spread far and wide, it was unavoidable that he should be suspected of many serious burglaries that were unrelated to him, or of aiding and abetting others in the commission of such acts. Once, when a dozen or more gold ingots were lost from the Suzhou treasury, the investigators concluded, "They must have been stolen by Lazy Dragon since there is no trace of how they were removed."

In truth, Lazy Dragon had not taken the ingots, but when he learned that he was under suspicion of having done so he felt he must get to the bottom of the matter. He suspected that the culprit might be the treasury commissioner himself, so he went in the night to eavesdrop at the commissioner's residence. Once there, he overheard the commissioner say to his wife, "I took the ingots, and now others suspect Lazy Dragon. This is my good fortune. But Lazy Dragon will never admit to doing this thing. Tomorrow I shall write up Lazy Dragon's history as a thief and submit it to the authorities. Then there is no doubt he will take the blame."

When Lazy Dragon heard of this, he thought, "This is not good! I had nothing to do with this theft, but now the commissioner intends to accuse me before his superiors. All officials are of the same feather, and I am not without blemish. I shall never be able to clear myself. The best course for me is to take myself away and avoid a beating I do not deserve." He left Suzhou at once and went to the city of Nanjing where he pretended to be a blind man and told fortunes in the streets.

There was at the national vault at Suzhou a certain Zhang Xiaoshe who was well known for his ability to discern thieves among the populace. He happened to be in Nanjing at the time, and when he came across Lazy Dragon he at once thought, "There is something peculiar about this blind man!" On closer inspection he saw that it was Lazy Dragon in disguise. Seizing the false fortuneteller by the arm, he led him to a quiet spot and said, "You have stolen the ingots from the treasury and the authorities are after you. So you have come here and disguised yourself in this manner to escape attention. You cannot fool me!"

Lazy Dragon took Xiaoshe's hand in his own and declared earnestly, "You know me for what I am, and you should help me clear myself of this false accusation. So why do you, too, speak in this way? The ingots were stolen by the commissioner. I clearly heard what he told his wife in bed that night. He said he intended to put the blame on me and smear my reputation before the authorities. I have sought refuge in Nanjing because I feared the authorities would believe his words. Now, if you go to the authorities and tell them what you have learned, you will not only receive a reward but also clear my name. And I shall of course give you a humble token of my gratitude. So please do not betray me now."

Xiaoshe had, in fact, been entrusted by the authorities to investigate the matter of the ingots, and now that he obtained this information he let Lazy Dragon go and returned to Suzhou where he reported his findings. The ingots were indeed brought to light at the commissioner's home and Lazy Dragon was exonerated. Zhang Xiaoshe, whose information had resolved the case, was rewarded by the authorities.

A few days later, Zhang Xiaoshe went again to Nanjing and came upon Lazy Dragon, still walking the streets disguised as a blind fortune-teller. Intentionally bumping shoulders with him, Xiaoshe said, "That matter in Suzhou has been cleared. Have you forgotten what you promised me last time?" Lazy Dragon replied, "I have not forgotten. Look in the pile of cinders at your home, and you will see an insignificant expression of my gratitude." Pleased, Xiaoshe declared, "Old Dragon never goes back on his word!" So saying, he parted company with Lazy Dragon.

At home, he searched the pile of cinders and uncovered a package containing some gold and silver as well as a sharp, gleaming knife. Xiaoshe stuck out his tongue in astonishment and exclaimed, "What a ruthless thief! He feared I might blackmail him, and while thanking me, he left this knife as a threat. But when could he have placed this package here? His skills are indeed marvelous. From now on I must be careful not to offend him in any way!"

As for Lazy Dragon, he knew the matter of the ingots was over after he encountered Zhang Xiaoshe the second time. Nonetheless he feared someone else might scheme against him, so he washed his hands of his risky calling and thereafter made his living by telling other people's fortunes. He lived out his last years at Changgan Temple where he eventually died a natural death.

Although he had been notorious as a thief during his lifetime, he was never punished by a tribunal; nor had he had his arms tattooed like other thieves. And to this day, people in Suzhou delight in telling stories about his crafty mischief-making. He might well be called a man of integrity among thieves, for he was certainly a cut above those hypocritical, money-grubbing gentry who forsake all honor when they smell profits. And had he been able to apply his phenomenal skills to launching surprise attacks on enemy camps or to spying out enemy intrigues, he would no doubt have been acclaimed as a hero. The pity of it is that in these times of peace and tranquility his talents found no outlet more worthy than the devising of paltry artifices that merited little more than a good laugh!

Glossary

Dates of Some Chinese Dynasties:

Tang dynasty — AD 618–907

Song dynasty — AD 960–1279

Yuan dynasty — AD 1271–1368

Ming dynasty — AD 1368–1644

Titles Conferred By China's Imperial Examinations:

tongsheng — Candidate for the lowest degree in the imperial examination system.

xiucai — One who has passed the imperial service examinations at the county level in the Ming and Qing dynasties.

juren — One who has passed the imperial service examinations at the provincial level during the Ming and Qing dynasties.

jinshi — One who passed the highest imperial service examinations.

zhuangyuan — Title conferred on one who came first in the highest imperial service examinations.

Some Chinese Weights and Measurements

li — A unit of distance equivalent to approximately one third of a mile.

mu — A unit of land measure equivalent to approximately one fifth of an acre.

tael (or *liang*) — a unit of weight roughly equivalent to 1½ ounces, used, among other purposes, for measuring silver.

qian — One tenth of a *liang*.

fen — One tenth of a *qian*.

Miscellaneous

yamen — The headquarters or residence of an official or government department in imperial China.

"watches" — In older times, the night was divided into five two-hour periods. These began at dusk and ended at dawn. The third watch, for example, corresponded to about midnight, and the fifth watch to the hours just before dawn. The beginning of each watch was usually marked, in cities, with the beating of a drum in the city's drum tower.

Lao Zi — Philosopher in the Spring and Autumn Period (770–76 B.C.) of Chinese history, founder of Daoism.

Miao people — An ethnic minority group of people in Southwest China , known historically for their steadfastness and warlike temperament.

Nine Fountains — In Chinese mythology, the place where the spirits of the dead reside.

Mid-Autumn Festival — The 15th day of the 8th lunar month, when families got together to thank the gods for the year's harvests. People still observe it today by partying and eating "moon cakes."

Qingming (or Pure Brightness) — one of the 24 solar periods, occurring on April 4, 5, or 6. On this day, people traditionally visit, or "sweep," the graves of their ancestors.

Literary Terms

Make clouds and rain — A poetic allusion to the act of love-making.

Jade stalk — A Chinese literary term for "penis."

Apply the five-finger (or hand) funnel — Euphemism for "masturbate."

THE ABBOT AND THE WIDOW
Tales from the Ming Dynasty
Ling Mengchu

Ling Mengchu (1580–1644) a Ming dynasty scholar and writer, wrote down hundreds of stories in two volumes called *Slapping the Desk in Astonishment*—or "Two Slaps"—in China's famous teahouse storytelling tradition.

Ted Wang majored in English and Russian at Yanjing and Beijing universities. An experienced translator both from English to Chinese and Chinese to English, his main works are translations of Chinese novels, plays, screenplays, and a vast number of social science papers in Chinese studies.

Chen Chen was a musicologist in her youthful years in China. She became a translator and editor in the late 1970s, working both in China and the United States. She is the author of the critically proclaimed memoir *Come Watch the Sun Go Home* (1998).

EastBridge
SIGNATURE BOOKS
Doug Merwin, Imprint Editor

Signature Books is dedicated to presenting a wide range of exceptional books in the field of Asian and related studies. The principal concentrations are texts and supplementary materials for academic courses, literature-in-translation, and the writings of Westerners who experienced Asia as journalists, scholars, diplomats, and travelers.

Doug Merwin, publisher and editor-in-chief of EastBridge, has more than thirty years' experience as an editor of books and journals on Asia and was the founding editor of the East Gate Books imprint.